D1221753

FINANCIAL

RISK
MANAGEMENT
IN BANKING

THE THEORY & APPLICATION OF ASSET & LIABILITY MANAGEMENT

DENNIS G. UYEMURA

DONALD R. VAN DEVENTER

McGraw-Hill

New York San Francisco Washington, D.C. Auckland Bogotá
Caracas Lisbon London Madrid Mexico City Milan
Montreal New Delhi San Juan Singapore
Sydney Tokyo Toronto

McGraw-Hill

A Division of The McGraw·Hill Companies

BANKLINE

A Bankline Publication

© 1993, Bank Administration Institute Foundation

ALL RIGHTS RESERVED. No part of this publication may be reproduced, stored in a retrieval system, or transmitted by any means, electronic, mechanical, photocopying, recording, or otherwise, without the prior written permission of the publisher and the copyright holder.

This publication is designed to provide accurate and authoritative information in regard to the subject matter covered. It is sold with the understanding that the publisher is not engaged in rendering legal, accounting or other professional service.

Authorization to photocopy items for internal or personal use, or the internal or personal use of specific clients, is granted by BANK ADMINISTRATION INSTITUTE FOUNDATION, provided that the US$7.00 per page fee is paid directly to Copyright Clearance Center, 27 Congress Street, Salem MA 01970, USA; Phone: 1-(508) 744-3350. For those organizations that have been granted a photocopy license by CCC, a separate system of payment has been arranged. The fee code for users of the Transactional Reporting Service is: 1-55738-353-7/93/$0.00 + $7.00

ISBN 1-55738-353-7

Printed in the United States of America

BC

8 9 0

TABLE OF CONTENTS

List of Figures

List of Tables

INTRODUCTION

We have conducted several informal surveys of banking school students about how well bankers perform asset and liability management (ALM) activities. Specifically, these students were asked to grade the banking industry on a scale from "A" to "F" in terms of how well bankers understand ALM and how well they manage ALM risks. The results were consistently about 25% "C" and 75% "D" with an occasional "F" now and then. Clearly, these samples of bankers are not very impressed with the "state of ALM" today.

In thinking about these results we speculate that, rather than reflecting a lack of understanding of issues or methods, these attitudes derive from a more fundamental frustration about ALM. Everyone talks around the subject. Everyone asserts that they understand it and have some level of expertise at it. Everyone hints that there exist powerful and mysterious (or mystic?) techniques to "maximize profits and minimize risks." If such magic exists, why is it that the perceptions of the field are so poor?

We assert that no such magic exists . . . that the emperor has no clothes. The practice of ALM is not a mystic art, nor is it a virtuoso skill, only to be perfected by years of diligent study, apprenticeship, and heavy doses of rocket science.

Rather, ALM is an application of basic corporate finance as taught in any MBA program. Yes, there are subtleties and nuances resulting from the role of banks as intermediaries, as well as from bank regulatory activities. However, the fundamentals are the same. Understand them and you have taken the first essential step in demystifying the "art" of ALM.

It is the objective of this book to present a comprehensive framework for understanding ALM. It results from over 25 years of collective experience in theorizing and applying these ideas to real banking organizations. Most importantly, it addresses practical decision-making situations that every financial institution faces and suggests approaches that have proven effective in our experience. While we will discuss many of the actual approaches that we have found successful in practice, we are not claiming that ours are the only correct methods. Indeed, this material is some of the most difficult and challenging in all of corporate finance. We offer our ideas for your consideration and hope that they will stimulate a more open debate about all of ALM.

We have found ALM to be one of the most rewarding and satisfying of all banking disciplines. To practice ALM effectively, one needs a good understanding of the entire balance sheet structure and dynamics of the bank: its pricing strategies, the preferences and behavior of its customers, the money and capital markets, the regulators, senior management, and shareholders.

This seems like a weighty undertaking, and it is. But it is also fun. We hope to convey this excitement by concentrating on an intuitive rather than rigorous understanding of the issues. After all, we have always viewed the task of an A/L manager to be part analyst and part teacher/mentor/communicator. Success at analysis means nothing without effectively conveying the essence of the issue and the tradeoffs that must be made to the rest of the bank.

This book will be helpful for a number of potential readers:

- Senior executives (particularly CEOs) who want a basic financial understanding of the major controversies and dilemmas facing the industry today;

- Financial analysts responsible for ALM activities who want to understand how other banks have managed to get their ALCOs to deal with all of the most difficult financial subjects; and,

- Banking school students who want a solid foundation and reference guide to aid them in their ALM and funds management courses.

COMMENT ON MATHEMATICS

The mathematics of stochastic processes is difficult and, for the most part, not accessible to the vast majority of bankers. Given our intended audience, we will not attempt a rigorous mathematical treatment of the subject matter presented. We have chosen to trade off some analytics for the sake of comprehensibility by a wider readership. However, for those who desire such material, we are developing a follow-up book that will provide a detailed and rigorous treatment of this most difficult of ALM topics.

CHAPTER 1

What Is Asset and Liability Management?

Asset and liability management (ALM) is the financial risk management of any financial institution. This includes risk assessments in all dimensions—policy setting, structuring of the bank's repricing and maturity schedules, undertaking financial hedge positions, capital budgeting, and internal profitability measurements. It also includes contingency planning in the sense that the bank must analyze the impacts of unexpected changes in the environment (e.g., interest rates, competitive conditions, economic growth) and how it will respond to those changes.

While the last paragraph is admittedly not the product of Ernest Hemingway, we will try to breathe some life into this critical subject in the rest of the book. To get started, it is interesting to ask what other bankers think of ALM. When bankers (including many CEOs) are asked to define ALM, invariably phrases like "maximize profits" and "minimize risks" are offered. Such concepts are in the correct arena, but they still miss the point. Indeed, they can be dangerously wrong by implying that it is possible to devise strategies that increase the expected profitability of the bank while minimizing its overall risk structure at the same time.

Unfortunately, life is not quite so simple. In all of finance, risks and returns are linked in very well-defined ways—ways that are the financial counterpart of the "no free lunch" rules of basic finance. Generally, any action to increase the expected returns of any organization will also increase its risk structure. ALM has more to do with understanding those risk/return tradeoffs and exercising them well than with the alchemy implied by the "maximize profits and minimize risks" illusion. Indeed, the best ALM practitioners are experts at making these risk and return tradeoffs clear so that the board of directors and senior management of the institution can make informed business judgments about the best course for the bank. A few years ago one of us made the mistake of telling a chief executive officer that we had a 60% chance of winning an important piece of business. He replied that anyone who wasn't 100% certain about getting the business could not possibly be a good banker. This book is not for that kind of chief executive officer, because there are no simple answers between the covers of this book. Those who search for simple answers and grand slams should return this book for a refund at their earliest opportunity. For those of you who are still with us, we offer some simple truths as a substitute for simple answers.

1.1 THE RISK AND RETURN TRADEOFF IN ALM

This book relies upon a common depiction of the risk and return tradeoff as taught in any business school finance course. Figure 1.1 shows three possible risk and return positions that a bank might face, with risk shown on the x-axis and return on the y-axis. There are three possible positions the bank may attain as shown in Figure 1.1. Position A has the lowest risk, position C has the highest expected return. Position B has the same expected return as A and the same risk level as C. If confronted with a decision about which position to adopt, it is simplest to make some comparisons two-at-a-time.

In comparing positions A and B, it should be clear that A is superior to B because they have the same expected returns, but A is less risky than B. It is also clear that position C is better than B. Both have the same risk, but C displays a larger expected return. Therefore, under no circumstances will position B be adopted.

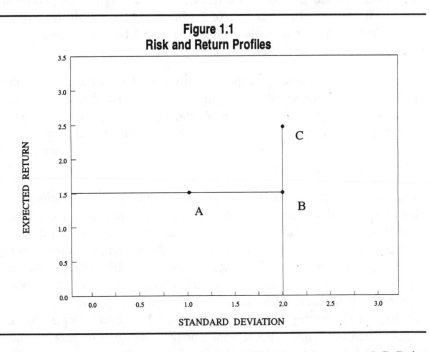

Figure 1.1
Risk and Return Profiles

The situation is not as simple when comparing positions A and C. Point C has a higher expected return and more risk than A. Which should a bank adopt? The answer is purely a function of the risk/return preferences of the shareholders and management of the bank. Either A or C are perfectly legitimate options among the three potential positions considered.

The point here is that there is no way to simultaneously maximize returns (or profits) and minimize risks. Banks can only make risk/return tradeoffs and attempt to maximize returns for whatever aggregate level of risk they choose to undertake.

1.2   THE GOAL OF ALM

From this discussion, a definition of the ultimate purpose of ALM emerges:

Goal of ALM: *To maximize the risk-adjusted returns to shareholders over the long run.*

This definition has three important components:

Risk-adjusted returns. This phrase relates to the strong positive correlation between the expected profitability of the bank and its overall risk structure. This linkage as it was depicted in Figure 1.1 will be emphasized over and over again throughout this book.

Shareholders. Bank managers speak loudly and often about their emphasis on shareholder value and their adopting more of a shareholder perspective. If so, then very specific behavior should be forthcoming. We shall see what this implies and whether most bankers are truly working in the interests of shareholders, in the interests of themselves, or whether they are simply placating regulators.

Long run. American industry and financial institutions are routinely criticized for their short-term focus. Ask any banker about his or her forecast of earnings and he or she will invariably talk about the current quarter or current year. As we will learn, the markets do not react favorably to high current earnings if that performance is not sustainable. What is the "long run"? This should be considered a period long enough to encompass at least one full business cycle. In baseball language, a player builds an outstanding career batting average by doing his best every single day. Like sophisticated investors, team general managers will pay players for consistent excellence, not on the basis of a few four-hit games.

To achieve our stated goal requires a much broader set of policies and methods than found in more conventional ALM discussions. To create value for shareholders with a practical asset and liability management approach, one must go beyond accounting earnings, beyond short-term forecasts, and beyond relying only on the simplest analytical techniques. ALM is a multidimensional set of activities. Decrease risk in one dimension and you have probably increased it in several others! Learning to cope with this is one of the major goals of this book.

1.3 TYPES OF RISK

What are the generic types of risks that bankers face? They can be classified into six popular categories: credit risk, interest rate risk, foreign exchange risk, liquidity risk, operating risk, and capital adequacy risk.

Credit risk. This is by far the most important of risk categories in banking. It is also the one risk area that traditionally has a large group of staff dedicated to its administration. A critical issue to examine is how credit administration and ALM should be coordinated to insure proper returns to shareholders. These linkages are growing stronger over time as more and more disciplines originating in asset and liability management are being applied in credit management, an area just as critical in the last decade as asset and liability management was in the 1975-1985 period in the United States.

Interest rate risk. This is the conventional ALM topic. Concerns about interest rate mismatches seem to rise when interest rate volatility increases or when the general level of rates is high. Like the options market, people often do not pay any attention to this discipline until it is too late to hedge the risk no one anticipated when times were good.

Foreign exchange risk. In this era of globalization and international activities, many banks are encountering significant exchange rate risk. Most international banks have multiple currency exposures, and all major industrial corporations do. This area promises to be very important in asset and liability management in the years ahead.

Liquidity risk. This refers to the risk that there will not be sufficient cash for normal operating requirements. It is probably the least understood of all the ALM risk areas, yet one of the most important.

Operating risk. This refers to the risk of losses or unexpected expenses associated with fraud, check kiting, litigation, etc.

Capital adequacy risk. This is a misnomer. Capital is merely a funding source, not a source of risk. Moreover, the emphasis on "capital adequacy" is very much a creation of the regulatory agencies and public policy considerations. Corporate financial theory asserts that the financing structure of any firm is irrelevant for a broad range of assumptions. However, considerable time will be devoted to the topic of capital both because we believe there is an "optimal capital structure" and because capital must be properly allocated in order to gauge whether returns are sufficient to satisfy shareholders or not. Hence, according to this framework, the primary risk associated with capital is that it is oftentimes improperly allocated (especially using regulatory allocations), resulting in misleading signals, poor pricing, and bad strategic decisions.

1.4   WHICH RISKS CAUSE BANKS TO FAIL?

Although not a specific focus of this book, it is useful to ask which of the risk areas just delineated most often lead to bank failures. From analyses we have seen, it is very clear which of the risk types is least responsible for the failures of banks and savings and loan institutions—and that is capital. Clearly, a bank funded solely with equity will have a difficult time going bankrupt, but saying a bank failed for lack of capital is a truism that provides little insight into the true original source of risk. This should not be surprising since we have already asserted that capital adequacy is not a bona fide risk type. Hence, inordinate attention to capital ratios may not be very effective in terms of improving the safety and soundness of the industry, unless those ratios are linked in a much more precise way to assess risk than they are in the current regulatory environment.

At least among large banking institutions, there are two main factors for failures: (1) the effects of significant credit losses, which in turn cause (2) a loss of liquidity when the marketplace realizes that these two risks have reduced the true market value of assets to levels where there is insufficient "cushion" to insure payment of liabilities. Credit losses alone will not cause a bank to fail if the depositors expect the government to support the institution or if the bank has little exposure to the wholesale markets for its funding needs. In the latter case, a bank can have enough losses to result in negative capital and still operate normally, as evidenced by many savings and loans, because retail investors tend to be less sensitive to bank credit quality. As long as it has funding (i.e., as long as suppliers of funds do not fully perceive the institution's risk), a financial institution will be viable. Like the greater fool theory, this is not a sound basis for long-term financial strategy, but it can be used to buy time in a crisis.

Can liquidity risk alone cause a bank to fail? Probably not. High liquidity risk can only arise in the first place if the markets have enough confidence in the bank to allow it to develop a large dependence on volatile funding sources. Indeed, "confidence" is almost a synonym for "liquidity." Without any other sources of risk, that confidence should not change. (One exception would be a general run on the banking industry as experienced in the 1930s, which can be viewed as a loss in confidence in the central bank. In that scenario, high liquidity risk banks would indeed fail before low liquidity risk banks.) To lose liquidity, some other source of risk must become apparent. Hence, liquidity risk alone would not lead to bank failures. Bankers often cite false rumors about a strong bank with an aggressive funding strategy. Such a bank will not fail if it proves the market wrong by repaying liabilities as scheduled. The biggest names in Hong Kong banking face this test regularly, and American bankers should be prepared to as well. It's the Missouri "show me" approach to liquidity risk management.

Among smaller banks, there are also numerous examples of fraud as a major factor in failures. Of course, among savings and loan institutions, interest rate risk has played a substantial role in the number of failures during the 1980s. A universally more conservative posture in the United States has made people less concerned about interest rate risk for the same reason that people no longer worry about tetanus and whooping cough: they take the proper precautions. Nonetheless, government "regulatory accounting" practices in the 1980s helped postpone the day when the people finally saw that the emperor of the savings and loan industry had no clothes. These clothes were not stolen. For the most part, management lost them placing bets at the interest rate casino. When you lose in that casino playing 30-year fixed rate mortgage roulette, you do not pay when you leave, you pay every year for 30 years. As a matter of fact, some savings and loans played double-or-nothing by lending in areas where risks were almost 100% correlated with interest rates (like real estate development and construction lending).

1.5   FINANCIAL ORGANIZATION STRUCTURE: WHO DOES ALM?

Three financial departments are usually very actively involved in various aspects of asset and liability management activities. They are the Controllers Department, the Budgeting (or Financial Planning) Department, and the ALM (or Financial Analysis or Forecasting) Department. Their responsibilities are defined as follows:

Controllers: Reports historical financial performance, and therefore establishes the current base balance sheet and income statement from which all risk analyses will be determined.

Budgeting: Establishes the current year financial objectives of the bank in terms of balance sheet volumes and revenues and expenses based upon a "most likely" set of assumptions for interest rates, market trends, and local economic and business cycle trends. This is usually a *bottom-up* process whereby individual units commit to specific financial objectives and the sum of the units determines the total bank goals.

ALM: Forecasts the bank's balance sheet, cash flows, and income statement given changes or variances in the bank's budget assumptions. That is, this area simulates the bank's financials should the base case assumptions turn out to be wrong—which is almost always the case! It gauges the sensitivity of the bank's earnings and balance sheet strength (in terms of asset quality, liquidity, and capital ratios) to *unexpected* changes in interest rates or market conditions. With such knowledge, the bank's management team can anticipate unfavorable circumstances and be ready to respond to them should they arise.

ALM is normally a *top-down* process. That is, it undertakes all analyses at the total bank level and sends signals to lower levels of the organization if adjustments are desired.

To summarize, it has been stated that:

- Controllers tell us where we have been;
- Budgeting tells us where we want to go; and,
- ALM tells us how we are going to get there!

1.6   THE ALM PROCESS

The last section reviewed the specific responsibilities of three of the departments typically found in a finance group or division of a bank. This section describes the overall steps involved in ALM as a process rather than as functions.

Policies and guidelines. This refers to setting up operating limits or boundaries for the risk-and-return trade-offs within which the bank feels it can safely operate. This establishes the risk tolerance of the organization. ALM risk limits and policies should be explained to and ratified by the board of directors. They should be recommended to the board by the Asset and Liability Committee (ALCO).

Analysis. This refers to determining the bank's current position in every risk dimension and where it is forecast to be for all future time periods. The critical issue is this: Is the bank currently outside of its risk limits? Or is it forecasted that the bank will move outside of its risk boundaries at some point in the future? These analyses are normally the responsibility of the ALM department.

Decisions. This is the responsibility of the bank's ALCO. If the bank is currently outside of its limits, or is forecasted to migrate outside of its limits, then a decision must be made as to how to correct the situation. There are two types of decisions that could conceivably be made. One is to attempt to adjust the current or future risk position of the bank by taking on some incremental securities positions or to alter the maturity structure of the future balance sheet through new pricing strategies or investment decisions. Hence, the ALCO could decide to alter the bank's balance sheet structure to prevent the risk measure in question from going beyond a risk limit.

Another legitimate, although rarer, decision is to determine if the old risk limits are still appropriate for the bank. Perhaps the business environment has changed, making the risk less hazardous. Or perhaps technological improvements allow more effective management of the risk. For whatever reason, it is possible that the ALCO recommend to the Board that the risk limits be permanently or temporarily altered due to new circumstances. Periodically, all risk limits should be reviewed for their appropriateness given constantly changing business conditions and strategies.

Execution. Whenever the ALCO decides to alter the risk profile of the bank, a set of incremental securities or off-balance sheet positions must often be undertaken. In such instances, it is normally the treasury, funding, or trading unit that would be responsible for executing the transactions. These are departments that normally interface with the markets and conduct such activities for the bank or its customers.

Evaluation. One of the major themes of this book is that proper accountability and performance measurement is critical to the successful implementation of ALM. The success or failure of the attempted adjustment to the bank's risk profiles must be determined in a timely, objective manner. This is usually done by either the ALM Department or Controller's Department. Never should the unit responsible for execution of positions be asked to provide the performance evaluation of their actions.

1.7   THE CHARACTERISTICS OF A SUCCESSFUL ASSET AND LIABILITY MANAGER

The successful asset and liability manager is a rare individual. As discussed in the Introduction, the general perception about the effectiveness of ALM in banks is very low. A common mistake many banks make is to oversimplify the task. Many banks will seek out or appoint one of three types of individual to assume the ALM responsibilities:

> Controller: An individual with a strong accounting background.

> Investments/Funding: A "street-wise" individual with significant market or "deal" experience.

> Rocket Scientist: An individual who can derive the Black-Scholes option pricing formula from scratch.

While all these backgrounds are helpful, none are sufficient for the task. ALM requires a unique blend of skills and characteristics. Some of the most important attributes are as follows:

Analysis. The individual must have a solid basic grasp of corporate financial theory and the concepts of economic risk and economic value. To achieve this actually involves attributes of all three of the types of individuals listed earlier. Good analyses should reveal all of the risk-return tradeoffs the bank must assess and manage. It also involves determining the risk aversion profile or risk preferences of the board and senior management. Basically, it addresses the questions: "How much risk are we willing to take in every dimension? Given our decision, how do we maximize long-term shareholder value within those limits?"

Accountability. The person should be meticulous and fair-dealing in reporting back to the ALCO and board of directors about the success or failure of the bank's risk management policies, strategies, and activities. Organizations that are open and frank about their failures will learn from them and become stronger in their ability to manage future similar situations. Of course, more often than not, the chances of achieving such an open atmosphere are very much a function of the management style of the CEO. In an ALCO situation, shooting messengers will definitely result in a less effective organization (as well as a scarcity of good messengers).

Teaching. ALM suffers from its veneer of esoteric theory. The best ALM practitioners are those who can convey the essence of risk and return trade-offs to the ALCO and board of directors such that all participants develop a proper understanding of how the risk profiles of the organization stand relative to its approved risk limits. This means that the asset and liability manager must be part educator as well. To do so well, strong verbal and written communications skills are a definite plus.

To put it succinctly, the asset and liability manager must be a person who is competent in basic theory, someone who is willing to be held accountable for his or her analyses and recommendations, and someone who can help others develop an intuitive understanding of the main issues and tradeoffs.

1.8 TAKE-HOME MESSAGES OF THIS BOOK

There are four main take-home messages that are summarized here. They will be reinforced throughout the remainder of this book.

1. Risk is multidimensional (risk types, conceptual approaches, target accounts, analytical techniques, time horizons, etc.).
2. Returns should always be assessed on a fully risk-adjusted basis.
3. Markets provide reliable and readily available measures of the "price" of risk.
4. Risk-adjusted return methods should be applied consistently across all assessment activities, including ALM studies for the total bank, new business proposals, capital budgeting analyses, unit performance measurement, product profitability, product pricing spreadsheets, incentive programs, etc.

1.9   SUMMARY

This chapter presented an overview of the goal of ALM, the types of risks that banks face, the organizational structure that addresses various aspects of ALM for the bank, and the process involved in the management of ALM. Later chapters will deal with more subtle aspects, including pitfalls of the process and its interrelationships with other important organizational activities, such as incentive setting and performance measurement.

An important distinction made in this chapter is that ALM is related more with understanding how individual business decisions and aggregate portfolio composition affect the bank's overall risk profiles, and how to risk-adjust a business unit's performance, than it is with identifying new profit opportunities for the bank or increasing its profitability. Better understanding of ALM theories and practices, implemented on a consistent basis across all financial decision-making in an organization, can lead to improved long-term profitability and shareholder value (stock price) performance. The remainder of this book is devoted to explaining these concepts.

CHAPTER 2

The Nature of Risk, Return, and Performance Measurement

Before delving into the analysis of the risk areas outlined in Chapter 1, it is important to establish clear, general definitions of the concepts of risk and return. These definitions will be applied to each of the risk types presented in the last chapter. These concepts will provide a critical foundation for all subsequent discussions on asset and liability management.

2.1   WHAT IS RISK?

This section will deal with a definition of **risk**. Later, this chapter will discuss the concept of **return**. Risk in any formal sense must reflect some concept of uncertainty. For our purposes, a simple definition is as follows:

> *Risk*: **The volatility (standard deviation) of net cash flows of a business unit.**

A business unit might be a department of the bank, such as a branch; a product type, such as residential mortgage loans; a single customer relationship; or the entire bank.

To illustrate the concept of volatility, consider two banks that have the same expected average net cash flows over the long run. While the averages are the same, the volatilities are quite different, as shown in Figure 2.1 and Figure 2.2.

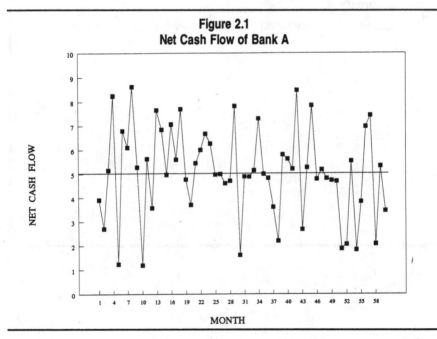

Figure 2.1
Net Cash Flow of Bank A

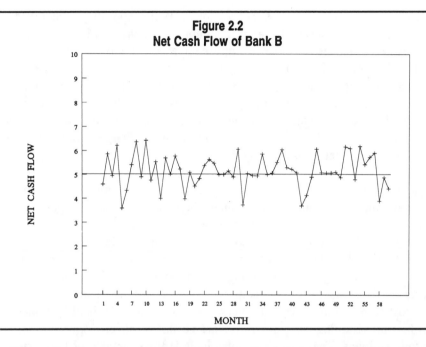

Figure 2.2
Net Cash Flow of Bank B

From the figures, it should be clear that Bank A has more "riskiness" in its financial results than Bank B. The "riskiness" attribute for each of these banks can be quantified as the standard deviation of the net cash flows over a long period (at least one business cycle).

The concept of net cash flow deserves explanation through a definition that reflects actual cash transactions as simply as possible. Instead of referring to the conventional definition of cash flow as required by FASB #95 or as discussed in accounting textbooks, it is suggested that all noncash accounting entries be removed from every business unit's financial results, and that many of these be replaced by their cash counterpart. Some of the most important of these include the provision for credit losses (replaced by actual chargeoffs), FASB #91 loan fee deferrals (replaced by total cash fees collected during the period), goodwill amortization, amortization of other intangibles, any mark-to-market entries such as for assets held for sale, and the provision for income taxes (replaced by the taxes derived from the current marginal tax rate).

Some readers may have noticed that we have not yet mentioned depreciation, which is usually the first item to be discussed when adjusting financial statements to determine cash flows. Ideally, the net cash flows of any business unit should be adjusted as if all fixed assets, especially premises, were leased on a month-to-month basis where the lease rate is adjusted to current market rates every month. While appropriate in theory, this is simply not practical for a large number of business units, such as the hundreds of branches in some banking companies. A simple alternative is to classify each facility into one of four or five current price ranges for leases and to impute an estimated lease cost for each branch based upon its square footage. An even simpler alternative is to go ahead and recognize the actual lease payments or scheduled depreciation as rough approximations for current market lease rates. (Some form of charge should be estimated on any property that is fully depreciated.)

It is highly recommended that the financials for all business units be prepared on a cash basis for budgeting and performance measurement purposes, and that all accounting adjustments be booked in one segregated unit in the Controller's Department. (The one exception could be premises expense, where the adjustments are sometimes maintained in a property management unit.) Numerous situations exist where business managers have recommended changes in accounting assumptions or methods because the effects on their financial statements would be favorable in the near term. The most common of these controversies usually centers around how much loan loss provisioning or loss reserves are needed to cover a specific unit's portfolio of loans. Two other examples include the estimates of loan origination expense to be deferred under FASB #91 and the assumptions used in recognizing excess servicing rights or for accreting discounts. Such decisions should not alter the perception of the perfor-mance of any line unit. To prevent line managers from spending unproductive time debating such points, their units should be viewed on a purely cash basis so that they neither benefit nor lose because of the specific accounting assumptions adopted.

The mathematical definition of volatility recommended is the standard deviation of net cash flows. This is one of the most elementary statistical definitions of volatility. It is calculated from the following equation:

$$Standard\ Deviation = \sqrt{\frac{\sum_{i=1}^{n}(CF_i - CF_{avg})^2}{n-1}}$$

$$where\ CF_i = Cash\ Flow\ at\ Period\ i$$
$$CF_{avg} = Average\ Cash\ Flow$$

Fortunately, most financial calculators and computer spreadsheet software contain automatic functions to calculate this equation.

For those readers conversant in corporate financial theory, a more rigorous definition of risk would be something like "the covariance matrix of returns with the market." This technical definition would encompass the notion that markets only expect returns based upon the systematic, or non-diversifiable, risks when compared to the full range of investment alternatives in the entire marketplace. Unfortunately, such a concept is difficult and laborious to evaluate for all business units, whereas net cash flows are much more readily available. Some of the subtleties of correlation coefficients and diversification will be explored at some length in Chapter 4.

2.2   What Is Return?

Most bankers associate the concept of "returns" with the following common measurements: net income, return on assets, and return on equity. They then go on to debate which of these three is the best indicator of return. Each of these measures has serious weaknesses as a measure of performance. Returns should be measured in terms of cash flows or market values, rather than in accounting terms. To facilitate this presentation, we will discuss each of the conventional concepts, then expand the discussion for a shareholder-oriented alternative.

Keep in mind that the perspective here is twofold: decision-making (ex ante) and performance measurement (ex post). Thus, we are seeking a measure of return that can be used when confronted with a set of new business opportunities, and all we have are expected, or forecasted, risks and returns. With each of the measures of return we consider here, we will assess the type of behavior that would reasonably result if that particular measure was the primary performance measure.

Net Income. First consider this most common of all measures of return or profitability. It is presumed that virtually all proposed business transactions show positive expected earnings over the life of the activity, or they would not be considered. (For now, do not consider complicated multi-product relationships.) As a consequence, using net income as the performance measure results in business units accepting essentially all opportunities. Hence, everything will be accepted. This simplistic behavior violates the stated goal of ALM, which is to maximize **risk-adjusted returns** to shareholders. Net income, especially on an accounting basis, tends to ignore or understate the risk consequences, at least in the early phases of the activity.

Return on assets. This return concept has traditionally been of considerable importance because of the banking industry's fixation with asset levels or "footings." The problems with taking the ratio of earnings to total assets are twofold. First, some activities do not have conventional balance sheet measures. Examples include trust, cash management, securities sales, and the sale of cashier's checks or safe deposit box rentals. For these, there is no "A" in ROA.

The second problem is that the simplest and fastest way to improve ROA is to shrink one's portfolio of business. There is little incentive to seek out any new business, unless the new opportunity improves the average ROA of the unit. Therefore, the new activity must demonstrate an expected ROA above the average for the current portfolio, which is, at best, an arbitrary standard.

Return on equity. This measure has some intrinsic advantages over net income and ROA, but it also has some serious pitfalls, too. Its strength is that it is a step toward a risk-adjusted return concept. However, as with using ROA, the easiest way to improve ROE is to shrink one's portfolio and return the equity that supported that forgone business. Again, no new business will be accepted unless it surpasses the current average ROE of the business unit.

To summarize, net income is a signal to grow without proper recognition of the long-term risk implications involved, whereas ROA and ROE are signals to shrink or forgo opportunities to achieve higher ratios. Is there any measure that overcomes these defects? Fortunately, the answer is yes.

2.3   SHAREHOLDER VALUE ADDED

This section is a variation on the work of Joel Stern and Bennett Stewart, who popularized the "economic value added" concept. For a discussion of economic value added, see *The Quest for Value* by Stewart.

> *Shareholder Value Added ("SVA"):* **Dollar earnings in excess of the hurdle return on "economic" capital.**

This definition leads to some new concepts, such as the hurdle rate and "economic" capital. Both are discussed below.

Hurdle rate. The hurdle rate is composed of a risk-free rate (often repre- sented as the yield on the current Treasury long bond) and a risk premium. The average risk premium for the aggregate marketplace of equities is around 7% to 8%. Assume for the sake of discussion that it is 7%. Since large banks represent a cross section of the economy in their aggregate lending and investment activities, their risk premiums will be close to that of the aggregate marketplace. Finally, given that current long bond yields are around 8%, this implies that the hurdle rate for typical large banks is about 15%. Again, for simplicity, assume that this is a good approximation of the hurdle rate for banks. (Refer to Chapter 4 for further discussions on administering the hurdle rate concept.)

Return on economic capital (ROEC). This concept revolves around the no- tion of economic capital allocations to business units. It implies that one should ignore both the actual accounting equity of the bank as well as current regulatory capital standards in determining performance. This issue will be covered considerably in Chapters 3 and 4. Assuming that the capi- tal allocation reflects some estimate of the risks being undertaken by the business unit, then ROEC represents the earnings of the unit divided by the capital allocated to it. (See Appendix 2A for a detailed example of the calculation of ROEC and SVA.)

Since the SVA concept is related to a dollar amount of earnings above a threshold, it does not suffer from the shrinkage syndrome of ratio meas- ures such as ROA and ROE. It promotes finding good opportunities as well as ceasing inadequate activities. Since it establishes a hurdle concept, it recognizes the risk attributes of the potential activity up front. We shall learn how these features drastically alter the decision-making process by the use of a case study in the next section.

2.4   CASE STUDY ON PROFITABILITY MEASURES

Let us now illustrate the various profitability measures presented above by creating a new business unit from scratch. On the first day of business, there are six new one-year lending opportunities that are presented by the account officers. They are summarized as follows in Table 2.1:

Table 2.1
List of Case Study Opportunities

Opportunity Number	1	2	3	4	5	6
Loan Amount	$100	100	100	100	100	100
Economic Capital	$5	5	5	5	5	5
Net Income	$2.00	1.00	0.50	0.25	0.10	0.05

To simplify further, assume that all of these opportunities have exactly the same credit risk and operating expenses. All of the proposed borrowers are in the same business and will use the loans for the same purpose. The different earnings expectations result only from the different pricing (yields) on the loans. (This could be attributed to the competitive pricing situation in six different geographic locations.) Hence, it is reasonable to assume that the volatility of net cash flows will be identical. Thus, the allocated economic capital will be the same for all six opportunities.

The issue faced is to decide which, if any, of the proposed activities should be accepted by the business unit. We can accept none of the six, only one, or any number up to all six. To aid the decision, calculate the expected profitability of each under all of the measures discussed, starting with SVA. Calculate the expected shareholder value added from each proposal using the following procedure used in Table 2.2.

Table 2.2
Calculation of SVA

Opportunity Number	1	2	3	4	5	6
Hurdle Rate	15%	15%	15%	15%	15%	15%
Economic Capital	$5	5	5	5	5	5
Hurdle Income	$0.75	0.75	0.75	0.75	0.75	0.75
Net Income	$2.00	1.00	0.50	0.25	0.10	0.05
SVA	$1.25	0.25	(0.25)	(0.50)	(0.65)	(0.70)

Notice that the hurdle rate and allocated capital are identical in every opportunity. Again, this is consistent with the identical risk characteristics of each. From the hurdle rate of 15% and the economic capital of $5, it is clear that the hurdle income level is the product of the two, or $0.75. The SVA in this simple case study is the difference between the expected net income and hurdle income for each proposal.

Summarize the expected profitability of each transaction using each of the profitability measures shown in Table 2.3.

Table 2.3
Profitability of Each Opportunity

Opportunity Number:	1	2	3	4	5	6
Net Income	$2.00	1.00	0.50	0.25	0.10	0.05
ROA	2.00%	1.00%	0.50%	0.25%	0.10%	0.05%
ROE	40.0%	20.0%	10.0%	5.0%	2.0%	1.0%
SVA	$1.25	0.25	(0.25)	(0.50)	(0.65)	(0.70)

First, all three measures give a consistent ranking of the opportunities from the most desirable (#1) to the least (#6). This simplifies the decision-making process. Accepting the first three opportunities and forgoing the others is possible, but never accept numbers 4, 5, and 6 while forgoing 1, 2, and 3. Hence, limit possible decisions to the following six portfolios, or combinations, of loans in Table 2.4.

Table 2.4
Summary of Profitability Measures

Portfolio #:	1	2	3	4	5	6
Number of Loans	1	2	3	4	5	6
Total Assets	$100	200	300	400	500	600
Total Capital	$5	10	15	20	25	30
Net Income	$2.00	3.00	3.50	3.75	3.85	3.90
ROA	2.00%	1.50%	1.33%	0.94%	0.77%	0.65%
ROE	40.0%	30.0%	23.3%	18.8%	15.4%	13.0%
SVA	$1.25	1.50	1.25	0.75	$0.10	($0.60)

Given these outcomes, the decisions under various profitability measures are clear. Using net income, the unit would accept all six proposals. Under the ROA or ROE measures, only the first transaction would be undertaken. To accept any more would lower the unit's apparent ROA or ROE profitability. Notice that both net income and ROA/ROE send extreme signals to the organization to either grow as much as possible or stay as small as possible.

In contrast, the SVA signal tells the unit to accept the first two opportunities and forgo the rest. As is evident from Table 2.2, the first two proposals are the only ones with positive incremental SVA. The rest show negative SVAs; that is, they lose shareholder value.

The concept that SVA represents is that it is not sufficient for each new business opportunity to show positive expected earnings. Shareholders require a minimum rate of return on their investment in the bank, and that is the hurdle or required return on capital. This is the return they need to compensate them for the risk they take by investing in the bank.

Therefore, every set of activities undertaken by the bank should be expected to return something above and beyond this minimum return: SVA. In this sense, SVA represents the earnings expected by the bank in excess of that needed to cover the hurdle or required level. **Only with positive incremental SVA is the bank being properly compensated for the risk it undertakes with any potential business opportunity.**

Later chapters will show how to determine the hurdle rate and how to allocate capital and will deal with such issues as business opportunities with different risk levels or different hurdle rates.

2.5   DISTINCTION BETWEEN SVA AND PORTFOLIO ROE

At this point, it is worthwhile to discuss the difference between using the SVA measure compared to using a "minimum portfolio ROE" concept. That is, why not simply announce that the hurdle ROE for all business units is, for example, 15%, and that the goal of the unit is to maximize net income while maintaining a minimum portfolio ROE of at least 15%?

To discuss this, refer back to Table 2.4. To maximize earnings while establishing a portfolio ROE above 15%, this line unit would be expected to accept the first five proposals, ending up with a portfolio ROE of 15.4%. However, we have already established that alternatives #3, 4, and 5 lose shareholder value, since they do not provide sufficient earnings to cover the required hurdle rate.

The correct decision was to accept only opportunities #1 and #2. This results in a portfolio ROE of 30%. Indeed, whenever the SVA signal is utilized, the portfolio ROE will usually be substantially higher than the hurdle rate, in this case 15%. Furthermore, it is not possible to predict what the value-maximizing portfolio ROE should be. That will be a function of all of the specific value-creating opportunities available to the bank.

2.6   SUMMARY

This chapter shows that the most rational performance measure is not the simple dollar amount of earnings, such as net income, since that will result in accepting virtually all proposals that hint at the prospect of any profit at all, regardless of risk. Nor is it ROA or ROE, which are simple ratios, and which often result in simply attempting to shrink or forgo potentially good opportunities.

The best measure is a hybrid concept: to maximize the dollar amount of earnings in excess of the hurdle return on capital. It is no accident that this definition is the only one that is consistent with the goal of ALM: to maximize the risk-adjusted return to shareholders over the long run. **SVA is a valid measure of the risk-adjusted return to shareholders. It will be consistent with our goal of ALM as long as it is applied as a long-run concept.** This will be discussed further in Chapter 4.

APPENDIX 2A: DETAILED CALCULATION OF SVA CASH FLOWS

This appendix offers a detailed calculation of the cash flows needed for SVA calculations and capital allocations. It simply lists the adjustments that may be undertaken to arrive at a more economic concept of "earnings" than normally used in calculating ROE.

Start With: **Accounting Pretax Income**

Remove: Any allocated or actual loan loss provision

Add In: Current chargeoffs net of recoveries

Remove: Depreciation and historic lease cost on all fixed assets

Add In: Current market lease rate on all fixed assets

Remove: Goodwill amortization expense

Remove: Other amortizations such as loan fees, servicing rights

Add In: Adjustment for equity in excess of target at a marginal
              cost appropriate for the bank to fund in the national
              funding markets

Remove: Book tax provision

Add In: Income tax expense at full marginal cash tax rate

Results In: **Cash flow for capital allocation calculations**

In our experience, all of these adjustments are simple with the possible exception of the lease and depreciation adjustments. These are only refinements that should not skew the capital allocations and can easily be ignored if they prove to be too burdensome.

CHAPTER

3

Capital Regulation

Chapter 2 established that capital represents the bank's cushion against unexpected losses or cash flow volatility. Proper assignment of capital is critical to establishing a correct hurdle and measuring shareholder value added (SVA).

Many bankers believe that capital allocations are important, but when confronted with the task, they become confused by regulatory capital standards. This chapter will review some of the background leading up to the current situation of regulation by capital, and will point out some of the pitfalls of blindly following regulatory capital standards to determine pricing and performance hurdles. The next chapter will offer simpler and more effective approaches to capital allocations and value determination.

3.1   FOUNDATIONS OF BANKING SAFETY AND SOUNDNESS

Until about 1980, the basis for banking safety and soundness was a three-tiered system designed in the 1930s in response to the last major run on the nation's banking system. That concept worked quite well for about 50 years. It is depicted in Figure 3.1.

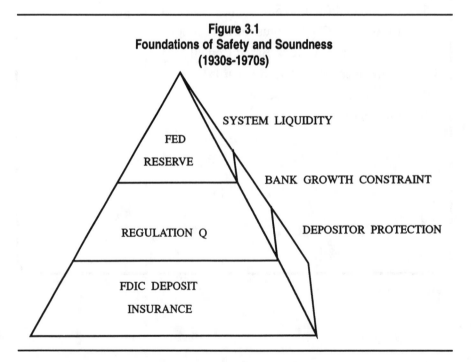

Figure 3.1
Foundations of Safety and Soundness
(1930s-1970s)

SYSTEM LIQUIDITY

FED
RESERVE

BANK GROWTH CONSTRAINT

REGULATION Q

DEPOSITOR PROTECTION

FDIC DEPOSIT
INSURANCE

At the highest level, the Federal Reserve banks provide emergency liquidity to the entire banking system. This "lender of last resort" function is designed to maintain market confidence at both national and international levels. Whenever a short-term financial disruption occurs, such as the deposit run on Continental Illinois in 1984 or the market crash of 1987, the Federal Reserve provides additional liquidity to the financial sector to reassure investors and depositors that they will continue to have normal access to their funds and will have the ability to conduct their desired financial transactions.

At the next level, the national banking laws created a measure intended to prevent "unsafe" or speculative growth by individual banking organizations. Specifically, Regulation Q limited what banks and savings and loans could pay for deposits under $100,000. For many years, these limits were about 5.00% or 5.25% and were applied to savings accounts. The theory was that if banks were prevented from offering high rates for deposits, they would not be able to grow in a speculative or an irresponsible manner.

Finally, the concept of federal insurance on deposits was implemented so that individual savers would not need to be concerned about the financial stability of their local bank or savings institution. This was the responsibility of the FDIC and FSLIC.

Notice that safety is assured at three critical levels or tiers: confidence by individual savers, constraints at the level of risk-taking by individual banks, and confidence in the general banking system. This structure functioned quite well from the mid-1930s, when it was created, through the entire 1970s.

Unfortunately, events in the 1970s set into motion the demise of Regulation Q as a viable approach to constraining bank risk. The emergence of technology and communications to allow Money Market Mutual Funds (MMMFs) to sweep up small deposits and invest them in large certificates of deposit (over $100,000) to earn a higher interest rate started massive disintermediation within the banking industry after inflation led to a sharp rise in interest rate levels.

A whole new industry emerged whose main function was to gather small deposits away from local banks and deposit them at a much higher interest rate, wherever the highest rate could be found in the country. Of course, what was preventing banks from paying open market rates for small deposits was Regulation Q. To reverse the disintermediation, Regulation Q had to be phased out and a substitute found as a regulatory growth constraint.

3.2   CAPITAL REGULATION REPLACES REGULATION Q

The concept of official minimum capital standards was created in the early
1980s as the new risk-constraining mechanism in the banking industry.
The necessity for this action arose from the official phase-out of Regulation Q with the 1980 passage of the Financial Deregulation and Monetary
Control Act. Hence, the post-1980 concept for the safety and soundness of
the banking industry is depicted in Figure 3.2 as follows.

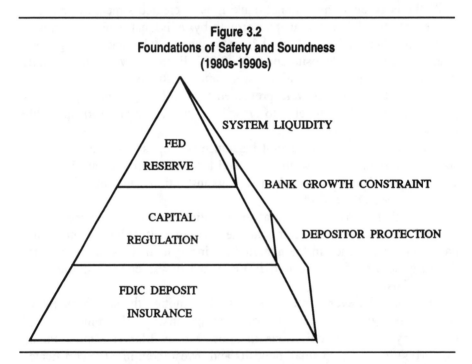

Figure 3.2
Foundations of Safety and Soundness
(1980s-1990s)

SYSTEM LIQUIDITY

FED
RESERVE

BANK GROWTH CONSTRAINT

CAPITAL
REGULATION

DEPOSITOR PROTECTION

FDIC DEPOSIT
INSURANCE

Rather than relying on deposit price restrictions to limit the growth rate
of banks and savings institutions, the regulatory agencies decided to focus
on capital standards as their primary risk-constraining mechanism.

The first issue that the regulators had to face was a definition of capital.
Since many of the larger regional banks and most of the money center
banks were very highly levered in the 1970s, the regulatory agencies opted
for a definition of capital that would facilitate an orderly buildup of the
regulatory capital ratios. To do so, they devised the notion of "primary
capital."

3.3   PRIMARY CAPITAL: A PRESCRIPTION FOR HIGHER RISK

To simplify this discussion, concentrate on the main components of primary capital, rather than its many details and complexities. (This will be true of the treatment of all regulatory capital concepts. These simplifications do not materially alter the conclusions reached.) The major components of primary capital were:

- Common Equity and Retained Earnings
- Perpetual Preferred Stock
- Loan Loss Reserve
- Mandatory Convertible Notes (MCNs)

The last item in this list was most indicative of the regulator's intent to allow for the orderly buildup of capital ratios. These MCNs, which were split between equity contract notes and equity commitment notes, were long-term debt instruments that would either be redeemed directly by an exchange of common stock or indirectly from the proceeds of the issuance of stock. In other words, MCNs were nothing more than "plain vanilla" debt coupled with the promise of the future issuance of stock. Of course, the debt itself had absolutely no loss absorption potential, and therefore, did not represent capital in any conventional sense, just the promise of new capital to be issued sometime over the next 10 to 12 years.

What happened to the banking industry as a result of the implementation of the primary capital standards? Ironically, all of the evidence suggests that a much higher risk structure resulted. That is, rather than acting as a risk constraint, this concept may have contributed to even riskier bank balance sheets.

The major trends that emerged as a result of primary capital are summarized as follows:

Decrease in liquid assets. The pressure to improve capital ratios while improving earnings streams led to a predictable decline in the holdings of lower-yielding liquid assets, such as federal funds sold, Treasury bills, and short-term Eurodollar placements. Hence, there was a significant decline in the asset liquidity of the industry. Chapter 11 will discuss the critical importance of balance sheet liquidity to the stability of the banking industry.

Sale of fixed assets. During the early 1980s, many banking companies decided to cash in on their holdings of major real estate assets. A common occurrence was the sale of the headquarters building with a concomitant booking of a large loan loss provision to absorb the gain. This strategy contained a double benefit in that it converted the hidden equity in the building into regulatory capital, but it also avoided the book tax provision on the gain and got the entire pretax gain into primary capital. (A corollary to this action was the sale of any other long-term assets, such as certain investment securities, at a gain.)

Increase in off-balance sheet activities. This period saw the explosion of off-balance sheet risk by banks as sources of revenue that did not require capital. Standby letters of credit, loan commitments, interest rate swaps, foreign exchange contracts, among others, were all "competitively" priced (i.e., underpriced) and sold in large quantities. There is little doubt that the rush to find off-balance sheet sources of revenues ensured that banks would not be properly compensated for the risks they were taking.

All in all, it does not appear that the interests of safety and soundness were at all well served by the implementation of primary capital. Indeed, one could make a strong case that the riskiness of the industry increased as a direct result of this concept.

Why did primary capital not work? Simply, the concept did not reflect actual financial risk. Any capital measure that ignores true economic risk is bound to misfire, as this one did. As another piece of evidence about bank safety and soundness in the 1980s, consider Figure 3.3.

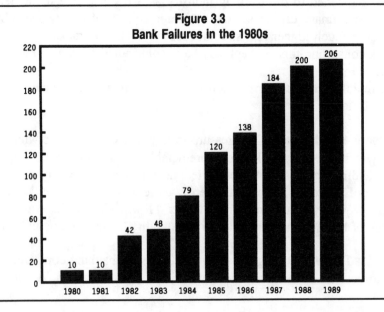

Figure 3.3
Bank Failures in the 1980s

Figure 3.3 shows that the rate of bank failures increased dramatically during all of the 1980s. (Of course, the S&L situation was even worse.) For comparison, Figure 3.4 illustrates that the failure rate of insured institutions outstripped any decade since the 1930s. (*Note*: This figure only shows the failures of FDIC insured banks. During the early 1930s, many thousands of uninsured banks failed as well.)

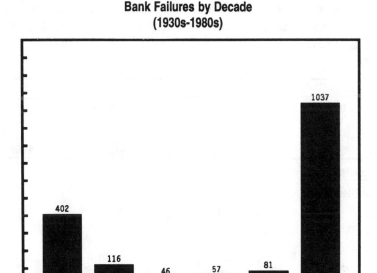

Figure 3.4
Bank Failures by Decade
(1930s-1980s)

Although primary capital should not be solely blamed for these results, this form of regulatory capital did not have any significant effect in decreasing the number or rate of bank failures. The next chapter will offer a view of the major reason for the dramatic increase in bank failures during the 1980s.

3.4   THE DESIRE TO LEVEL THE INTERNATIONAL PLAYING FIELD

By the mid-1980s, a number of problems with primary capital and the use of regulatory capital in this country were being voiced. Among them were some of the points already discussed:

■ Decrease in liquid assets

■ Increase in off-balance sheet risk

■ Sale of long-term assets to recognize gains

Another common complaint among U.S. bankers at the time was the "unfairness" of U.S. regulators in adopting any capital regulations at all while the large international banks in other countries were allowed to lever significantly more than U.S. banks. On numerous occasions, it was common to hear senior executives from the money center banks complain about their loss of stature and competitiveness as supported by exhibits such as Table 3.1.

Table 3.1
Largest 25 Banks in the World by Country

Country	1970	1980	1987
North America:			
United States	8	4	1
Canada	3	1	0
Asia:			
Japan	4	7	17
Europe:			
United Kingdom	3	3	2
West Germany	2	3	1
France	2	6	4
Italy	3	0	0
Other:			
Brazil	0	1	0

Invariably, they cited the ability of foreign banks to lever their balance sheets more than U.S. banks. As one piece of evidence, consider the data in Table 3.2 showing the book capital ratios of the largest banks in the world. The argument asserted that the West German and Japanese banks had a competitive advantage due to their propensity to lever up their book equity, as evidenced by the low book equity ratios of their largest banks.

Table 3.2
Capital Ratio Summary for Large International Banks
(As of December 31, 1986)

Country	Book Equity Ratio	Market Capital Ratio	Market/Book Ratio
Switzerland	5.7%	18.9%	330%
United States	5.6%	4.9%	88%
United Kingdom	5.2%	4.8%	92%
Canada	5.1%	4.3%	84%
W. Germany	3.0%	8.6%	287%
Japan	2.6%	17.0%	654%

Note: Averages for largest 100 banks in the world.

However, book equity ratios are hardly the entire story. Notice in Table 3.2 the market capital ratios. (*Note*: The concept of market capital ratios is defined in Chapter 4. For now, this column may be interpreted as an estimated market value of capital divided by an estimate of the mark-to-market value of assets.) This column tells an entirely different story . . . and it is one of the important themes of this book. **Accounting balance sheet values are oftentimes seriously misleading and should not be used to evaluate or manage risk!** Market prices and market capital provide far more effective indicators of risk and value than accounting or "book" values, an idea which will be expanded upon in Chapter 4.

Table 3.2 indicates that the equity markets were discounting the value of U.S. bank assets relative to the asset values in Japanese or West German banks. The markets were estimating that the true (mark-to-market) equity positions in both Japanese and West German banks were significantly stronger than those in large U.S. banks. Thus, U.S. banks turn out to be more highly levered than the very foreign competition most complained about!

Nevertheless, bankers in the United States perceived that they were at a competitive disadvantage and were quite vocal about it. These authors do not agree with that assessment.

3.5   RISK-BASED CAPITAL: SALVATION OR PANACEA?

In 1986, the Federal Reserve Bank and the Bank of England issued the first regulatory capital proposal to address all of the weaknesses in primary capital. It was called "Risk-Based Capital" (RBC). This was the first example of a potential multinational accord on capital standards.

It is beyond the scope of this book to go into the many details of these calculations and guidelines. However, to explain the concept, we will present a highly abbreviated overview of the rules as they will exist after December 31, 1992. Readers should not rely on this presentation as being comprehensive—it is not. RBC rules are extremely complex in practice due to their detail and volume.

Before assessing the prospects for the success of RBC, do not lose sight of the reasons for its creation: the specific shortcomings of primary capital. They can be summarized as follows:

■ To distinguish among the general riskiness of the major asset classes.

■ To reflect off-balance sheet risks in capital ratios.

■ To achieve consistency in capital standards among international banks.

While RBC does address these specific defects, there remain other more subtle and equally serious shortcomings with RBC. However, before proceeding, consider an illustration of the RBC procedures and calculations.

3.6   RISK-BASED CAPITAL: ILLUSTRATIVE EXAMPLE

To illustrate the concept of RBC, consider a bank with the simplified balance sheet components shown in Table 3.3.

For conventional book equity-to-asset ratio, simply divide shareholders' equity by total assets. In this example, GAAP total assets would be $400 million and the equity ratio is 5.00%.

There are three steps in calculating the risk-based capital ratios. First, assign the risk weightings to the different assets. Second, assign conversion factors and risk weightings to the various off-balance sheet items. Third, determine the capital accounts. Table 3.4 summarizes the first two steps for the illustrative example.

The risk weighting categories under the RBC guidelines are the four listed in the table: 0%, 20%, 50%, and 100%. All asset and off-balance

Table 3.3
Risk-Based Capital Illustrative Example
ABC Bank ($ millions)

Assets:

Commercial Loans	$200
Mortgages	100
Loan Loss Allowance	(5)
Funds Sold	50
Treasury Notes	55
Total Assets	$400

Off-Balance Sheet Items:

Unused Loan Commitments	$50
Standby LCs	20

Capital Components:

Common Equity & Surplus	$20
Loan Loss Allowance	5

Table 3.4
Calculation of Risk-Adjusted Assets
($ Millions)

	Nominal Amounts	Conversion Factors	Risk Weightings	Risk-Weighted Asset Equivalents
Assets:				
Commercial Loans	$200	—	100%	$200
Mortgages	100	—	50%	50
Federal Funds Sold	50	—	20%	10
Treasury Notes	55	—	0%	0
Off-Balance Sheet Items:				
Unused Commitments	$50	50%	100%	$25
Standby LCs	10	100%	100%	10
		Total Risk-Weighted Assets . . .		$295

sheet categories treated by RBC are assigned to one of these four weightings.

To convert the nominal amount of off-balance sheet contracts (including futures, swaps, and foreign exchange contracts) to an on-balance sheet equivalent, conversion factor procedures were developed. The illustrative example in Table 3.4 avoids some of the more difficult conversion procedures. Suffice it to point out that the risk-adjustment for off-balance sheet items is a two-step process: conversion factors and risk-weightings.

The third step in calculating the risk-based capital ratios is determining the capital accounts. There are two classifications of capital under risk-based capital: Tier 1 and Tier 2. Tier 1 capital is also referred to as "Core Capital." Tier 2 capital is called "Supplementary Capital." The sum of Tiers 1 and 2 is referred to as "Total Capital."

For our purposes, define Tier 1 capital as tangible common equity. Tier 2 capital is composed of all other qualifying forms of capital, such as perpetual cumulative preferred stock, the loan loss allowance, and qualify-

Table 3.5
RBC Calculations for Illustrative Example ($ Millions)

	Core Capital	Total Capital
Capital Components:		
Common Equity	$ 20.00	$ 20.00
Loan Loss Allowance		5.00
Less: Disqualified Allowance	_____	−1.31
Totals	$ 20.00	$ 23.69
Asset Components:		
Risk-Weighted Assets		$295.00
Less: Disqualified Allowance		−1.31
Net Risk-Weighted Assets		$293.69
Capital Ratios:	6.81%	8.07%

ing forms of long-term debt. Unfortunately, there are a plethora of rules and limitations regarding how much of each of the Tier 2 components may be included as capital.

In our example, one of the more important limitations takes effect. This one limits the amount of the loan loss allowance that qualifies as Tier 2 capital to 1.25% of total risk-weighted assets. Since risk-weighted assets were $295 million, the qualifying amount of allowance that qualifies is 1.25% of that amount, or $3.69 million. The residual, disqualified amount is $5.00 million − $3.69 million, or $1.31 million of the loan loss allowance. This amount is excluded from the capital accounts. Finally, whatever amount of allowance that is excluded or disqualified from Tier 2 capital is also deducted from risk-adjusted assets. The final calculations of the RBC ratios for this example are shown in Table 3.5.

The minimum RBC ratio standards are 4.00% for core capital and 8.00% for total capital. This example bank would meet both standards.

3.7 SHORTCOMINGS OF RISK-BASED CAPITAL

RBC does specifically address the weaknesses of primary capital in that it does begin to reflect risk, capture some off-balance sheet activities, and standardize international capital standards. However, there remain serious additional shortcomings. Some are summarized as follows:

Credit is not the only risk. RBC reflects only one risk type: credit risk. For example, both 90-day Treasury bills and 30-year Treasury bonds are given 0% risk weightings. This is accurate and acceptable if credit risk was the only risk type in existence. However, no portfolio manager would assign the same riskiness to a T-bill and a Treasury "long bond." The interest rate risk differential between these two items is massive and should not be ignored. Indeed, RBC completely ignores interest rate, liquidity, foreign exchange, and operating risks. Regulatory agencies are certainly aware of these omissions. They promise to release future additional rules to capture at least some of these other risk types.

Credit risk among loans is (almost) ignored. RBC only addresses "generic" credit risk. That is, it acknowledges that cash or T-bills have lower credit risk than commercial loans, or that general obligation bonds have lower credit risk than revenue bonds. However, it almost totally ignores the riskiness of the loan portfolio. Exceptions are that it gives a 50% weighting to residential mortgages and it recognizes loans collateralized by cash or government securities, but all other loans to the private sector are classified in the 100% category. Hence, the only social benefit gained from the complicated machinations of RBC is to remove the incentive to decrease liquid assets. It does not attempt to assess the major credit risk area of the bank: the loan portfolio. (*Note*: Regulatory agencies have always endeavored to avoid any hint of credit allocation; hence, their reluctance to deal with this issue.)

Accounting capital definitions are used. This point will be the topic of the next chapter. Briefly, financial statements simply do not provide reliable estimates of true capital or risk. Indeed, it is recommended that GAAP equity levels be ignored for all true risk assessments! Capital market participants expend large amounts of time and energy attempting to understand the overall risk profile of all publicly traded entities. Hence, market capital ratios are easier to obtain and far more reliable than ratios based on variations of GAAP values. This will be expanded in the next chapter.

Due to these shortcomings, blind application of the RBC guidelines can lead to misleading capital allocations and pricing hurdles. Although the intentions of the regulatory agencies in these various capital standards are good and well-founded, and the risk-based capital concept is a major improvement over primary capital, the good intentions of the regulatory agencies to shore up the safety and soundness of the industry could backfire, as they did with primary capital. That is, they could inadvertently lead to worse risk-management and pricing decisions than if the RBC regulations were never implemented. Chapter 4 explains this position in detail.

3.8   CONSEQUENCES OF RBC STANDARDS

What does RBC portend for the banking industry? Some results are apparent and predictable. They can be classified as follows:

Cost of implementing and using RBC. The first consequence to the industry is the cost of measuring RBC ratios. Literally thousands of "person-hours" are being spent in every major banking organization, and hundreds of thousands of dollars are being spent modifying applications and accounting systems in many banks, just to perform the RBC calculations. It is estimated that the total expenditure being incurred by the United States (including banks, regulators, analysts, investors, and journalists) is in the billions of dollars to measure, assess, and comply with these capital standards. Do the benefits outweigh the costs? These authors are somewhat skeptical about this issue.

Yet more emphasis on accounting measures of capital. If regulatory agencies insist on playing in the GAAP arena, banks will naturally focus only on those rules. The next chapter expands on this point. For now, let us assert that in the long run, economics and market efficiency must prevail. The sooner bankers focus their endeavors on true market concepts and values, the sooner they can begin to reverse the adverse trends that have developed.

The loophole game. As with any regulatory constraint on doing business, there is a direct incentive to "minimize" the consequences of RBC on bank activities. One example will suffice. Many loan commitments contain clauses that pricing on the facility may be increased to reflect the cost of additional regulatory burdens, such as reserve requirements or capital rules. Neither banks nor their customers want to see such provisions invoked. Hence, they both have an incentive to renegotiate their loan agreement to minimize the consequences of RBC. One way to do this is to institute "evergreen" 364-day loan commitments. This is due to the conversion factor for unused loan commitments that is applied only to facilities with an original maturity of one year or more. Therefore, a commitment for 364 days, but which rolls over every day for another 364-day period, technically escapes any capital burden. Who wins in this game? Neither banks nor their corporate customers are better off; the only winners are the lawyers who renegotiate these loan contracts!

So, where does this leave the industry? The results are as follows: a lot more cost; attention to accounting measures rather than market or economic values; and full employment for lawyers. What are the benefits? Well, in the spirit of "misery loves company," U.S. bankers can take solace in the fact that many of their international competitors are now forced to deal with these same capital issues and costs.

Now, while that has been said, we do not question the intent or integrity of the regulatory agencies. Although the regulators' intentions to constrain risk-taking and irresponsible growth are good and well-placed, and risk-based capital is a significant improvement over the primary capital concept, the approaches being used are neither cost effective nor truly risk-constraining.

Any capital standard that does not efficiently reflect all risk types cannot succeed. Moreover, any use of accounting concepts to measure risk or capital cannot succeed. It is always easier to criticize than to offer practical alternatives, but in this case, alternatives that are simpler and cheaper to administer, and that reflect all risks exist and will be the topic of Chapter 4.

3.9 ADMINISTERING THE RBC STANDARDS

Now that we have argued that regulatory capital rules should not be used to allocate capital or in measuring returns, what should banks do about the RBC standards? The answer is simple:

> **Always comply with the minimum regulatory capital standards.**

Keep in mind that compliance with minimums is not the same as using the regulatory measures in loan pricing models or in calculating shareholder value added.

What if economic capital allocations are less than the regulatory minimums? There are methods to compensate for this inefficiency that will be described in Chapter 4. This is not an unusual situation.

3.10 SUMMARY

Regulation by capital was adopted as a replacement for Regulation Q as a growth and risk restraint on the banking industry in the United States. Unfortunately, all regulatory capital initiatives suffer from two serious weaknesses: they do not adequately reflect all of the risks and they rely on accounting measures of capital ratios. Risk-based capital was proposed to remove the disincentives to hold liquid assets, to capture off-balance sheet activities, and to "level" the international playing field. While it does address these specific problems, it is simplistic in reflecting credit risk and it is very labor- and cost-intensive to administer.

CHAPTER
4

Using Market Signals in Loan Pricing and Capital Allocations

Chapter 3 presented the reasons for the emergence of capital as a major focus of bank regulation. Capital standards replaced Regulation Q as a growth and risk constraint on banking organizations. While such efforts are laudable and well-intended, they are difficult to implement if accounting measures are utilized, and risk is not reflected in its entirety.

Now that some of the difficulties with regulatory capital have been presented, it is incumbent to propose a viable alternative. Fortunately, more than one exist. The basic criteria concerning alternative capital measures are clear: the alternatives should be less costly to administer, reflect all risks, and utilize market value rather than accounting concepts. The first suggestion is to use market capital instead of accounting or regulatory capital measures. Indeed, whenever possible, market signals should be incorporated into the fabric of decision-making in all aspects of banking.

Before expanding upon the use of market capital, it is important to consider one digression on the theme of using market signals. The topic is no less than a fundamental problem with banking today. Understanding this issue and dealing with it could be critical to the future profitability, and even survival, of the U.S. banking industry!

4.1   ONE FUNDAMENTAL PROBLEM WITH BANKING

The title of this section is admittedly presumptuous. But this is a serious issue and represents a major message of this entire book! In our opinion, a fundamental problem with banking today is this:

> **Banks are not properly compensated for the credit risks they take.**

How can we know this? The answer is schematically illustrated by Figure 4.1.

The solid line shows what the bond markets require as risk premiums for corporate bonds by credit rating. Notice that the premiums become extremely large as the credit rating goes below investment grade (BBB). Contrast the bond market line with the dashed line indicative of bank yields for loans to similar credits. Notice that bankers are much less discriminating than the corporate bond markets. That is, the risk premium differential between AAA-rated credits and "junk" credits is far less in bank portfolios than in the open market.

This mispricing at both ends of the credit spectrum is the main cause of the industry's ills today. Further, this problem is not new. Indeed, it has been going on for decades! Therefore, we must explain why the industry

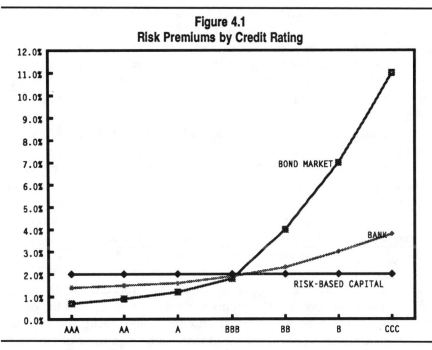

Figure 4.1
Risk Premiums by Credit Rating

only experienced such massive failures in the decade of the 1980s, and not in the 1950s, 1960s, or 1970s.

The key to the argument is that prior to the 1970s, bankers had a virtual "monopoly" on commercial short- and intermediate-term credit extension in this country. Hence, even though banks did not price credit risk properly within each rating class, they did manage to achieve average yields across their entire portfolios that were adequate. Emphasis must be placed on the concept that pricing was adequate **on average, but not within each rating category.** This situation is not unusual in regulated industries with effective barriers to entry to prevent more competitive pricing.

As long as that monopoly power was maintained, the industry was viable. However, as soon as alternatives to bank credit became available, mainly in the 1970s, there was a steady loss of the highest-rated, and thus highest-quality, customers. Specifically, direct access to the money and capital markets resulted from advances in technology and communications (the same advances that allowed the creation of the Money Market Mutual Funds). Hence, many corporations found that they could directly issue commercial paper or shelf-registered notes as substitutes for their bank lines. Of course, referring back to Figure 4.1, the initial companies to gain access to such alternatives were the highest-quality companies, who happened to be the ones being overcharged for their bank lines.

It is no secret that banks systemically lost their most creditworthy customers during the 1970s and 1980s. However, if banks had been pricing rationally, i.e., similarly to the corporate bond markets, then this trend would have been fairly inconsequential, and the yields on their remaining portfolio of higher risk credits would have risen substantially. Unfortunately, bankers were left with the more risky subset of their former relationships, but without the subsidy that the AAA and AA borrowers had been providing, and without proper spreads for the riskier credits left in their portfolios. Hence, the 1980s were the first full decade where the industry was left openly exposed to the consequences of its relatively indiscriminate pricing practices. The result was a dramatic increase in bank failures.

The fundamental problem with banking is clear: Banks have not charged high enough yields to their lower-rated credit relationships and they charged yields that were too high for their strongest customers. Now, what will the new risk-based capital standards do to this situation? Unfortunately, it will drive banks in exactly the wrong direction! Blindly applying RBC rules to conventional loan pricing models will result in the dotted line in Figure 4.1. The RBC line is absolutely horizontal; that is, RBC suggests that all loans should be priced identically, regardless of the credit rating of the customer! It is now apparent that instead of providing an incentive to price loans more rationally, RBC will tend to move the current insufficient pricing practice in the wrong direction, toward even less discrimination rather than greater!

The moral of the story is that bankers must adjust their pricing expectations to be more consistent with the clear signals offered by the money and capital markets. To do otherwise means that banks will continue to fail and confidence in the industry will continue to erode. And why have bankers not adjusted their pricing? Historically, the most often used argument was that "the competition (i.e., another bank) is forcing us to price this way." If true, then it is now evident that this impersonal "competition" is pricing itself out of existence.

Actually, the "credit crunch" of the early 1990s was consistent with a fundamental and correct adjustment in the pricing practices of banks regarding their higher risk credits. Of course, pricing adjustments are only part of the story. The credit crunch also reflected a return to such fundamentals as insisting on positive project cash flows and real equity. These trends are all essential for the long-term viability of the industry.

4.2 USE OF MARKET SIGNALS IN CAPITAL MANAGEMENT

Regarding alternatives to current regulatory capital practices, it has been suggested that market capital be used in the place of the complexities and incompleteness of risk-based capital. What is meant by market capital?

The amount of market capital of a banking company with publicly traded stock is simply the market capitalization of the banking company, which is calculated as the number of shares outstanding multiplied by its price per share. Normally, this figure will be somewhat lower or higher than the bank's book equity level. This difference may be treated as a crude mark-to-market adjustment of the assets of the bank. Hence, a formula for the market capital ratio of a bank is as follows:

$$\text{Market Capital Ratio} = \frac{\text{Market Capital}}{(\text{Total Assets} + \text{Market Capital} - \text{Book Equity})}$$

where Market Capital = Number of Shares Outstanding × Price per Share.

This concept satisfies the criteria established for a more effective alternative to regulatory capital:

Less expensive. For publicly traded entities where reliable stock prices are readily available, there simply could not be a less expensive calculation. For the price of a newspaper, market capital can be determined. (A suggestion for privately held banks is offered in Section 4.4.)

Encompasses all risk types. Stock prices reflect all anticipated risks facing any firm, including credit risk, interest rate risk, currency risk, market share risk, or operating risk. In this sense, market capital is far superior to the RBC rules that only deal with some aspects of credit risk.

No loopholes. Rather than provide job security to those who look for loopholes rather than create value, markets are not fooled by stratagems to obfuscate a company's true risk structure. Indeed, any company that expends resources to "paper over" any weaknesses will be negatively impacted in the marketplace.

Utilizes market values rather than accounting concepts. This is almost too obvious to point out. Not only is there a market value estimate of capital, there is also a market value adjustment to the asset base. Since market values are used, market capital ratios automatically provide a shareholder perspective, which is consistent with the stated goal of ALM from Chapter 1.

Additional advantages of this approach are that:

- It is fast: market capital may be determined instantly by referring to the latest stock market transaction.

- It is simple compared to the complexities of the risk-based capital calculations.

- It is objective.

4.3   OBJECTIONS TO AND DISADVANTAGES OF USING MARKET CAPITAL SIGNALS

Most large bank CEOs will probably cringe at the suggestion regarding market capital, which, while not perfect, has advantages over the complexities and incompleteness of current regulatory efforts. Here are some positions concerning expected objections and apparent disadvantages.

Many banks are not publicly traded. Even within large multibank holding companies, there is only one stock price available, and that is only applicable to the consolidated company. How can capital be assessed within the various individual bank subsidiaries? What about the thousands of privately held banks that have no market quotes? A relatively simple alternative measuring the volatility of historical cash flows of the bank will be described in Section 4.4 of this chapter.

"The market does not understand us" syndrome. Some large bank CEOs have significant frustrations with the marketplace. They believe that the markets either do not understand their situation, or are not sophisticated enough to be able to understand their organizations or their complex strategies. By this argument, market prices are unreliable indicators of risk or value. These authors have little sympathy for this view. If the markets do not understand a major banking company, then that must be a criticism that can only be directed at the management of that company. Markets are the best estimators of risk and value. Market analysts devote large amounts of time, effort, and money endeavoring to understand and convey the risk and return prospects of publicly traded companies.

Market prices are too volatile to be usable. The very responsiveness of stock market prices to altered expectations is often cited as a reason not to use them. However, it is a straightforward matter to smooth out market price volatility by using a moving average concept instead of the spot price. For example, a 90-day moving average, one-year moving average, or even a three-year moving average may be used without any significant problems.

4.4   AN ALTERNATIVE APPROACH FOR MARKET CAPITAL

For banks that have no publicly traded stock, or for subsidiaries of multibank holding companies, an alternative to market capital ratios is needed. To be consistent with the principles established in the first two chapters, capital assessments should be based on the volatility of historical cash flows.

The procedure would be as follows: The financial statements for the bank would be converted into economic cash flows, as discussed in Appendix 2.A, on a quarterly basis. The standard deviation of cash flows would be calculated for the prior three or five years. This value would be divided by the average cash flow level. The result is called the **normalized standard deviation**, and is expressed as a percentage value.

The regulatory agencies would then establish a schedule of minimum capital ratios as a function of ranges of the normalized standard deviations. Banks with relatively high risk, regardless of the source of risk, will show higher normalized standard deviations and should be required to attain higher capital ratios.

The advantages of this procedure over current regulatory approaches include the following:

Captures all sources of risk. The volatility of cash flows derive from all sources of risk: credit, interest rate, liquidity, operating, foreign exchange. Hence, this procedure is comprehensive.

Broad applicability. This method is universal and may be applied to any type of financial institution: foreign or domestic, trust company or finance company. In this sense, it is applicable for banks as they are empowered today, or as they may be expanded into securities or insurance activities in the future. It may also be adopted by regulators in other financial industries.

Simplicity. This procedure is relatively simple as compared to the cost and labor associated with risk-based capital.

Robust. This procedure does not have to be modified for the emergence of new securities. Under the current regulatory approach, considerable effort had to be expended to expand risk-based capital for interest rate swaps and currency options. This would be unnecessary with the standard deviation approach.

A critical issue in this type of approach is the length of the historical time period used to calculate the standard deviations. An extended period (greater than two years) is probably advantageous to provide some historical averaging effect. A three- or five-year calculation is recommended so that banks may improve their standard deviations within a realistic timeframe. Using a 10-year period would leave high-risk banks under a heavy "drag" of the longer historical period so that even if they could smooth out their cash flows, the improvements would not lower their overall standard deviation calculation for many years.

4.5   CAPITAL ALLOCATIONS

Within every bank, the reasons to estimate capital allocations are numerous, including:

- Unit or departmental profitability reports,
- Product or service-line profitability analyses,
- Loan pricing spreadsheets,
- Acquisition or divestiture decisions, and
- Capital budgeting analyses.

In seeking an appropriate measure, opt for simplicity and objectivity. As a hint, what is the lowest common denominator for any definition of "business unit" from Chapter 2 (any product, organization unit, customer relationship, or subsidiary)? This must be **cash flow** as discussed in the appendix to that chapter; hence, our measure of allocated capital must be some volatility measure of historical cash flows.

Again, we recommend the concept of the annualized **standard deviation of cash flows**. This is a straightforward calculation that does not require any special analytical capabilities. Many hand-held calculators will perform the calculation. All that is needed are the monthly or quarterly cash flows for the business unit over the past several years.

The standard deviations obtained by this procedure are directly comparable across any definitions of business units. They directly represent approximate relative capital allocations. The advantage of this approach is that it is objective, relatively easy to calculate, and allows allocations across all product types, including those that are not depicted on the bank's balance sheet, such as trust or corporate cash management.

Once these relative allocations are obtained across the entire bank, they should be added up and each should be divided by the gross total of standard deviations across all products or units so that a percentage allocation exists for every business unit. These percentages should then be multiplied by the **target capital level** for the bank, as established by the senior management team and the board of directors. Note that the target capital level is not the same as the accounting equity level. The target level is the amount of capital that the bank aspires to maintain over the long run.

Refer to Table 4.1 for an illustration of the calculations for a simplified bank that only has three business units.

Some readers will have noticed that the standard deviation of cash flows for the three products of the bank add up to a value of $18, but the standard deviation for the total bank is only $12! This is normal. When different types of activities are combined in a single company or in a portfolio, the volatilities of the individual activities will tend partially to offset one another. This is an effect known as portfolio diversification, and it is discussed in the next section. For now, it is important to note that the line labeled "Percentage of Sum of Standard Deviations" takes each of the standard deviations from the line above it and divides by $18, not $12. Thus, in the column for commercial loans, the standard deviation of $10 is divided by the gross sum of the three columns, or $18, to obtain the 55.6% value. Also, the total bank standard deviation of $12 is divided by $18, resulting in the 150% value. This is an indication of the degree of diversification that exists with this combination of activities.

4.6   SOME OBSERVATIONS ON THE STANDARD DEVIATION METHOD

This suggested methodology for allocating capital is the simplest imaginable. Its advantages are that every business unit has cash flows which are relatively simple to measure, that cash flow volatilities reflect all risks, and

Table 4.1
Illustration of Capital Allocation Calculations
for ABC Bank

	Commercial Loans	Checking Deposits	Trust Accounts	Total Tank
Adjusted Cash Flows:				
Year 1	$101	$70	$53	$224
Year 2	95	68	48	211
Year 3	89	73	61	223
Year 4	110	71	50	231
Year 5	104	66	59	229
Year 6	98	72	45	215
Year 7	83	71	55	209
Year 8	88	69	50	207
Year 9	78	63	53	194
Year 10	101	71	57	229
Average	$94.7	$69.4	$53.1	$217.2
Standard Deviation	$10.0	$3.0	$5.0	$12.0
Percentage of Sum of Standard Deviations	55.6%	16.7%	27.8%	150.0%
Target Capital				$24.00
Allocated Capital	$13.33	$4.00	$6.67	

Notes:

■ All dollar amounts are $ millions.

■ All cash flows adjusted as described in Appendix to Chapter 2.

■ Assumes that ABC Bank only offers these three products.

■ Target Capital level differs from actual book equity from Table 3.3.

■ Allocated Capital = Percentage of Total Standard Deviation x Target Capital.

that cash flows are the basis for market valuations, so that this measure is consistent with a desire to use market signals or their closest substitute.

For those with a background in corporate finance, there are probably a few questions that may arise at this point. (Anyone not conversant with corporate financial theory may wish to skip this section.) The issues are as follows:

Diversification effects. The recommended procedure seems to ignore the detailed effects of diversification. In fact, a superior, although more complicated, approach would incorporate the use of a covariance analysis of historical cash flows rather than the simpler variances or standard deviations. Covariances reflect the diversification phenomenon in the way that the capital markets do. We would argue, however, that our simpler weighting of the targeted capital level by the standard deviations automatically compensates for diversification effects, but it spreads the benefit (in terms of a decreased capital burden) across all activities of the bank, rather than assigning it to a possibly small number of activities.

From a practical point of view, the focus on the standard deviation of each unit instead of the standard deviation of the entire company (which nets out the diversified risks) represents an "every tub on its own bottom" approach. If capital is not allocated in this way, nonsensical results could ensue. For example, if two units happen to show a strong negative correlation coefficient, then both will show an unusually low capital allocation which is completely dependent upon the existence of both activities continuing into the future. If, for whatever reason, the bank decided to exit one of those activities, then the other unit would suddenly find that it has a large, unexpected increase in its equity allocation. This would be a disastrous side-effect and would be extremely unfair to the unit so burdened in terms of its performance measurement. One of the cardinal rules recommended in profitability measurement (Chapter 13) is that all critical parameters that could cause an unexpected negative variance for a unit should be under the direct control of that unit. In this case, a decision to exit one activity has a large negative effect on another. This side-effect problem is minimized with the standard deviation approach described.

Another argument in favor of the standard deviation method is that while markets only look at covariances to price risk, companies must use variances to allocate capital. To understand why this must be, consider a company that has a zero or negative covariance with the market. If covariances were used to allocate capital, then this company would target either zero or negative capital levels! Clearly, this cannot happen. Every company on a stand-alone basis should have some positive level of equity to absorb unexpected cash flow volatility, regardless of whether its individual cash flows are positively or negatively correlated with the rest of the marketplace. See Chapters 10 and 11 for further explanation of this point.

Capital exists as a buffer against unexpected losses. Just because a company has zero or negative covariance with the market does not mean that it faces zero or negative risk. Every actual company will have a positive standard deviation of cash flows. By this argument, standard deviations are superior to covariances for allocating capital, whereas the markets use covariances rather than standard deviations to set risk premia for valuation purposes.

Expected versus unexpected losses. A very common question involves the distinction between the loan loss reserve and equity. Is the loan loss reserve a form of capital, and how should its level be determined with respect to capital? The answer is that capital is a buffer against *unexpected* losses, whereas the loan loss reserve exists to absorb expected chargeoffs. To illustrate this distinction, consider two different loan categories whose only source of risk is chargeoffs, as shown in Table 4.2.

Table 4.2
Illustration of Distinction Between Reserves and Equity

	Category A	Category B
Average Chargeoffs	1.50%	0.50%
Standard Deviation of Chargeoffs	0.50%	2.00%

By our reasoning, loan category A would have a loan loss reserve allocation three times larger than category B because its average chargeoff level is three times that of B. However, the equity allocation to category A loans would only be one-fourth that of category B, since its volatility of chargeoffs is correspondingly lower.

Do not view loan loss reserves to be capital, much in the same way that manufacturing companies do not consider their allowance for uncollectible receivables to be capital. How should an allocation for the loan loss reserve be estimated for profitability measurement purposes? This will be explored at some depth in Chapter 13, but a general idea is that the reserves should equal the present value of expected future chargeoffs.

Allocating capital to start-up business units. Another common question regards the "fairness" of our recommended approach to capital allocation with respect to new, start-up ventures. Suppose a new activity that is only four years old shows the following pattern of adjusted cash flows: 100, 150, 225, 340. This unit would have a standard deviation of about 104 from the historical information given. However, when looking at the pattern of cash flows, it is evident that this unit is showing a remarkably stable compounded growth rate of cash flow at about 50% per year. Indeed, the unit manager could make a good argument that there is little if any uncertainty in his results, and therefore, to use the standard deviation of the raw values would unfairly burden the unit with excessive equity.

While it would be rational for any bank to "detrend" this data to remove that source of volatility, a case can be made for leaving the calculation as it stands. Any special treatment for a unit leaves the way open for other specialized treatments such as deseasonalizing the data. Are strong trends or seasonality behavior sources of volatility or not? We believe so. Remember, Chapter 2 asserted that risk should reflect all sources of volatility. Hence, in practice, we have tended to resist such requests for special treatment. However, there is no doubt that some banks will disagree with this attitude.

A large equity allocation is reasonable for start-up enterprises given the bank's lack of experience with the activity, the fact that start-up activities tend to show a higher rate of failure than mature activities, and the expectation in this example that the activity is undergoing an exponential growth phase that does warrant a larger equity allocation in anticipation of that continued growth.

Now that a case for allocating capital has been stated, consider the issue of establishing the hurdle rate (return on economic capital) that is needed for calculating SVA as well as for loan pricing analyses.

4.7   ESTABLISHING A HURDLE RATE ON ECONOMIC CAPITAL

Earlier, the seminal studies of Ibbotson and Sinquefield were cited in establishing the average risk premium over Treasury bonds that the marketplace requires. Section 2.3 used a crude estimate of about 15% for the hurdle rate, which was composed of a 7% risk premium and an 8% risk-free T-bond rate. How critical is it to have an exact hurdle rate, and how often should the calculation be updated?

The discussion of the case study in Section 2.4 noted that the portfolio ROE that results from any application of the SVA performance measure is usually substantially higher than the hurdle rate. In that example, the optimal portfolio ROE that maximized SVA was 30% after applying a 15% hurdle rate for the SVA calculations. Likewise, any bank's actual results after using SVA should be well in excess of the hurdle.

Therefore, it is not essential to have an up-to-the-minute hurdle rate for the bank to achieve consistently superior returns. **What is much more important than whether the hurdle rate on any given day is 14% or 18%, is that the bank avoid activities that have returns that are negative or substantially below the hurdle (e.g., below 10%).** For this reason, a common practice is not to adjust the hurdle rate more than once per year. (More frequent revisions may be required in periods of extreme interest rate or inflation volatility.) Select a reasonable hurdle, such as 15%, and leave it alone for as long as possible, provided that the risk-free rate stays within a reasonable range on a moving average basis.

The advantage of a stable hurdle rate is that it is much easier to convey throughout the organization. It is important that such a critical signal be as stable as possible so that account officers and managers can develop a strong, intuitive comfort level with the general characteristics of the SVA performance measure and can concentrate on avoiding very bad decisions rather than worry about activities that are close to the threshold. Moreover, using a stable hurdle is consistent with our position that managers should not be subjected to unexpected volatility in their performance measure that is beyond their control.

Although banks don't have to use a stable hurdle rate, there are some attractions to the idea that should be given serious consideration, and a bank that did so would not find itself in serious trouble. If two banks utilized the SVA measure, one that adjusted the hurdle every day and the other that adopted a set 15% hurdle, both would show superior financial performance over time. The bank with the variable hurdle would expend more resources conveying the current hurdle throughout the bank and educating its staff about why it is important to constantly adjust the rate. Either approach would be a vast improvement over simple net income or ROA measures.

For other comments on the cost of capital, refer to Appendix 4A.

4.8   ACCESS TO NEW CAPITAL

One of the consequences of regulatory capital standards is to force many large banking companies to the capital markets to raise new equity. Unless the banking company has recently shown very strong results, this can be a lose-lose situation in the following sense:

- Shareholder value is lost at least by the amount of the underwriting fee, which can be as high as 5% of the new issue. This is a dead-weight loss to the shareholders that should not be incurred without concrete offsetting benefits.

- The transactions may give management the luxury of not addressing more fundamental issues like the level of interest rate and credit risks that the institution is incurring. Remember, capital is not a source of risk, just a buffer against unexpected volatility. To improve the safety and soundness of the industry, regulators should look toward loan pricing and capital ratios based on market signals and economic risks.

An equity offering can be important when the bank has taken a gamble and lost, bringing the bank's capital cushion far below the level desired given its level of risk. This is the case for much of the savings and loan industry in the United States. If capital has been impaired, management has no choice but to move back to the "right" capital ratio or it runs the risk of imposing the costs of bankruptcy on shareholders, depositors, and employees.

The moral of these observations is that banks should not try to raise more equity unless they can convince the markets that they will use the new capital to create shareholder value. An equity issue is no substitute for reducing risk to manageable levels. An equity issue will be very difficult if the track record for the bank is only to show negative SVA.

The marketplace is one of the most efficient distribution mechanisms for capital in existence. An important point to understand is that any bank that demonstrates positive, sustainable SVA will have access to all the capital it could possibly use through the marketplace. Positive SVA is not easy to achieve or sustain. Such banks trade at large premiums of market price to book value. They can access new equity without lowering or diluting the wealth of their existing shareholders.

Basically, the industry should first fix its risk/return profile to be properly compensated for the risks taken, then access to new equity for expansion will naturally ensue. To seek new equity before establishing a track record of value creation is usually very damaging to existing shareholders, and not in their interest. Indeed, for banks with consistently negative SVA, the value maximizing strategy would be to reduce their bank's activities and return any released capital to their shareholders!

4.9   ISSUES IN IMPLEMENTING MARKET CAPITAL MEASURES

Now, suppose that we have persuaded the regulatory agencies to adopt market signals in their evaluation of capital adequacy. Just how would this work? The simplest approach would be to utilize market capital ratios based upon 90-day moving averages of market closing prices. If a bank's market capital ratio were to drop below a prescribed target level, then it would have to file a plan to improve its ratio over no more than 12 months. As long as it adhered to its plan to correct the situation, there would be no further action taken.

However, if further deterioration results, then at some point, the regulators should do some combination of the following:

■ Increase the FDIC insurance premium rate;

■ Announce a reduction in the percentage coverage of deposits under $100,000, such as coverage of only 90% of all qualifying deposits, which would become effective in 12 months from the date of the announcement; or

■ Close the bank.

In those cases where market signals do not exist, the standard deviation method may be utilized. When applied to legal entities, the relative standard deviations for a particular bank would have to be compared against an index of banks with publicly traded stock to establish a reference scale against which to determine an estimated market capital ratio. Alternatively, a schedule of thresholds based directly on the normalized standard deviations could be established for evaluation purposes.

4.10   HOW NOT TO IMPLEMENT A MARKET APPROACH

Certain regulatory agencies have been very vocal about forcing banks to perform mark-to-market adjustments on their investment portfolios, but not on the rest of the balance sheet. We strongly disagree with this piecemeal concept. Such adjustments to any bank's profit and loss statement serve no useful purpose. Moreover, marking any segment of the balance sheet to market is totally meaningless and deceptive.

If a mark-to-market adjustment is desired, it should be done on the entire range of on- and off-balance sheet activities engaged in by the bank. This sounds like a difficult undertaking, but it is really quite simple. This is exactly the adjustment described in Section 4.2 as the difference between the market capitalization of the bank and its total book equity. Therefore, market signals provide current, complete adjustments for all sources of volatility from every known activity of the organization.

However, to subject one subset of the bank's activities to a mark-to-market estimate serves no useful function at all. Chapter 5 shows that interest rate risk cannot be estimated at all without fully considering the entire spectrum of effects on all on- and off-balance sheet instruments, which often tend to offset or hedge one another. Any mark-to-market estimate on the investment portfolio will be dominated by interest rate effects which are meaningless taken alone, and can only be interpreted when considered along with the interest rate repricing characteristics of all other activities of the bank.

4.11 SUMMARY

Capital allocation is one of the most important of all financial activities. It provides a critical mechanism in "risk-adjusting" performance measures. If done properly, the organization will be in a position to benefit its shareholders by finding opportunities that properly compensate the bank for the risks undertaken and create true shareholder value. Market signals provide the best set of benchmarks to utilize in gauging the propriety of either loan pricing or capital allocations.

The advantages of market signals are that they are accessible, respond quickly to changes in circumstances or expectations, and fully encompass adjustments for all sources of risk or volatility. It is recommended that such signals be incorporated into all aspects of analysis and decision-making of the organization.

APPENDIX 4A: COMMENTS ON THE COST OF CAPITAL

For readers trained in theoretical finance, the cost of capital calculation is a key calculation. It is essential for many bankers, particularly the most analytical, to use the tools of modern portfolio theory and its ancestor, the capital asset pricing model, to make the cost of capital calculation as precise as possible. We agree with this approach and encourage it. As an exercise in political economy, however, we always prefer the Spike Lee approach to dialogue with senior management: "Do the Right Thing." The objective for the ALCO is to succeed in adopting a hurdle rate for the organization that is roughly correct and universally accepted as reasonable. There are many tools useful in the exercise.

For the most analytical of senior management, the best quantitative tools are the most effective, and no self-respecting asset and liability manager would want to admit that he had not at least looked at the bank's "beta" in calculating the cost of capital. For most members of senior management, however, a graph like Figure 4A.1 clearly communicates the link between "returns" and the universally followed "market-to-book ratio." Something like the graph below is worth 1,000 betas in most asset and liability management committees. At the same time, we would never use it unless it depicted a number that we knew analytically to be "the right thing."

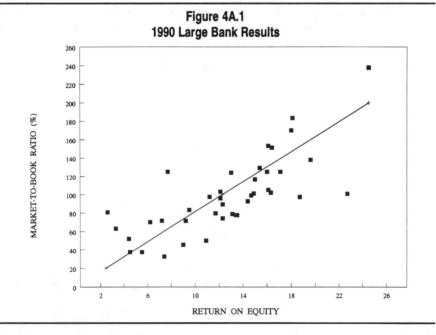

Figure 4A.1
1990 Large Bank Results

CHAPTER 5

Interest Rate Risk Overview

Interest rate risk is one of the traditional focal points of ALM. To many, it is the only ALM topic. Chapter 1 established the goal of ALM to be the maximization of the risk-adjusted returns to shareholders over the long run. How can one think about this goal in the context of interest rate risk management? This chapter will address the problem of goal identification and definitions of parameters. The following critical question will be discussed: **Is there an optimal interest rate sensitivity position?**

Chapter 6 will further develop the practical issues of interest rate positioning in terms of understanding the yield curve, changing a bank's interest rate sensitivity, the use of hedging instruments, and procedures for facilitating the decision-making process within the Asset and Liability Committee (ALCO) setting. Chapters 7 and 8 will review the major interest rate risk measurement techniques and discuss how to handle some of the complexities and pitfalls of specific bank products.

In reviewing the existing literature on interest rate risk management, writings tend to fall into one of three general categories:

■ The strengths and weaknesses of the three main analytical techniques: gap analysis, simulation modeling, and duration (which will be discussed in Chapter 7).

■ The "rocket science" approach that claims that unless exact duration, convexity, and higher order analyses are conducted using ultra-sophisticated techniques, then the bank is fooling itself and could inadvertently jeopardize its existence.

■ An overview of hedging instruments, with numerous charts and diagrams of the latest options on futures on cross-index currency swaps.

While there are elements of useful (i.e., practical) material in all of these approaches, they do not address the predicament of most bank ALM practitioners. That is, how can one think about these issues, and how can one provide a logical framework within which the ALCO and board members can realistically understand what the interest rate risk of the bank ought to be and why it should be that way? Providing such a framework is the objective of the next three chapters.

5.1   TARGET ACCOUNTS: AN EXAMPLE OF MULTIDIMENSIONALITY

Before we can address whether there is an optimal interest rate risk position, we must understand how to measure that risk. With regard to all

ALM risk types, there are multiple "target accounts" that should be considered. This is another aspect of the multidimensionality of ALM risks mentioned in Chapter 1.

Three of the most common types of target accounts associated with the management of interest rate risk are net interest income (or net income), market value of net equity, and economic equity ratio.

Net interest income (or net income). This is the most commonly considered category of target account. These measures are accounting concepts and are usually the major focal points of analyses in most banks. There is a tendency to concentrate attention on near term earnings effects due to rate shifts; that is, the effect of rate changes on earnings over the next 3 to 12 months. Hence, this is a short-term, accounting, earnings-oriented target.

Market value of net equity. This is the market capitalization concept presented in Chapter 4. That is, how does the market capitalization (i.e., stock price) of the banking company change if there is an unexpected change in interest rates? This is a balance sheet oriented concept on a market value basis. Since market capitalization also represents a rough net present value of all future cash flows or dividends, it also is a long-term, economic earnings concept.

Economic equity ratio. This is the market capital ratio also presented in Chapter 4. That is, how would a shift in interest rates change the ratio of equity to assets when both are measured on a market value basis? As such, this is a market value-oriented, capital ratio concept. Again, long-term cash flow expectations are used in developing this target.

Notice that these target accounts span a number of dimensions:

- Income statement versus balance sheet dimensions;

- Market value versus accounting dimensions;

- Capital amount versus capital ratio dimensions; and

- Short-term versus long-term dimensions.

These are not the only target accounts that might be considered. However, they are by far the most prevalent and present an ideal mix of dimensions for this discussion.

5.2   CASE STUDY ON INTEREST RATE RISK MANAGEMENT: THE PROBLEM

To convey some of the most important concepts in interest rate risk management, this section will use an illustrative example of a highly simplified bank in the form of a case study problem. In fact, assume that we are starting a *de novo* bank at the beginning of a new year that will be the simplest bank ever formed! Here are the start-up assumptions and conditions:

- The bank will have one asset (a $1,000 loan), one deposit (an $800 certificate of deposit), and $200 of start-up equity.

- The loan is a six-month "bullet" loan (i.e., all interest and principal are payable at maturity) that is priced at the current six-month CD rate (assumed to be 6%) plus a spread of 2%. Therefore, on January 1, the loan is booked at a yield of 8%. It is also assumed that the loan will continuously roll-over for subsequent six-month periods and that its yield will be reset on the roll-over dates to whatever the new CD rate is at those times plus the credit spread of 2%.

- The CD is booked on January 1 at the current CD rate of 6%. The bank is in the fortunate position that it can issue a CD with any initial maturity it desires. The initial maturity may be one day or five years, or any maturity between those values. However, once the bank selects an initial maturity, it is committed to rolling over the CD upon its maturity into a new CD with the same initial maturity as the first one. That is, it is committing to a set funding strategy for at least one year. For example, if the bank chose to fund its balance sheet with a three-month CD, then it must continue to roll over the initial CD for three more three-month periods for the rest of the first year.

- The CD yield curve is assumed to be "flat," that is, the rate for all maturities from one day through five years is 6%. Furthermore, the entire yield curve will unexpectedly shift once, on January 2, to a new flat value. This is referred to as a parallel shift in interest rates. It is further assumed that the yield curve will not change from its January 2 level for the remainder of the year.

- All earnings are paid out as dividends semi-annually. (This assumption is needed because the only source of cash to pay dividends is the bullet loan whose cash flows occur every six months.)

■ For simplicity, ignore taxes, FDIC insurance, reserve requirements, and other operating expenses.

This may seem like an imposing list of assumptions. However, it is the simplest case study that we can imagine. Table 5.1 is a summary of the starting balance sheet, and a formal statement of the case study problem follows.

Table 5.1
Interest Rate Risk Case Study
Starting Balance Sheet on January 1:

Assets:

    $1,000   Six-Month Loan Priced at CD + 2%

Liabilities and Equity:

   $ 800   CD of Any Desired Maturity

   $ 200   Equity

Problem. Imagine that you are the asset and liability manager for this bank and the ALCO and board of directors have issued you one instruction: Please minimize the interest rate risk of this bank. Your only choice is to pick a CD maturity that will be set for the rest of the year that will minimize the bank's rate risk. What CD maturity would you pick and why?

5.3 DISCUSSION OF CASE STUDY RESULTS

As simple as this case study is, there is no "best" solution. That is, there is no single CD maturity that "minimizes" the interest rate risk profile of this simple bank. Many readers will undoubtedly believe that there is one clear answer. Let us rephrase the problem to illustrate the most popular reasoning: If the objective is to minimize interest rate risk, what maturity CD should be used to fund this six-month loan?

Surprisingly, if the objective is to minimize earnings risk, then you should not use a six-month CD! To see this point, consider the full range of effects of an arbitrary 1% rate rise on the three important target accounts presented in Section 5.1. They are shown in Table 5.2.

Table 5.2
Interest Rate Risk Case Study Results
(Effects of a 1% Rise in the CD Yield Curve on January 2)

CD Maturity (Months)	Annual Net Interest Income ($)	Market Value of Equity (%)	Economic Equity Ratio (%)
3.0	$ −1.0	−1.4%	−0.9%
4.5	0.0	−0.9	−0.5
6.0	+1.0	−0.5	0.0
7.5	+2.0	0.0	+0.5
9.0	+3.0	+0.5	+0.9

Notice that there are three columns of effects summarized in Table 5.2 for various possible choices of CD maturity: annual net interest income, market value of equity, and economic equity ratio. Also, notice that the effects pertain to a 1% rise in interest rates. This particular rate shift is used for convenience only. We have no idea how rates will really change on January 2.

To understand this table, let us discuss one line of values for one CD maturity in detail. If the ALM manager had chosen a three-month CD to fund the bank, and if rates rise 1% on January 2, then the bank's net interest income would decrease by $1 compared to the situation if rates had remained unchanged.

To prove this, we can easily calculate the bank's total net interest income for the entire year under the two interest rate assumptions. If rates remain stable for the entire year, then the bank will earn 8% on the $1,000 loan, or $80 in interest income. The interest expense of the CD would be 6% times the balance of $800, or $48. Thus, net interest income would be $80 minus $48, or $32.

If rates rise 1%, then the bank's interest income, interest expense, and resulting net interest income by quarter would be as shown in Table 5.3. (Please note that to simplify the calculations, we have assumed that every quarter has exactly 91 days.)

Notice that the loan reprices to reflect the new higher rate environment in quarters three and four, after it matures and rolls over in the 7% CD environment for a total yield of 9%. However, the CD matures after the first quarter and rolls over at the new higher 7% rate at the start of the

Table 5.3
Quarterly Net Interest Income
Using a Three-Month CD Maturity
and Rates Rise 1% on January 2

	Quarter 1	Quarter 2	Quarter 3	Quarter 4	Year
Loan Yield	8.00%	8.00%	9.00%	9.00%	8.50%
Interest Income	$20.00	$20.00	$22.50	$22.50	$85.00
CD Rate	6.00%	7.00%	7.00%	7.00%	6.75%
Interest Expense	$12.00	$14.00	$14.00	$14.00	$54.00
Net Interest Margin	3.20%	2.40%	3.40%	3.40%	3.10%
Net Interest Income	$8.00	$6.00	$8.50	$8.50	$31.00

second quarter. Hence, net interest income is temporarily squeezed in the second quarter, but then attains its highest level in quarters three and four.

It is a simple matter to show that if rates were to increase by 2% instead of 1% on January 2, then annual net interest income would decline by $2 instead of $1. That is, the effect of any rate shift is the rate change (in % points) multiplied by –$1. Therefore, if rates happen to decrease by 1% on January 2, then net interest income would **increase** by $1 (which is the –$1 from Table 5.2 multiplied by the rate change of –1%) to $33 for the year. Now we see the utility of analyzing the effect of a 1% rate rise; value can be multiplied by any rate change for a simple estimate of the total expected effect with any rate change.

Going back to the three-month CD line in Table 5.2, now consider the effect on the market value of equity shown there of –1.4%. The market value of equity is always the residual when the market value of liabilities is subtracted from the market value of assets. Assume that the 2% spread that the loan carries is the appropriate risk premium over CD rates that the market would require for the credit quality of the borrower. If rates rise 1% on January 2, then the new market value for the loan (as well as that for the CD) would decrease as shown in Table 5.4.

The column labeled "New Market Value" is a mark-to-market calculation of the loan and the CD. For example, the loan will repay $1,040 of

Table 5.4
Market Value Calculations for Case Study Problem
Using Three-Month CD and Rates Rise 1%

	Maturity (Months)	Original Balance	Original Discount Rate	New Market Value	New Discount Rate	Percent Change
Loan	6.0	$1,000	8.0%	$995.22	9.0%	−0.48%
CD	3.0	800	6.0%	798.03	7.0%	−0.25%
Equity		200		197.18		−1.41%
Economic						
Equity Ratio		20%		19.81%		−0.94%

interest and principal at six months. When that value is discounted back at a 9% rate, the new market value is $995.22. A similar calculation was performed for the CD. The new market value of equity is simply the difference between the new market values for the loan and the CD. The new economic equity ratio is the new equity value of $197.18 divided by the new loan value of $995.22.

From Table 5.4, it is evident that the market value of equity decreases from $200 to $197.18 if rates rise 1%. This is a 1.4% decline, as indicated in Tables 5.2 and 5.4. Table 5.4 also shows that the economic equity ratio decreases from 20% to 19.81%, which is a 0.9% decline. Conversely, if rates were to drop 1% instead of increasing by that amount, then the market value of equity and economic equity ratio would both **increase** by the same respective magnitudes.

Now that we understand the meaning of the results shown in Table 5.2, we should repeat the original problem: Which CD maturity minimizes interest rate risk for this bank? From an examination of Table 5.2, it becomes evident that there is no solution—even for what is probably the simplest hypothetical bank in the world! The reason we claim that there is no answer is that there is no CD maturity that insulates the bank in all target account dimensions, which is to say that there is no CD maturity in Table 5.2 that displays zeros for all three target accounts. That is, minimizing the risk in one category causes increased risk in one or the other category.

Let us review each target account individually:

Net interest income. This account can be stabilized for the one-year time horizon against a shift in interest rates only if a 4.5 month CD is utilized. This is probably not intuitively obvious, but we suggest that the skeptical reader work through the arithmetic as an exercise. The reason that a six-month CD (matching the maturity of the loan) does not stabilize annual earnings is that matching maturities only works if balances are matched as well, and in this example, the volume of the loan is larger than the volume of the CD. (Please note that in most banks, the volume of earning assets is usually larger than the volume of interest-bearing deposits.)

Market value of equity. This is stabilized against interest rate changes only if a 7.5-month CD is selected. This difference in funding needed to hedge the market value of equity compared to trying to protect net interest income is the major message of this entire chapter and will be expanded upon in Section 5.5.

Economic equity ratio. Eureka! Most readers have a tendency to suggest a matched CD maturity compared to the loan. This is what is stabilized against rate risk if a matching of maturities between the loan and the CD is effected! When readers assert that using a six-month CD is the correct strategy for this case study, few realize that they are implicitly protecting the bank's economic equity ratio. This is no accident. It can be proven that this must occur. We will provide the proof for this assertion in Appendix 5C.

5.4   THE TRADITIONAL PRIORITIES OF SOME IMPORTANT CONSTITUENCIES

To add another perspective to our case study discussion, consider which constituencies might lobby the ALM manager to give more importance to particular target accounts. Historically, the senior management of the bank has focused on the earnings target account, which is net interest income in this case. It is not at all uncommon for management to want their earnings to be invariant to unexpected changes in interest rates for the current year. Hence, it would be very common for the management of the bank to recommend using the 4.5-month maturity choice.

The market value of equity is synonymous with the bank's market capitalization. Of course, the constituency most concerned with the risk (volatility) characteristics of the market capital or stock price of the bank would be the shareholders. If they wanted the bank to minimize interest rate risk, they would probably choose the 7.5-month CD option. Only in this way would the value of their investment in the bank not be subject to interest rate risk.

Finally, the constituency most concerned about equity ratios is the regulators. Recall that Chapter 3 suggested that regulators shift their attention away from accounting definitions toward market value concepts of capital ratios. For this case study, the appropriate capital ratio to use is the economic equity ratio. Hence, any regulator that wanted to minimize the interest rate risk of this bank would probably want to do so in the economic equity ratio dimension, and would recommend that the bank use a six-month CD to fund itself.

Thus, we see that the three important constituencies (management, shareholders, and regulators) would all want different CD maturities to be utilized to accomplish the goal of minimizing interest rate risk. What should the ALM manager do? Even for this, the simplest of all possible balance sheets, there is no clear solution. Indeed, this is one of the major reasons that ALM is often called an art and not a science.

But do not give up too easily. There are rational approaches to the interest rate risk dilemma that can be relied upon. Before we expand upon them, let us first bring our simple case study to closure by exploring two important analogies: fixed and floating-rate bonds.

5.5 THE BOND ANALOGIES

The two most important strategies that every ALM manager should consider are the two exemplified by the 4.5-month and 7.5-month CDs in our case study. They represent the "hedge the bank's earnings" and the "hedge the bank's stock price" strategies. That is, those are the two funding strategies that stabilize the bank in two critical target accounts: net interest income and the market value of equity. (As it happens, the riskiness of the economic equity ratio is usually intermittent between the risks to market equity and earnings. Therefore, if those two targets are managed within prudent bounds, then the economic equity ratio will be controlled, too.) In fact, these are probably the two most important strategies for any ALM manager, CEO, or board member to understand. We will emphasize this point by employing analogies to two simple bonds. The relationship we want to understand is illustrated by extracting a few of the results from Table 5.2 as depicted in Table 5.5.

Table 5.5
The Two Most Important Funding Strategies
(Effects of 1% Rate Rise)

Maturity Months	Annual Net Interest Income ($)	Market Value of Equity
4.5	0.0	−0.9%
7.5	+2.0	0.0

If the 4.5-month CD is used, then earnings for the year are not subject to interest rate shifts. However, the market capitalization of the bank is vulnerable, such that for every 1% rise in rates the stock price of the bank would fall by 0.9%. This is qualitatively true for all banks (and for any cash flow stream for that matter). If earnings (or cash flow) are hedged against interest rate changes, then the stock price or market capital of the bank (or net present value of the cash flow stream) must fall if interest rates rise.

If the 7.5-month CD were selected, then the stock price of the bank would not vary if interest rates changed. However, its earnings would rise whenever rates increased. Again, this is qualitatively true for all banks and for all cash flows.

To reinforce the last two paragraphs, consider analogies to two long-term bonds. These analogies are important in that they are intuitively simpler to understand, and they illustrate that the risk and valuation characteristics of any financial concept are universal. They are applicable in all situations, whether considering bank ALM or the purchase of investment securities or hedging with sophisticated derivative products, such as options or swaps.

Any analogy for the 4.5-month CD position in the case study must have the characteristics that its cash flows do not vary with interest rate shifts, and that its market value must decline whenever interest rates rise unexpectedly. The simplest bond with this characteristic is the long-term, fixed rate Treasury bond, often referred to simply as the "long bond." (*Note*: The analogy applies only to the two critical characteristics of a fixed cash or earnings pattern and a drop in market value if rates rise. Please do not confuse this analogy to imply that all the assets of this type of financial institution must be long-term, fixed rate. They might all be short term, with appropriate short-term funding, so long as net interest income is hedged against rate shifts.)

Most bankers understand all too well that the cash flows of any fixed-rate long bond are set; i.e., they do not change under any circumstances, and certainly not when market interest rates move up or down. However, as with any fixed cash flow stream, its market value is highly sensitive to any fluctuations in interest rates. This is because the market value of a fixed cash flow stream, such as the long bond's, is nothing more than the net present value obtained by discounting the expected future cash flows with the corresponding current discount rates. So when market interest rates move up, the discount rates are higher, and the discounted present value declines.

The analogy for the 7.5-month CD funding is a bond whose market value is stable, but whose cash flows rise whenever market rates increase. This is similar to a floating-rate bond whose coupon rate is reset at regular intervals, normally every three or six months, based upon a short-term index rate, such as LIBOR or Treasury bill rates. Clearly then, whenever interest rates rise the cash flow associated with this instrument increases. Because of this attribute, floating-rate bonds always trade near their par or full face value, since when rates rise, the increase in coupon offsets the increase in the discount rate, leaving the net present value unchanged.

Table 5.6 summarizes the important features of these two analogies. Hopefully, it is now evident why the results in Table 5.5 must qualitatively be as they are. The use of a 4.5-month CD is equivalent to fixing net interest income for the year. As with any fixed cash flow, the associated market value must show the characteristic that it will decrease whenever rates rise, since a fixed cash flow is now being discounted with a higher discount rate.

Table 5.6
Effects of a Rise in Interest Rates:

	Cash Flow	Market Value
Fixed-Rate Bond	Unchanged	Falls
Floating-Rate Bond	Increases	Stable

On the other hand, with the 7.5-month CD, cash flows increase whenever interest rates rise. The amount of this increase is exactly sufficient to compensate for the new higher market discount rates. Hence, the market value of the firm will not be affected.

Hopefully, it is also clear that **no bank can hedge both earnings and the market value of equity (stock price) at the same time.** Thus, every asset and liability manager and every ALCO must make a decision about its interest rate risk positioning that implies volatility (i.e., risk) in at least one dimension. There is no interest rate sensitivity position for any real bank that removes risk from all target accounts. The fundamental choices for the bank are identical to those outlined in Table 5.6. That is, either stabilize the stock price and have earnings (i.e., cash flows) that rise when rates go up (this is referred to as being "asset sensitive," since in this position, assets will reprice faster than liabilities), or stabilize earnings but have a stock price that falls whenever rates rise.

5.6   A REVIEW OF ALL POSSIBLE INTEREST RATE RISK STRATEGIES

Does corporate financial theory give any insights as to whether either of these two risk positions is better than any other? Actually, we should now generalize beyond these two example positions and consider the entire range of possible risk positions. They are summarized in Table 5.7. A simplified quantitative model is presented in Appendix 5B.

Table 5.7
Summary of All Possible Interest Rate Risk Positions—
Effects of a Rise in Interest Rates:

Sensitivity Type:	Earnings or Cash Flows	Stock Price or Market Value
1. Liability Sensitive Bank	Decreases	Falls Drastically
2. Fixed Earnings Bank	Fixed	Falls
3. "Hybrid" Bank	Small Increase	Small Decrease
4. Stable Stock Price Bank	Increases	Stable
5. Very Asset Sensitive Bank	Large Increase	Small Increase

Section 5.5 discussed positions 2 and 4 in detail. Table 5.7 fills in the alternatives with a simple qualitative description of all other possible risk positions. Notice the graduations of effects in both the cash flow and market value dimensions with the various alternative positioning strategies.

Before proceeding, we will now describe the "hybrid" and the two "extreme" positioning strategies.

Strategy 3—"Hybrid" bank. This strategy covers all the intermediate positions between the "fixed earnings" strategy 2 and the "stable stock price" strategy 4. In terms of the case study, it would apply for any CD maturity greater than 4.5 months and less than 7.5 months. The main characteristic of strategy 3 is that the earnings and equity risks change in opposite directions. That is, for a bank using this strategy, any incremental increase in funding maturity (or duration) would be expected to increase its volatility of earnings but decrease its stock price volatility. Furthermore, a "hybrid" bank will always have earnings that increase if rates unexpectedly rise and a market value of equity that declines with rate increases. It is important to note that the "stable economic equity ratio" position falls within this strategy type. For the case study, it was the six-month CD that prevented any change in the ratio of equity to assets (when both are expressed in market value terms). The six-month CD falls within strategy 3.

Strategy 1—Liability sensitive bank. The term "liability sensitive" refers to the situation where earnings decrease whenever interest rates unexpectedly rise. (Chapter 6 will explain why we must stipulate the term "unexpectedly" in the last sentence.) This condition is associated with balance sheets where the weighted average repricing of liabilities is less than that for the assets. This was the predominant positioning of most savings and loan institutions in the 1980s.

Strategy 5—Very asset sensitive bank. This applies to any bank where the market capital increases with an unexpected increase in interest rates. In terms of the case study example, it would apply to the use of any funding of maturities greater than 7.5 months.

These last two strategies (1 and 5) are referred to as "extreme" because they refer to situations where ALL target accounts increase or decrease in the same direction, rather than with strategies 2, 3, or 4 where the risks will increase in one dimension, but decrease in another.

5.7   INTEREST RATE RISK AND THE COST OF BANKRUPTCY

Now, based on the principles we have established, we should ask if there is an optimal positioning from among the five possibilities listed in Table 5.7. This issue is equivalent to asking the question: Is it possible to create shareholder value consistently over the long-run by taking interest rate risk, i.e., intentionally mismatching, the bank?

We firmly believe that the answer to the last question is **NO**. However, we do believe that it is possible to destroy shareholder value by taking interest rate risk outside certain parameters.

We will justify our opinion in Chapter 6, when we discuss speculating (i.e., betting) on interest rate movements. If the answer is no, then the markets will not reward any bank for taking rate risk. Indeed, banks can only lose value by doing so, since taking rate risk beyond prudent limits will increase the probability that the bank will become insolvent. If forced into bankruptcy, there will be considerable costs imposed on shareholders (not to mention management, employees, depositors, and taxpayers) that is not offset by any compensating benefit from taking the risk in the first place. In game theory terms, rate risk beyond certain limits is a "minus sum" game for shareholders.

Therefore, we are back to the original question of the case study: Which strategy creates the most shareholder value and maximizes the share price? The answer is that strategies 2, 3, and 4 are all equally acceptable to share-holders. They all result in the same stock price. How can we come to such a simple conclusion?

The answer is as simple as the time-honored observation that "there is no free lunch." We start with the premise that the management of the bank in question is no better at forecasting interest rates than the average financial institution or institutional investor. (Any individual who can consistently outguess the markets in predicting interest rates will be independently wealthy and have no need of bank employment or this book!) Shareholders will not pay or reward the bank to do something they can do just as well themselves, but they will CHARGE the bank (with a lower stock price) if the bank destroys value. Consider the following three examples:

Scenario A:

The bank chooses strategy 2 and issues a 4.5-month CD to fix net income for the year. Shareholders disagree and prefer strategy 4, or the 7.5-month strategy.

The shareholder buys $200 of the bank's stock and raises $800 by issuing its own 7.5-month CD and invests the proceeds by purchasing a 4.5-month CD at another bank. (If the investor cannot issue a CD, the equivalent transaction is available in the futures market, as explained in Chapter 6.) This combination of transactions allows everyone to achieve their objectives. Management fixes earnings and shareholders stabilize their net portfolio value. Therefore, shareholders are indifferent to this management decision.

Scenario B:

> The bank chooses strategy 4 and issues a 7.5-month CD. This will cause net income to increase if interest rates rise and net income to fall if rates decline. However, shareholders disagree with this strategy and prefer strategy 2.

The shareholder buys $200 of the bank's stock, raises $800 by issuing a 4.5-month CD, and purchases an $800 7.5-month CD from another bank. As in scenario A, the CD effects may be duplicated with futures transactions. Once again, the shareholder achieves the objective of stable portfolio "earnings" or cash flow, while management achieves its desire to stabilize the bank's stock price. Both are satisfied.

Scenario C:

> The bank sells the six-month loan, buys $1,000 of 30-year fixed rate bonds, and funds the bank with $800 of six-month CDs. The bank runs a significant risk of a negative net worth. Shareholders disagree with the strategy and prefer stabilizing the economic equity ratio.

As in scenarios A and B, shareholders can offset the interest rate mismatch taken by the bank through the issuance of $1,000 of 30-year bonds and the purchase of six-month CDs with the proceeds. (As above, futures transactions may be used in place of these "cash" bond and CD transactions.) These transactions would, indeed, achieve the correct strategy 3 position desired by shareholders with one crucial difference.

Unlike scenarios A and B, in scenario C there is a realistic chance that the bank will go bankrupt, thereby incurring significant legal, regulatory, investment banking, litigation, and liquidation fees. How can the shareholder recover such potential costs? There is no way as long as the bank's stock is held.

The only remedy for the shareholder in this situation is to SELL the stock. The markets will lower the market price of the stock to a level that recognizes the probability that this unhedgable cost will be incurred. The management of the bank has DESTROYED value by taking interest rate risk to such a degree that bankruptcy is a real possibility. If they had stayed with scenarios 2, 3, or 4, there would have been zero probability of bankruptcy due to interest rate shifts.

5.8   THE INTEREST RATE RISK "SAFETY ZONE"

From the previous discussion, we arrive at an important conclusion. To be precise, there is no probability of bankruptcy due to interest rate risk:

- If management succeeds in completely stabilizing the stock price no matter what happens to rates (strategy 4), or

- If management succeeds in completely stabilizing the net interest income no matter what happens to rates (strategy 2), or

- If management pursues any intermediate strategy (strategy 3).

We define these strategies as the interest rate risk "safety zone." If management is outside the "safety zone," then they are destroying shareholder value by taking a risk that shareholders cannot protect themselves against.

The classic illustration of the negative effects of a strategy outside the safety zone is the savings and loan industry in the late 1970s and early 1980s. These institutions were extremely liability sensitive with deposits that repriced much faster than their asset mix, which was dominated by 30-year, fixed-rate mortgages. Therefore, strategy 1 was being adopted. However, with the increase in interest rates experienced in the early 1980s, the industry lost a significant percentage of its net equity value. In response, adjustable-rate mortgages were heavily marketed in an attempt to move toward the safety zone. While substantial progress was achieved, interest rate risk was nevertheless a significant contributor to the "S&L crisis."

Among bankers, a popular notion exists that a primary function of banks is to "borrow short and lend long." This concept implies that there is a liquidity premium in the yield curve, such that, over long periods of time, banks can "capture" the liquidity spread by doing so. Again, this would be a strategy 1 approach, but on a lesser scale than with the S&Ls. Whether one "captures" the liquidity spread or not is not the issue. Whether there is a spread, how big it is, and whether it is positive or negative is a debate for mathematical economics. The key issue is whether the shareholders will pay a premium for the stock of a bank that is doing something that the shareholders can do for themselves. Unfortunately, there is no Santa Claus and there is no free lunch. "Gapping" or "short funding" to capture the spread in the yield curve doesn't benefit the shareholders for the reasons outlined in scenarios A, B, and C. For a margin payment in the thousands (not millions) of dollars, even individuals can buy Treasury bond futures and sell Eurodollar futures if they want to "gap" based on their own interest rate forecast. Therefore, a bank that "gaps" may increase its net income but doesn't increase its stock price. As explained above, it may decrease its stock price because of the increased risk of going bankrupt.

The primary conclusion from this chapter is that bank managements should endeavor to either hedge their earnings against interest rate risk, or be slightly asset sensitive. They should not attempt to maintain a liability-sensitive position over sustained periods. Nor should they be so asset-sensitive that their stock price would actually increase if rates rose.

This is not to say that banks should NEVER attempt a liability-sensitive position. There may be circumstances under which such a position is appropriate. Chapter 6 presents the criteria that should be met for such actions. However, we do believe that banks should not routinely adopt significantly liability-sensitive balance sheet strategies. We would roughly define a "significant" liability-sensitive position as one that would lower net interest income by more than about 1% for a 100-basis point adverse movement in interest rates.

Also, it would be unfair if we ignored those savings banks that do intentionally and prudently run significantly liability-sensitive positions. Keep in mind that it is the threat of bankruptcy that loses shareholder value. We are generally advocating adopting those interest rate risk strategies that cannot threaten the solvency of a bank or S&L. However, it is possible to adopt a riskier strategy, assuming that the S&L has enough capital to decrease the risk of bankruptcy to negligible levels. In our opinion, this is an exceptional situation, but it does exist.

5.9   SUMMARY

We have now presented the first example of a true risk management issue utilizing the generalized risk/return framework developed in Chapters 1 and 2. We have seen that risk cannot be treated as a unidimensional concept. Within the realm of one risk type, interest rate risk, there are at least three target account dimensions and three critical positioning strategies that should be considered.

It is not possible to eliminate interest rate risk from all three dimensions simultaneously. Therefore, any realistic strategy for the bank will entail leaving risk in one or more dimensions. Management should always understand all of these tradeoffs before adopting any long-term strategy.

It was argued that the expected risk-adjusted returns from aggressive interest rate mismatching are zero or negligible and do not nearly compensate the bank for the additional volatility and possible bankruptcy costs that are associated with such strategies. Therefore, banks should attempt to minimize interest rate risk over the long run. This can best be accomplished by adopting a mildly asset-sensitive risk structure.

APPENDIX 5A: IS INTEREST RATE RISK DIVERSIFIABLE?

For those who are familiar with corporate financial theory, one common source of confusion is the issue of whether interest rate risk is a systematic or nonsystematic risk. That is, is interest rate risk diversifiable?

There is no doubt that interest rate risk can be efficiently modified or hedged by the use of a huge array of specialized instruments, some of which were designed for just this purpose. These instruments include government bonds, financial futures, put and call options, interest rate or basis swaps, forward rate agreements, etc. Hence, any shareholder who understands the interest rate sensitivity of a particular stock can easily alter that risk characteristic to whatever final net sensitivity position is desired. This is usually most efficiently accomplished on a portfolio basis, rather than for each stock held.

Because of this facility, many analysts have argued that interest rate risk is "diversifiable." However, this is an inaccurate use of the term, as it was adopted in the Capital Asset Pricing Model. In that framework, diversification relates to volatility characteristics that vanish from the economy when securities are combined into a portfolio. But when interest rate risk is "hedged" through the use of another instrument, the risk does not disappear. It is just transferred to the counterparty on the other side of the hedging transaction. Therefore, interest rate risk is not diversifiable, but it is very easily transferred and changed to whatever final level any individual shareholder desires. Transactions that transfer interest rate risk are now among the most cost effective of any in our society, and they are available to individual shareholders of moderate means as well as the largest institutional shareholders.

In an academic finance sense, interest rate risk in this case is a lot like debt in the famous Modigliani and Miller model of capital structure, where it was proven that capital structure was irrelevant because the shareholder can offset any capital structure position the company may take. In the Modigliani and Miller model, it was assumed that there was no cost of bankruptcy. If, in the arguments above, bankruptcy cost is zero, then ANY interest rate risk level would be acceptable to shareholders and neither creates nor destroys shareholder value. Since there are definite costs of bankruptcy, both capital structure and interest rate risk decisions have the power to destroy value, whether or not they can create it.

When there is bankruptcy cost, even if interest rate risk is diversifiable, the bank's stock takes on the characteristics of a put option (at a price slightly below zero when there are bankruptcy costs). Like the Black-Scholes option model, in this circumstance it is the total volatility of the bank's stock price that matters, not just the portion of volatility that can be diversified away.

APPENDIX 5B: THE RELATIONSHIP BETWEEN THE INTEREST RATE VOLATILITY OF NET INTEREST INCOME AND THE MARKET VALUE OF EQUITY

The case study example results in Table 5.2 should not be literally extrapolated to represent the actual risk relationships for the "real world." To begin to understand some of the risk relationships between earnings and equity, we may utilize a more realistic model of a bank. This appendix analyzes the dividend growth valuation equation from corporate financial theory, along with a hypothetical income statement model. From these, a table will be derived that displays the relative risk levels of net income, net interest income, and the market value of equity, and how they change with respect to one another.

For the relationship between net income and market capitalization, we will rely on the dividend model for smoothly growing dividends:

$$Market\ Capital = \frac{DPOR \times NI}{k - g}$$

where DPOR = Dividend Payout Ratio

NI   = Net Income

k   = Required Return on Economic Capital

g   = Expected Growth Rate of Earnings and Dividends

We have kept this model to basic algebra to illustrate a point as simply as possible. We caution readers that a higher interest rate risk position (apart from changes in cash flow and the market value of the underlying assets) increases risk, increases shareholders' required return, and therefore increases the cost of capital. As argued above, market capital will not increase from this source, but we have not incorporated the subtle links between risk and cost of capital in this example.

For example, if net income does not change with unexpected interest rate shifts, then it is possible to predict the effect on the market value of capital from the equation. If we assume that k = 15% and g = 5% and that DPOR and NI are unchanged in the new interest rate environment, we get the following equations for the market capital before and after the interest rate shift:

$$Market\ Capital_{bef} = \frac{DPOR \times NI_{bef}}{K_{bef} - g}$$

$$Market\ Capital_{aft} = \frac{DPOR \times NI_{aft}}{k_{aft} - g}$$

and dividing one by the other and rearranging terms we get:

$$\frac{NI_{aft}}{NI_{bef}} = \frac{MC_{aft}}{MC_{bef}} \times \frac{(k_{aft} - g)}{(k_{bef} - g)}$$

where MC is market capital.

To use this equation, assume that k_{bef} is 15%, k_{aft} is 16%, and g is 5%. Now, if market capital after the rate change remains unchanged compared to before the shift, we see that net income is predicted to increase by 10% due to the rate change. We can now solve for the change in net income associated with any magnitude change in market capital, or vice versa.

The relationship between net income and net interest income is modeled based on the following assumed income statement for a "typical" high performance bank (Table 5B.1). We wish to know how an arbitrary change in net interest income affects net income. In this case, we assume that a

---

Table 5B.1
Income Statement for a High Performance Bank
Stated as a Percentage of Total Assets

	Before Rate Shift	After Rate Shift
Net Interest Income	4.00%	4.20%
Loan Loss Provision	1.00%	1.00%
Noninterest Income	2.00%	2.00%
Noninterest Expense	3.00%	3.00%
Pretax Income	2.00%	2.20%
Income Taxes @ 40%	0.80%	0.88%
Net Income	1.20%	1.32%

rate shift increases net interest income by 5% and ask what effect this change has on net income.

From Table 5B.1, a 5% increase in net interest income is consistent with a 10% increase in net income if all other factors are held constant.

From the dividend equation and the model in Table 5B.1, it is possible to generate the following Table 5B.2, summarizing the changes in net income, net interest income, and the market value of equity with a variety of balance sheet mismatch positions:

Table 5B.2
Effect of a 100-Basis Point Increase in the Yield Curve
for Various Balance Sheet Mismatch Positions

Strategy Type	Net Income	Net Interest Income	Market Value of Equity
1.	−6.5%	−3.3%	−15.0%
1.	−3.2%	−1.6%	−12.0%
2.	+0.0%	+0.0%	−9.0%
3.	+4.5%	+2.3%	−5.0%
4.	+10.0%	+5.0%	+0.0%
5.	+15.5%	+7.8%	+5.0%
5.	+19.9%	+10.0%	+9.0%

Note: The numbers in the left-most column of this table correspond to the interest rate risk sensitivity/strategy types described in Table 5.7. There are two "1"s and two "5"s in the table because the former represents any strategy where all three target accounts decline with interest rate increases, and the latter is associated with any strategy where all three increase in value with a rise in rates.

APPENDIX 5C: DERIVATION OF THE HEDGING CONDITIONS FOR THE INTEREST RATE RISK TARGET ACCOUNTS

The results displayed in Table 5.2 for the case study problem are not accidental. They may be derived from equations that predict each number shown. Of particular interest are the conditions that result in zero risk for any one of the target accounts. For instance, it was asserted that when the maturities of the loan and CD are the same, then the equity ratio target is insulated against unexpected interest rate shifts. In this appendix, we will derive all of the equations needed to understand these relationships. These concepts were originally popularized by Macaulay more than 60 years ago, but they have gained renewed popularity thanks to the writings of George Kaufman, Alden Toevs, and others.

To proceed with these derivations, it is first necessary to introduce a new term: duration. For this discussion, it is sufficient to use the concept more specifically referred to as "modified duration" or "interest rate elasticity (IRE)." We will use this particular application of duration throughout this book.

IRE is defined as the percentage change in market value of a cash flow stream for a 1% increase in the yield curve. This definition is universal. It applies to any financial concept, security, or institutional entity: a Treasury bill, an options contract, or the equity of a bank. This definition may be stated in the form of an equation as follows:

$$IRE = \frac{\Delta MV}{MV \times \Delta r} = \frac{-D}{1+r} \qquad [1]$$

where   D   = duration in years of the cash flow stream

        r   = yield to maturity (or interest rate)

      MV   = market value of the cash flow stream

A detailed explanation of duration and a derivation of this equation will be presented in Chapter 7. For the bullet loan and CD presented in the case study example, the duration happens to be the same as the maturity of each. We will now derive all of the risk equations for the various target accounts. In all of the derivations, we will assign subscripts to the duration and market value terms, where A refers to assets, L to liabilities, and E to the market value of equity.

5C.1   EQUATIONS FOR THE MARKET VALUE OF EQUITY TARGET

In this section, we will derive the equation that specifies the change in the market value of equity when interest rates shift. We begin with the basic identity equation that the market value of equity is the difference between the market values of assets and liabilities:

$$MV_E = MV_A - MV_L \qquad [2]$$

This equation is differentiated with respect to the interest rate, r:

$$\frac{\Delta MV_E}{\Delta r} = \frac{\Delta MV_A}{\Delta r} - \frac{\Delta MV_L}{\Delta r} \qquad [3]$$

Rearranging equation [1] as it applies to the market value and duration of assets, we get:

$$\frac{\Delta MV_A}{\Delta r} = \frac{-D_A \times MV_A}{(1+r)} \qquad [4]$$

Substituting equation [4] and its counterpart for liabilities into equation [3] yields:

$$\Delta MV_E = (-D_A \times MV_A + D_L \times MV_L) \times \frac{\Delta r}{1+r} \qquad [5]$$

This equation describes the change in the market value of equity for a shift in the yield curve. We can modify it for the percentage change in the market value of equity by dividing equation [5] by equation [2]:

$$\frac{\Delta MV_E}{MV_E} = \left[\frac{-D_A \times MV_A + D_L \times MV_L}{MV_A - MV_L} \right] \times \frac{\Delta r}{1+r} \qquad [6]$$

This equation may be checked for the case study example. For example, Table 5.2 indicates that for a 1% rise in rates, using a three-month CD would lead to a 1.4% decline in the market value of equity. Substituting the appropriate values into equation [6], we get:

$$\frac{\Delta MV_E}{MV_E} = \left[\frac{-0.5 \times 1000 + 0.25 \times 800}{1000 - 800} \right] \times \frac{0.01}{1.06} = -1.4\% \qquad [7]$$

Please note that for both the loan and the CD, their respective durations are the same as their maturities (stated in years). This will always be the case for financial transactions that have only one future cash flow. Therefore, the duration of the six-month loan is 0.5 and the duration of the three-month CD is 0.25. As expected, the −1.4% value is confirmed.

A particularly important result was the "hedge condition" for the market value of equity. That is, what relationship must be maintained if the bank wishes to stabilize its equity value against shifts in the yield curve? This is revealed from an examination of equation [5] for the change in equity, which is always equal to zero whenever the following condition is met:

> Hedge Condition: Market Value of Equity
>
> $$D_A \times MV_A = D_L \times MV_L$$

[8]

This equation may also be checked for its consistency with the case study results shown in Table 5.2. We may rearrange its terms to solve for the CD duration that hedges equity:

$$D_L = \frac{D_A \times MV_A}{MV_L} = \frac{0.05 \times 1000}{800} = \frac{5}{8} \, yr = 7.5 \, months$$

[9]

Indeed, the 7.5 month CD value found here matches that given in Table 5.2.

5C.2 EQUATIONS FOR THE ECONOMIC EQUITY RATIO TARGET

For the effects of interest rate shifts on the economic equity ratio, we start with equation [2] and divide all terms by the market value of assets to obtain the following:

$$\frac{MV_E}{MV_A} = 1 - \frac{MV_L}{MV_A}$$

[10]

The left-hand side of equation [10] is the economic equity ratio. This equation is then differentiated with respect to the interest rate, r:

$$\frac{\Delta (MV_E/MV_A)}{\Delta r} = \left(\frac{MV_L}{MV_A^2}\right) \times \left(\frac{\Delta MV_A}{\Delta r}\right) - \left(\frac{1}{MV_A}\right) \times \left(\frac{\Delta MV_L}{\Delta r}\right)$$

[11]

This may be arranged as follows:

$$\frac{\Delta (MV_E/MV_A)}{\Delta r} = \left(\frac{MV_L}{MV_A}\right) \times \left[\frac{\Delta MV_A}{MV_A \times \Delta r} - \frac{\Delta MV_L}{MV_L \times \Delta r}\right]$$

[12]

The terms in the brackets may be replaced by variations of equation [1]:

$$\frac{\Delta\,(MV_E/MV_A)}{\Delta r} = \left(\frac{MV_L}{MV_A}\right) \times \left[-\frac{D_A}{(1+r)} + \frac{D_L}{(1+r)}\right] \qquad [13]$$

And rearranging terms, we get:

$$\Delta\,(MV_E/MV_A) = \left(\frac{MV_L}{MV_A}\right) \times (D_L - D_A) \times \frac{\Delta r}{(1+r)} \qquad [14]$$

This equation is divided by equation [10] and rearranged to obtain:

$$\frac{\Delta\,(MV_E/MV_A)}{(MV_E/MV_A)} = \frac{MV_L}{(MV_A - MV_L)} \times (D_L - D_A) \times \frac{\Delta r}{(1+r)} \qquad [15]$$

The left-hand side of equation [19] is the percentage change in the economic equity ratio. This equation may now be used to solve for the change in equity ratio for the case study example with the three-month CD funding:

$$\frac{\Delta\,(MV_E/MV_A)}{(MV_E/MV_A)} = \frac{800}{(1000 - 800)} \times (0.25 - 0.50) \times \frac{0.01}{(1.06)} = -0.94\% \qquad [16]$$

This is consistent with the –0.9% result shown in Table 5.2.

The hedge condition for this target is now apparent from equation [15]. The percentage change in the equity ratio will always be zero whenever the duration of assets equals the duration of liabilities:

> Hedge Condition: Economic Equity Ratio
> $$D_A = D_L$$

[17]

This is the proof of the statement made in Section 5.3 that matching durations of assets and liabilities is equivalent to hedging the economic equity ratio. This also confirms the result found in Table 5.2 that it is the six-month CD that hedges the economic equity ratio with a loan maturity of six months.

5C.3   EQUATIONS FOR THE NET INTEREST INCOME TARGET

The derivation of the equations pertaining to net interest income require separate equations for interest income and interest expense over the time period being analyzed. For interest income, start with an equation for a situation where interest rates change sometime early in the time period, as follows:

$$IntInc_{\Delta r \neq 0} = [MV_A \times D_A \times r_A] + [MV_A \times (T - D_A) \times (r_A + \Delta r)\,] \qquad [18]$$

where T is the total time period being analyzed. The first set of bracketed terms in equation [18] gives the interest income during the initial life of the asset(s) where the yield is fixed at the original interest rate. The set of terms within the second pair of brackets is the interest income during the rollover period(s) experienced at the new, shifted interest rate, where delta r is the amount of the rate shift. Clearly, if rates do not change, then equation [18] simplifies to the following:

$$IntInc_{\Delta r = 0} = [MV_A \times D_A \times r_A] + [MV_A \times (T - D_A) \times r_A] \qquad [19]$$

The effect of the rate shift on interest income is the difference between equations [18] and [19], or

$$\begin{aligned} \Delta IntInc &= IntInc_{\Delta r \neq 0} - IntInc_{\Delta r = 0} \\ &= MV_A \times (T - D_A) \times \Delta r \end{aligned} \qquad [20]$$

With analogous equations, the equation for the change in interest expense can be derived as follows:

$$\Delta IntExp = MV_L \times (T - D_L) \times \Delta r \qquad [21]$$

The total effect of the rate shift on net interest income (NII) may now be calculated from the difference between equations [20] and [21]:

$$\begin{aligned} \Delta NII &= \Delta IntInc - \Delta IntExp \\ &= MV_A \times (T - D_A) \times \Delta r \\ &\quad - MV_L \times (T - D_L) \times \Delta r \end{aligned} \qquad [22]$$

We may use equation [22] with the case study situation. For example, for the three-month CD and a 1% shift in interest rates, we get:

$$\begin{aligned} \Delta NII &= 1000 \times (1.0 - 0.5) \times .01 - 800 \times (1.0 - 0.25) \times .01 \\ &= \quad 5.0 \quad - \quad 6.0 \\ &= \quad 1.0 \end{aligned} \qquad [23]$$

This is the same value shown in Table 5.2. Also, from equation [22], it is possible to describe the hedge equation for net interest income:

$$\boxed{\begin{array}{c} \text{Hedge Condition: Net Interest Income} \\ MV_A \times (T - D_A) = MV_L \times (T - D_L) \end{array}} \qquad [24]$$

Equation [24] may be rearranged to find the CD maturity that hedges net interest income for the case study, as follows:

$$
\begin{aligned}
D_L &= T - \frac{MV_A \times (T - D_A)}{MV_L} \\
&= 1.0 - \frac{1000 \times (1.0 - 0.5)}{800} \qquad [25] \\
&= \frac{3}{8} \, yr = 4.5 \, months
\end{aligned}
$$

CHAPTER 6

Interest Rate Risk Mismatching and Hedging

Chapter 5 introduced the issue of interest rate risk management in terms of the multiple target accounts and the dilemma between attempting to stabilize earnings versus insulating the market value of capital against unexpected interest rate shifts. Chapter 5 argued that because the markets do not reward interest rate mismatching the amount of interest rate risk undertaken by banks over sustained periods should be small. This chapter poses another question: Are there any circumstances when intentional interest rate mismatching should be attempted?

To discuss this issue, this chapter first describes some of the fundamental theories of the yield curve and introduces the concept of implied forward rates. It will be demonstrated that balance sheet mismatching strategies should be based on forecasts of these implied forward rates, and not on whether interest rates are simply expected to rise or fall! Finally, this chapter demonstrate how a bank can utilize financial futures contracts to manage its net mismatches.

6.1   INTRODUCTION TO THE YIELD CURVE

The yield curve is usually depicted as a graph of market interest rates as a function of maturity. Technically, the interest rates and maturities should pertain to zero coupon bond equivalents. For most time periods, the yield

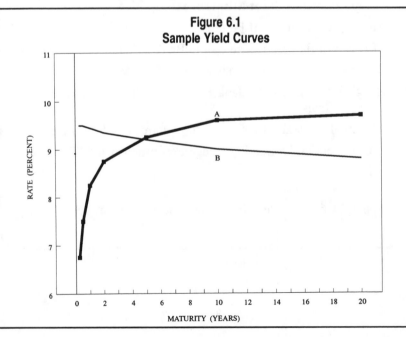

Figure 6.1
Sample Yield Curves

curve looks like the upwardly sloping yield curve labeled "A" in Figure 6.1.

On some occasions, the yield curve may become "inverted" like curve "B" in Figure 6.1, where longer term yields are lower than shorter term yields. This circumstance is associated with relatively high short-term yields. Finally, other more complicated shapes and patterns are possible, with peaks or valleys in certain regions.

What is the significance of the shape of the yield curve? One common explanation is that the yield curve's shape contains an implicit forecast of all future interest rates. These forecasted rates are called the "implied forward rates" and may be interpreted to be a consensus forecast of future interest rates by the marketplace. More controversial is whether a portion of these patterns is caused by premiums for interest rate risk and/or liquidity risk.

6.2   EXAMPLE CALCULATION OF IMPLIED FORWARD RATES

As an illustrative example, consider a simple yield curve in Table 6.1 that consists of four maturities.

Table 6.1
Hypothetical CD Yield Curve on January 1

CD Maturity	Maturity in Days	Maturity Date	Yield
3 Months	90	April 1	6.00%
6 Months	180	July 1	6.50%
9 Months	270	October 1	7.00%
12 Months	360	January 1	7.50%

Note: To simplify the mathematics, we will make the assumption that every month has 30 days and the calendar year consists of 360 days. Also, we will assume that the bid-ask spread, FDIC insurance premium, and reserve requirements are all zero.

From these four yields, it is possible to calculate a number of implicit interest rate forecasts. For example, from the three- and six-month yields, the three-month yield to occur in three months from today is forecasted to be 6.90%. That is, this yield curve is forecasting that a three-month CD issued on April 1 and maturing on July 1 will bear a 6.90% yield. This is called the "three-month forward three-month rate." This forward rate may be interpreted as the rate that permits a "break-even" condition to exist between the January 1 three- and six-month CD rates. To understand this point, consider the following hypothetical situation which makes the further simplifying assumption that all CDs are "bullet" transactions, where all interest is paid at maturity. (This bullet assumption is made to simplify the calculations and is not essential for the point being made.)

> Suppose that a bank issues a $100 CD with a three-month maturity and yield of 6.00% on January 1. It then invests the $100 proceeds by purchasing a six-month CD issued by another bank for a yield of 6.50%. At the end of the first three months, it must "roll over" the original three-month CD principal *and interest* for another three months. This is because the bank will not receive any cash flows from its purchase of the six-month CD until July 1. Hence, it has no choice but to issue another CD to pay off the principal and interest due on April 1 to the purchaser of the original three-month CD. This amount is $101.50 (which is the $100 principal amount plus the interest of $100 × 6% × 90 days / 360 days, or $1.50).

Finally, on July 1, the bank will collect $103.25 from its maturing six-month CD investment. For a break-even condition to result, this entire $103.25 will be paid as the interest and principal on the second three-month CD that was issued on April 1. These cash flows are summarized in Table 6.2.

Notice that the cash flows are exactly matched at every time point. This is how we adhere to the "break-even" condition and is the reason why the rollover CD pays out exactly $103.25 in principal and interest at the six-month point. That is the only amount that balances out the cash flows.

To calculate the rate on the rollover CD, we know that the initial principal amount was $101.50. That was the amount required to pay off the principal and interest of the original three-month CD at the three-month point. Therefore, the amount of interest that the rollover CD paid was $103.25 − $101.50, or $1.75. This represents a yield of 1.724% (which is $1.75 divided by $101.50) for three months, which is annualized by multiplying by four, resulting in a rate of 6.90%. The activities just described are shown in schematic form in Figure 6.2.

Table 6.2
Presentation of Cash Flows Used to Calculate
the Implied Forward Yield

At start of positions on January 1:
Issue $100 three-month CD at 6.00%.
Purchase $100 six-month CD at 6.50%.

After three months, on April 1:
Three-month CD matures, payout is $101.50 (principal and interest).
Issue rollover three-month CD for $101.50 principal amount.

After six months, on July 1:
Six-month CD investment matures and pays $103.25 to bank.
The rollover CD matures, payout is $103.25.

Figure 6.2
Calculation of the Three-Month Forward Three-Month Yield

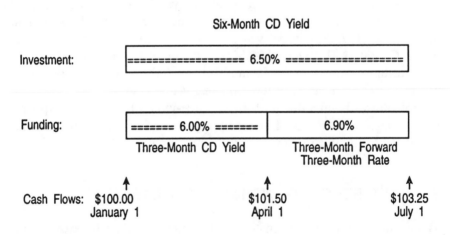

This 6.90% implied forward rate will be shown to be the critical factor in any decision to mismatch a bank balance sheet. We will illustrate this contention in the next section with a simple example.

Now that one example of a forward rate calculation is completed, all of the remaining implied forward rates may be presented in Table 6.3. Every pair of interest rates in the current yield curve will generate the implied forward rate applicable to the time interval between the two maturity dates being considered. The procedure is exactly the same as that described for the three-month forward, three-month CD rate.

Table 6.3
Implied Forward Rates from the Yield Curve in Table 6.1

CD Maturity	Current Rates on January 1	Three-Month Forward Rate Starting on April 1	Six-Month Forward Rates Starting on July 1	Nine-Month Forward Rates Starting on October 1
3 Months	6.00%	6.90%	7.75%	8.55%
6 Months	6.50%	7.39%	8.23%	
9 Months	7.00%	7.88%		
12 Months	7.50%			

We emphasize that every pair of current yield curve rates gives rise to one implied forward rate. For example, the three-month forward nine-month rate of 7.88% is derived from the current three-month and 12-month CD rates. This value of 7.88% is the predicted nine-month CD rate to occur three months in the future. This is a CD that is issued on April 1 and matures on January 1 of the following year.

In contrast, the nine-month forward three-month rate of 8.55% pertains to a CD issued on October 1 and maturing on the following January 1. It is calculated from the current nine-month and 12-month CD rates.

6.3   INTEREST RATE MISMATCHING CASE STUDY

Many bankers associate mismatching strategies with their forecast of interest rate movements. That is, if they believe rates will rise, then they tend to consider either lengthening their liability repricing structure or shortening their asset profile. If they think rates will decline, they will consider lengthening the repricing of assets or shortening their liabilities. As described, this approach may turn out to be incorrect.

To demonstrate why it may be wrong, and to illustrate the correct approach to mismatching activities, consider a variation on the illustrative case study presented in Section 5.2 of Chapter 5. In this example, assume that a bank is started on January 1, but with the single exception that instead of a flat CD yield curve at 6.00% that day, the yield curve is as displayed in Table 6.1. Initially, this example will only consider results over the first six months of the year. That is, the discussion will be limited to the life of the initial six-month loan period only. Later, the results for the entire year will be reviewed.

To further simplify the case study, consider only the three-month and six-month CD funding choices. The target account will be net interest income. Finally, since we will rigorously track every cash flow, assume that all earnings are paid out as dividends but only once at the end of the year.

When this case study was first presented in Chapter 5 with a flat yield curve, we focused our attention exclusively on the risk (volatility) impacts on the three target accounts. However, any mismatching decision a bank might undertake is usually driven by a return, or profit, motivation. Therefore, this chapter will shift the focus to maximizing the net interest income of this case study bank over the first six months of the year. Once complete, the volatility (i.e., risk) implications of these strategies will be considered.

The first step is to calculate the net interest income experienced by the bank for the two funding strategies over a wide variety of interest rate shifts on January 2. The simpler of the two strategies to analyze is that for the six-month CD funding. In this case, the net interest income of the bank is fixed for the entire time period being considered. Therefore, on January 1, the bank will extend the $1,000 six-month loan at a yield of 8.50% and issue an $800 six-month CD at a yield of 6.50%. The six-month earnings (on July 1) will be as displayed in Table 6.4.

Table 6.4
Summary of Net Interest Income: Six-Month CD Funding

On January 1:
    Extend $1,000 six-month loan at 8.50%.
    Issue $800 six-month CD at 6.50%.

On July 1:
Interest Income:	$1,000 8.50% loan	$42.50
Interest Expense:	$ 800 6.50% CD	$26.00
Net Interest Income (Six Months):		$16.50

These figures will not change over this time period no matter how the yield curve might shift on January 2, or at any other time during the first six months of the year. (Some readers will have noticed that for a six-month time period, a matched-maturity funding strategy does indeed hedge or stabilize net interest income. However, for a one-year time period, it is only a 4.5-month CD that hedges earnings. These results can be proved using the hedging equations derived in Appendix 5C.3.)

The alternative strategy under consideration involves "short-funding" with a three-month CD. In analyzing this funding choice, be careful to determine all of the cash flows, including any interest payments or receipts. To illustrate, Table 6.5 will calculate the detailed cash flows for a 1% rise in interest rates on January 2. Later, the results across a variety of potential rate shifts will be presented.

Table 6.5
Summary of Cash Flows: Three-Month CD Funding with a
1% Rise in the Yield Curve on January 2

On January 1:
> Extend $1,000 six-month loan at 8.50%.
> Issue $800 three-month CD at 6.00%.

On January 2:
> Yield curve shifts up by 1% for all maturities and remains there for the remainder of the year.

On April 1:
> First three-month CD matures, payout is $812.00 principal and interest.
> Issue rollover CD for $812.00 principal amount at 7.00% rate.

On July 1:
> Second three-month CD matures and pays $826.21 principal and interest.
> Loan matures and bank receives $1,042.50 principal and interest.

Summary of Net Cash Flows over First Six Months:

Interest Income:	$42.50
Interest Expense:	$26.21
Net Interest Income (Over Six Months):	$16.29

As with the implied forward rate example in Section 6.2, it is critical to consider the effect of the April 1 interest payment in determining the CD amount to issue on that date. The bank has no choice. It has no other source of cash flow to pay the $812.00 of interest due to the purchaser of the first thee-month CD, because the loan will not generate any cash flows until July 1. (Recall that both the loan and the CD have interest payable at maturity.) Therefore, it must "borrow" the $812 amount by issuing a CD with that amount of principal on April 1.

Using this methodology, the six-month net interest income for a wide array of possible new three-month CD yields may be calculated. These are shown in Figure 6.3, compared to the stable net interest income pattern obtained with the six-month CD funding.

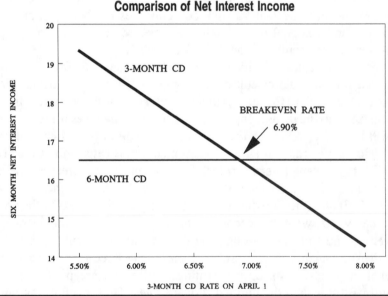

Figure 6.3
Comparison of Net Interest Income

It is now appropriate to reconsider the issue of whether or not to mismatch. Keep in mind that this question must be decided on January 1 as the new year commences with a new bank balance sheet. It is not known how rates will change on January 2. The "conventional wisdom" according to many bankers is that if they expect rates to rise, lengthen funding (i.e., use the six-month CD). If they expect rates to fall, shorten funding (i.e., use the three-month CD).

This maxim has two defects. First, it ignores the risk consequences of these actions. Therefore, the risk-adjusted profitability expected from the mismatching, even if positive, will probably be less than the hurdle rate of return required by shareholders. Thus, value may be destroyed.

Second, even if the shareholders did not care about the risk consequences of the funding decision, it may still turn out to be exactly the wrong thing to do from an expected profitability perspective! This becomes apparent upon a closer examination of Figure 6.3. Keep in mind that the thee-month CD rate on January 1 is 6.00%. Suppose that the ALCO for this hypothetical bank believes that interest rates will rise on January 2 by 50 basis points, or 0.50%. According to the conventional maxim, the hypothetical bank should then adopt the "lengthen funding" strategy and issue a six-month CD. However, the net interest income achieved by the bank, if it is correct and rates increase by 50 basis points, is less than if it had used the shorter term funding!

Indeed, Figure 6.3 reveals that if it is believed that rates will rise by 90 basis points or less, then the three-month funding strategy should be adopted. (Keep in mind that the risk consequences are being ignored for the moment and the goal is to maximize expected earnings.) The proper "break-even" three-month rate on April 1 is 6.90%.

It is no accident that this break-even rollover rate is 6.90%! That was the implied forward rate calculated in Figure 6.2 in the previous section. **The correct criterion for accepting an interest rate mismatch in attempting to maximize earnings is whether one believes that interest rates will be higher or lower than the appropriate implied forward rate in the yield curve, and not simply whether interest rates will rise or fall compared to current interest rates.** That is, one must forecast whether the three-month CD rate which will exist in April will be higher or lower than 6.90%. If you are convinced it will be higher than 6.90%, then you will probably not want to accept the three-month CD funding strategy. However, if you truly believe that the three-month rate will be less than 6.90% in April, then you will probably prefer the three-month strategy if your goal is purely to maximize earnings, since you are predicting that rates will be lower than the implied forward rates. Thus, even if you agree with the markets that rates will increase, but you believe that the extent of the increase will be less than that implied by the forward rates derived from the yield curve, then you would want to fund with the three-month CD.

A corollary to this conclusion is that if the implied forward rates turned out to be exactly right, then it would not matter what funding strategy your bank or any bank adopted. The implied forward rates are the rates that result in the same earnings levels regardless of any balance sheet matching or mismatching. This chapter will prove this for our three-month versus six-month funding case study situation. However, we will now expand our consideration to the entire 12-month time period.

We will calculate the net interest income for the case study situation under the two funding strategies for the four quarters of the year assuming that the implied forward rates turn out to be exactly right. To do this, we must utilize the implied forward rates displayed in Table 6.3. The results are displayed in Table 6.6.

Table 6.6
Summary of Quarterly Net Interest Income
if Implied Forward Rates Occur as Forecasted

	1st Quarter	2nd Quarter	3rd Quarter	4th Quarter	Total Year
Loan:					
Volume:	1000	1000	1000	1000	1000
Yield:	8.50%	8.50%	10.23%	10.23%	9.37%
Interest Income:	21.25	21.25	25.58	25.58	93.66
================	======	======	======	======	======
Funding Strategies:					
Three-Month CD Funding:					
Volume:	800.00	812.00	783.50	798.68	798.55
Yield:	6.00%	6.90%	7.75%	8.55%	7.30%
Interest Expense:	12.00	14.00	15.18	17.07	58.25
Net Interest Income:	9.25	7.25	10.40	8.51	35.41
Six-Month CD Funding:					
Volume:	800.00	800.00	783.50	783.50	791.75
Yield:	6.50%	6.50%	8.23%	8.23%	4.47%
Interest Expense:	13.00	13.00	16.13	16.13	58.25
Net Interest Income:	8.25	8.25	9.46	9.46	35.41

Notice that the CD yields for the three-month strategy are directly from the three-month row in Table 6.3. For the six-month CD strategy, the yield for the first two quarters are fixed at 6.50%. The rollover occurs on July 1 at the July 1 six-month forward rate of 8.23%. Similarly, the loan rolls over on July 1 at the six-month CD rate plus the credit spread of 2%, or 10.23%. Finally, we should explain the usual pattern of CD volumes, especially on July 1. Keep in mind that we must rigorously account for every cent of cash flow for these calculations to be meaningful. On July 1, the loan repays interest and principal of $1,042.50. We assume that the borrower only needs to borrow $1,000. Therefore, we have an extra $42.50 of interest income that lowers the amount of the CD we must issue on July 1. (Also, we assumed that dividends are only paid at the end of the year.)

As we guessed, the net interest incomes for both strategies are identical for the total year at $35.41. Therefore, from an economic perspective, the profitability levels are equal. However, there are two differences that should be noted: one minor and one major. The minor difference is that the pattern of net interest incomes by quarter are different in the two strategies. Whenever the implied forward rates differ significantly from current interest rates, then whichever strategy involves greater mismatching will show the greater volatility in its quarter by quarter sequence of forecasted earnings, as is indicated in Table 6.6. Therefore, even if you are convinced that the yield curve forecast is correct, you should be indifferent as to whether you accept mismatches or not. To accept mismatching implies not only leaving the bank at the mercy of future interest rate volatility, it also means subjecting the bank to greater net interest income volatility even if the implied forward rates are exactly right!

The major difference is that there are substantial risk differences between the two strategies. The mismatch (three-month CD) strategy involves far greater potential earnings volatility than the six-month CD approach, regardless of what unexpected changes occur in future interest rates. This is visualized in Figure 6.3 by the "slope" of the net interest income line with the three-month CD funding compared to the horizontal (stable) results with the six-month CD. This issue was discussed in Chapter 5. The three-month funding strategy is outside the interest rate risk safety zone. It should never be undertaken, at least not for the entire amount of the balance sheet. Practical mismatch limits will be presented in Section 6.5.

Remember: Always compare your forecast of interest rates with the implied forward rates derived from the current yield curve, and not with the current set of interest rates.

6.4   CRITERIA FOR INTEREST RATE MISMATCHING

We are now in a position to list the criteria that must be met to profit from any interest rate mismatching strategy:

Criteria for profitable interest rate mismatching:

- You must have a forecast of future interest rates that differs from the implied forward rates in the current yield curve (which represent the market consensus forecast.)

- You must be right and the marketplace must be wrong.

- You should be comfortable with the risk consequences of your mismatching activities.

Keep in mind that the yield curve is a true consensus of the best market professionals. They are willing to **guarantee** that you can lock in the implied forward rates in the yield curve. This is commonly accomplished by the use of futures or forward contracts. Therefore, you must be confident enough in your own forecasting skills that you can basically "beat the markets."

As should be abundantly clear from previous chapters, we do not believe that banks can systematically beat the markets. Even if one could, the profits achieved over sustained periods would have to be greater than the required rate of return for the additional volatility risk that would be experienced. We firmly believe that the markets are efficient enough to prevent systematic value creation through interest rate mismatching. All of the academic studies we have seen support this point of view. If you accept it, then you should not attempt to "outguess" or "outmaneuver" the markets by aggressive interest rate forecasting and positioning.

Having asserted this, we will also claim that modest levels of mismatching might be very healthy for most banking organizations! The following explains what we mean by "modest" levels of mismatching and why we say this.

6.5   TO MISMATCH OR NOT TO MISMATCH?

In Chapter 5, we demonstrated that there are multiple target accounts and that it is impossible to insulate the bank in all target dimensions and for all time periods against interest rate risk. Hence, the task for all banks is to find a range of risk levels for each target account that are acceptable and mutually achievable under normal circumstances. This means continuously living with modest amounts of volatility in several dimensions and constantly shifting the relative risk levels among the various targets within the safety zone defined in Chapter 5. Thus, we have no choice but to accept risk levels that are constantly increasing in one or more dimensions while we try to decrease them in others. This was one of the important conclusions of Chapter 5.

Also, even if there were only one target account and the bank wanted to have zero risk in that single dimension, this would be an equally impossible task, not for theoretical reasons, but for practical ones. That is, the repricing characteristics of bank products have large degrees of uncertainty in the cash flow characteristics associated with them, such as the basis risk of the prime rate, the balance behavior of demand deposits, and the prepayment rates of mortgages. Hence, it is impossible to structure a zero risk balance sheet in any single dimension no matter how skilled the asset and liability management staff or how perfect the data sources may be. This will be an important conclusion of Chapter 7, which presents a variety of practical measurement and analytical problems.

Given these theoretical and practical difficulties, why not just pick one of the three targets and attempt to minimize its risk? Our experience is that to do so becomes equivalent to issuing powerful sleeping pills to all of the ALCO members. That is, if they believe that the risk profile is being routinely minimized and is on automatic pilot, then they will lose their interest in understanding, monitoring, and questioning the management of that risk type.

We recommend that the ALCO remain on alert to all of its risk dimensions by actively questioning, managing, and adjusting those positions. To do this, they should constantly be faced with a series of analyses and decisions. They should believe that they are responsible for monitoring and managing the interest rate positions of the bank in more than one target dimension so that they do not lose sight of the tradeoffs inherent in that decreasing one increases another. The simplest way to accomplish this is to challenge the ALCO with a modest level of discretionary position-taking (mismatching) authority.

The benefit from such an approach is that it will keep the attention level of the ALCO high. It will promote active discussions and debate in the ALCO meetings. It will motivate the ALCO members who are not routinely involved with the markets to monitor market trends and to seek opportunities to integrate their incremental marketing and pricing strategies with the positioning objectives of the ALCO given anticipated market conditions. Besides, it is fun!

How much mismatching should be allowed by the ALCO? As a crude rule of thumb, we suggest that incremental mismatch risk be limited to no more than 2% of forecasted net interest income over a 12-month horizon. Also, we recommend that mismatching never be large enough to take the bank outside of the safety zone defined in Chapter 5. By definition, then, any incremental mismatch decision will modestly increase the riskiness of one target account, but it will also serve to decrease the riskiness of at least one other target. In this context, mismatches represent a form of fine-tuning of the relative risk levels among the targets.

Circumstances where all monitored target accounts increase in riskiness due to a proposed mismatch position means that the bank is wandering outside of its safety zone. This should be a truly exceptional situation and should only be attempted after a vigorous and complete discussion of the risk implications in the ALCO meeting. For the bank to be in such a position in the first place represents an extremely imbalanced starting position, analogous to position numbers 1 or 5 in Table 5.7. The proposed additional mismatching would take the bank even further away from the normal operating zone recommended by the authors. This is not necessarily bad, but should be well understood by the ALCO, and perhaps the board, as a rather speculative and aggressive "bet" on interest rate movements, rather than routine risk management.

6.6   HEDGING BALANCE SHEET MISMATCHES

We now return to the original case study presented in Section 6.3 and use it to illustrate the concept of hedging mismatches. Suppose that you have decided that you want to minimize all interest rate mismatches, but you find that there is only demand for a six-month loan maturity and a three-month CD maturity among your customers and you wish to accommodate these desires. Is there any way that you might accept those mismatched transactions and still manage to stay within the safety zone?

One approach was presented in Section 6.2. That would involve entering into a series of transactions in the national CD markets that offset the balance sheet mismatch. In this case, it would be necessary to purchase a six-month CD and issue a three-month CD, probably with a dealer or brokerage house. These transactions are presented in Table 6.7.

Notice that the bank has achieved its desired correction of the original mismatch. In the "after hedge" balance sheet, the three-month brokered CD asset is offset by the three-month customer CD, leaving the bank with

Table 6.7
Balance Sheet Hedging Example

Starting Situation (Before Hedge):

Assets:	Liabilities:
$1,000 Six-Month Customer Loan at 8.50%	$ 800 Three-Month Customer CD at 6.00%
	$ 200 Equity

Balance Sheet After Hedging:

Assets:	Liabilities:
$1,000 Six-Month Customer Loan at 8.50%	$ 800 Six-Month Brokered CD at 6.50%
$ 800 Three-Month Brokered CD at 6.00%	$ 800 Three-Month Customer CD at 6.00%
	$ 200 Equity

the $1,000 six-month loan funded by an $800 six-month CD and $200 of equity.

The type of hedge described here is referred to as a "cash" or "on-balance sheet" hedge. That is, actual (cash) purchases and sales of securities are transacted. Unfortunately, the difficulty of such an approach is that it significantly increases the size of the bank's balance sheet. In this example, the balance sheet has increased in size by $800. Therefore, many of the bank's profitability measures and capital ratios will decline as a result of the hedge positions. Moreover, a relatively small bank pays a high premium (both in lack of name recognition and lack of experience) in a market where it is an infrequent participant. Is there any alternative to this apparently inefficient ballooning of the bank's balance sheet that also requires executing wholesale transactions at the same rates and same brokerage commissions as Morgan Guaranty?

6.7   HEDGING WITH FINANCIAL FUTURES

This is an ideal situation for considering a simple futures hedge. Financial futures contracts are exchange-traded instruments that allow a firm to alter the repricing or maturity characteristics of a financial transaction. This discussion is intended to introduce the concept of hedging with financial futures. Those interested in understanding the detailed mechanics of accomplishing futures transactions are referred to a number of good reference books on the subject. Also, for the sake of clarity, we have assumed futures contract characteristics that most conveniently fit the parameters of our case study example. Although the concepts are correct, many of the technical details—such as the actual delivery dates—are not correct. Again, we refer the interested reader to those books dedicated to an in-depth treatment of this subject.

The futures rates that exist in the exchanges are conceptually identical to the implied forward rates calculated from the current yield curve (except for minor cash flow impacts of mark-to-market settlement on a daily basis). They are designed to permit the same economic effects as the cash hedge described in the last section. For this discussion, assume that there exist futures contracts based on the 90-day CD rate with expiration dates on the 1st, 91st, 181st, and 271st days of the year. These dates correspond to January 1, April 1, July 1, and October 1 of our hypothetical 360-day year. Therefore, assume that the January 1 futures rate applicable to the "April delivery" should be 6.90%.

(*Note*: There are times when the implied forward rate and the futures rate for a corresponding time period differ. This represents a theoretical arbitrage opportunity if the rational economic differences from mark-to-market settlement have been accounted for correctly. It is beyond the scope of this book to discuss this point.)

Exchange-traded futures contracts for 90-day instruments trade in increments of $1 million. However, to accommodate this case study, assume that contracts are available in increments of $100.

Since we are attempting to lengthen the maturity of a liability, we must "sell" or "short" eight of the hypothetical contracts for April 1 delivery. (The proper hedge ratio can be refined, as will be discussed in Section 6.10.) This means that we agree with the exchange that we will "deliver" or sell $800 worth of 90-day CDs to the exchange on April 1 with a yield of 6.90%. In practice, actual delivery of the underlying instrument is extremely rare and unnecessary. What is important is that the economic equivalent cash flows are achieved as if delivery actually did occur. This eight contract short positions would replace the two brokered CD transactions presented in Section 6.7.

The advantage of the futures transaction is that it will provide the counterparties with the economic effects of the cash hedge transaction in the last section, but without entering into any actual cash securities purchases and sales, and thus without the ballooning of the balance sheet. How is this accomplished?

As previously stated, an agreement is entered into with the futures exchange to deliver a 90-day CD on the delivery date in April carrying a yield of 6.90%. This agreement is then subjected to a simplified mark-to-market process for any interim changes in that specific futures rate on every business day between the opening of the position and its closure. In this case study example, the position would be opened on January 1 and closed on the 91st day of the year, or April 1. At the end of each trading day, the exchange notes the closing rate for each delivery and does the simplified mark-to-market calculation.

(*Note*: The mark-to-market calculation is simplified in that it does not take into account the time value of money. For the April contract, a one basis point change on January 2 causes the same mark-to-market calculation as one occurring on March 30. This aspect of the settlement process has very specific effects on the correct calculation of the theoretical hedge ratios, although these effects will be ignored in this book. We will assume that any futures gains or losses are settled only at the time of closing out of the position.)

For every one percentage point rise in the futures rate on each of our eight "short" $100 contracts, we expect to receive $0.25 from the exchange. For every percentage point fall in the futures rate, we would pay $0.25 to the exchange. This $0.25 amount is the approximate economic effect of a one basis point yield shift on a $100 90-day contract, calculated as 1% per year × $100 × 90 days maturity/360 days per year. (*Note*: For an actual $1,000,000 futures contract, the value of a one percentage point change would be $2,500.)

6.8   EFFECTS OF A FUTURES HEDGE ON THE BANK'S FINANCIAL RESULTS

To see how the futures contract affects our mismatched balance sheet to provide an effective hedge, consider three interest rate scenarios for the 90-day CD rate on April 1: 6.00%, 6.90%, and 7.50%. The case of the 6.90% scenario is one where the implied forward rates in the yield curve occur as predicted by the marketplace. The case of the 6.00% rate is one where the three-month CD rate remains unchanged from January 1 through April 1, despite the 6.90% implied forward rate that existed on January 1. Thus, in this situation, interest rates turn out to be lower than the implied forward rates that existed on January 1. The 7.50% case is one where interest rates move higher than was forecasted by the implied forward rates.

Table 6.8 analyzes the detailed cash flows for the 7.50% scenario. Please note that for all of the futures hedge examples presented in the remainder of this chapter, the hedge objective will be to decrease the mismatch between the six-month loan and three-month CD on the balance sheet. The specific item being hedged will be the three-month CD. There-

---

Table 6.8
Six-Month Cash Flow Analysis of Futures Hedge Example
For Three-Month CD Rate on April 2 of 7.50%

On January 1:

- Issue $800 three-month CD at 6.00%.
- Lend $1,000 for six months at 8.50%.
- Short eight CD futures contract for April 1 delivery.

On April 1:

- Pay $812 (interest and principal) to the holder of original CD.
- Close out futures position and receive $1.20 from exchange as the settlement gain on the position (calculated as 60 bp gain × $0.0025 per bp × 8 contracts).
- Issue a new three-month CD for $810.80 at 7.50%. (*Note:* This is the amount required to "refinance" the maturing CD net of the futures gain. Had the futures position not been undertaken, then the amount of the new CD would have been $812.00, as was shown in Table 6.5.)

On July 1:

- Pay $826.00 interest and principal to CD owner.
- Receive $1,042.50 interest and principal from the maturing six-month loan.

Six-Month Net Interest Income:

- Interest income = $42.50
- Interest expense = $26.00
- Net interest income = $42.50 − $26.00 = $16.50.

---

fore, all futures gains and losses will be netted into the CD funding transactions, as will be evident in all of the examples.

Notice that the futures gain incurred on April 1, the closeout date of the hedge position, is blended into the new financing requirement on that date in determining the amount of the next CD to issue. This must be done

since there is no other cash flow on that date. Recall that the loan in this
example is a six-month bullet loan where all principal and interest will be
repaid on July 1, hence there are no loan cash flows available in April.

The six-month net interest income of $16.50 is identical to the finding
in Table 6.6 for the three-month CD funding where the implied forward
rate of 6.90% is realized. In that table, the net interest income for the first
two quarters was $9.25 and $7.25, respectively. These add up to $16.50.
What the futures contracts accomplished was to "lock in" or guarantee that
the futures rate of 6.90% would be realized on April 1.

To illustrate this point, we will repeat the calculations shown in Table
6.8 for the other two rates: 6.00% and 6.90%. These are summarized in
Table 6.9 to derive the six-month net interest incomes for each scenario
for the two quarters both with and without the futures hedge.

Table 6.9
Effects of Futures Hedge on
Six-Month Net Interest Incomes

	Three-Month CD Rate on April 1:		
	6.00%	6.90%	7.50%
Without Futures Hedge:			
Interest Income	42.50	42.50	42.50
Interest Expense	24.18	26.01	27.22
Net Interest Income	18.32	16.49	15.28
With Futures Hedge:			
Interest Income	42.50	42.50	42.50
Interest Expense (Hedged)	26.01	26.01	26.00
Net Interest Income (Hedged)	16.49	16.49	16.50
Memo:			
New CD Amount on April 1	813.80	812.00	810.80

Notice that the effect of the hedge is approximately to "lock in" the
six-month net interest income so that it is essentially equivalent to the
6.90% scenario in the unhedged situation. That is, the effect of the futures
position is to ensure that the economic results are equivalent to a situation
where the forecast of implied forward rates comes true. The interested

reader is encouraged to work through these calculations for other possible three-month CD rates on April 1. Regardless of the rate used, similar net interest incomes will result.

6.9 ILLUSTRATING A HEDGE ANALYSIS AT AN ALCO MEETING

Now that you understand how to use financial futures as one mechanism to correct mismatches in your balance sheet, how do you persuade the ALCO to consider such a proposition? We will offer one suggestion that has proven to be the most effective in our own experiences.

This approach is consistent with all of the fundamentals presented in this book. It emphasizes the risk-return tradeoff of the hedging decision. Most importantly, it avoids the major pitfall of any such consideration—confusing hedging decisions with outright speculation on interest rate movements. Hedging should never be confused with a bet on future interest rate movements. To illustrate the distinction, consider the two approaches that might be used in presenting the hedge decision for our particular case study:

Approach 1: The Speculator

The asset and liability manager states the following: "Today, we will consider whether or not we should hedge our balance sheet mismatch. We understand that the correct comparison to make involves our forecast of interest rates in April versus the implied forward rate of 6.90%. Since we believe that the three-month CD rate in April will be higher than 7.00%, I recommend that we put on the hedge. However, if we believed that the CD rate in April would be lower than 6.90%, then we should not consider the hedge."

This asset and liability manager is correct in comparing the bank's rate forecast with the appropriate implied forward rate. However, he is doing a great disservice to his bank by asserting that the proper criterion for the hedge is whether or not it is expected to show a gain. He is really showing us that he is a bond trader in an asset and liability manager's clothing! For our case study example, this approach violates our limit that no more than 2% of the bank's annualized net interest income should be put at risk by any "positioning" decision.

In contrast to this speculative approach, consider the alternative approach.

Approach 2: The Risk and Return Manager

The asset and liability manager states the following: "Today, we will consider our forecasted interest rate risk profile and discuss whether or not we are still comfortable with it. We first want to confirm that the bank remains within its general policy limits. If not, then we should consider actions to correct those mismatches. We will assess this with a detailed position analysis using our primary target account: forecasted net interest income over the next six months. We may decide to fine-tune our balance sheet profile on a modest scale depending on our current feeling about interest rate movements."

This manager is being consistent with the recommendations put forward in this book. The point is to be sure that the bank is within its general risk limits first, and only then will the bank promote discussions about the outlook for interest rates within the context of modest "fine-tuning" adjustments.

For our simplistic case study example, we must assume that the ALCO decides to engage in corrective action to decrease the amount of balance sheet mismatching it faces on January 1 with the six-month loan and three-month CD. How can we facilitate a decision about how much of the mismatch to correct?

One effective approach is to conduct a simulation of a wide variety of possible yield curve shifts and to display the effects of these changes on the level and volatility of earnings. This is referred to as a Monte Carlo simulation. Table 6.9 displays the calculation procedure for a Monte Carlo simulation for a simple step probability distribution for the unhedged balance sheet and for one possible futures hedge position. It is important in any such simulations that a probability distribution consistent with the ALCO's expectations be employed. For this example, we assume that the bank's ALCO believes that the probability distribution for the 90-day CD rate on April 1 will center around 6.50%, which differs from the implied forward rate on January 1 of 6.90%. There is nothing wrong with this. Hopefully, the ALCO has plausible reasons for their difference from the market consensus. The assumed forecast is shown in Table 6.10.

With this distribution, it is possible to simulate the bank's net interest income over the first six months of the year in each of the three possible interest rate scenarios. The results of these simulations are summarized in Table 6.11. For the column labeled "Hedged Bank," the values pertain to the short eight futures contracts previously discussed.

In this simple case study, there is only one relevant yield—the three-month CD rate—on one date, April 1, that we must analyze. Therefore, it

Table 6.10
ALCO Probability Distribution for the April 1 90-Day CD Rate

CD Rate	Probability
6.00%	25%
6.50%	50%
7.00%	25%

Table 6.11
Calculation of Monte Carlo Results for the Unhedged
and Hedged (Eight Contract) Strategies

April 1 CD Rate	Probability	Unhedged Bank Six-Month Net Interest Income	Hedged Bank Six-Month Net Interest Income
6.00%	25%	18.32	16.49
6.50%	50%	17.31	16.49
7.00%	25%	16.29	16.49
Weighted Average Rate		17.31	16.49
Standard Deviation		0.72	0.00

Note: Values are net interest income forecasted for the first six months of the year.

is possible to calculate the results for every possible outcome. However, in a real situation, there would be literally thousands of plausible combinations of yields of a myriad of maturities on the various repricing dates that must be considered. Moreover, it is incumbent on the analyst to limit the yield curve distributions to those that do not allow large arbitrage opportunities. Therefore, highly specialized software is required to conduct these simulations. For a further discussion of Monte Carlo simulations, see Faye Kobashigawa and Donald R. van Deventer's commentary "PC Software Makes Risk Analysis Accurate, Fast, and Cheap," *American Banker*, April 5, 1991.

By this same procedure, results may be obtained for a wide variety of possible futures hedge ratios, for example from 0 contracts (unhedged) to 20 contracts. Once all of the potential averages and standard deviations are

calculated, they are displayed in a risk/return profile similar to that originally presented in Figure 1.1. For this case study, these results are presented in Table 6.12 and Figure 6.4.

Table 6.12
Simulation Results for Various Futures Hedge Ratios
(Values Are $ Thousands and Represent Net Interest Income for Six Months)

Number of Futures Contracts Shorted	April 1 90-Day CD Rates:			Weighted Average	Standard Deviation
	25% @ 6.00%	50% @ 6.50%	25% @ 7.00%		
0	18.32	17.31	16.29	17.31	0.72
2	17.86	17.10	16.34	17.10	0.54
4	17.41	16.90	16.39	16.90	0.36
6	16.95	16.70	16.44	16.70	0.18
8	16.49	16.49	16.49	16.49	0.00
10	16.04	16.29	16.54	16.29	0.18
12	15.58	16.09	16.60	16.09	0.36
14	15.12	15.88	16.65	15.88	0.54
16	14.67	15.68	16.70	15.68	0.72
18	14.21	15.48	16.75	15.48	0.90
20	13.75	15.27	16.80	15.27	1.08

Notice from Figure 6.4 that the risk minimizing position is indeed the
short eight futures contracts hedge. This should be expected since the characteristics of the hypothetical hedging instrument were tailored perfectly to
fit the mismatch situation in terms of volume, maturity of the underlying
position being hedged, and delivery date. As we shall see, real life is not
so straightforward.

The unhedged position in this figure is at the upper right-hand region of
the display. This is consistent with the unhedged position having very high
risk. It also has the largest expected net interest income. (Recall that our
probability distribution for the forecasted three-month CD rate was that
there was a 75% chance that the 90-day CD rate on April 1 would be

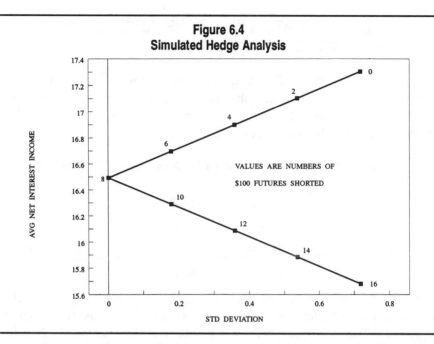

Figure 6.4
Simulated Hedge Analysis

below 6.90%, the implied forward rate. Therefore, the highest expected net interest income will be associated with the completely unhedged, mismatching strategy.)

From Chapter 5, one border of the safety zone is where net interest income is stabilized against rate shifts. The zone then extends into a modest asset sensitive region. In examining Table 6.12, the lines labeled 0 to 6 futures contracts shorted are all liability sensitive. That is, as the forecast of rates goes higher, net interest income decreases. The safety zone starts at eight contracts, since this is where net interest income is stabilized. The asset-sensitive region applies to hedges with nine or more contracts. (Although we do not prove it here, the safety zone includes those positions where eight through 12 contracts are employed.) Therefore, the ALCO should first decide to hedge with at least eight contracts just to get to the safety zone, then discuss whether it wants to use even more than eight contracts up to a maximum of 12.

Since the ALCO believes that interest rates will be lower than the implied forward rates, there is no incentive for them to attempt going beyond using eight contracts. To do so would only lower expected earnings. Therefore, a prudent ALCO in this situation would approve a hedge using a futures position where 8 $100 contracts are sold for delivery on April 1.

6.10   HEDGE SIMULATION WITH BANK FORECAST HIGHER THAN IMPLIED FORWARD RATES

Now, suppose that the ALCO for the case study bank has a forecast distribution different from that in Table 6.10, one where forecasted rates are higher than the implied forward rates from the January 1 yield curve. For example, consider the following distribution:

ALCO Probability Distribution for the April 1 90-Day CD Rate

CD Rate	Probability
6.50%	15%
7.25%	55%
8.10%	30%

Notice that this distribution is broader than that presented in Table 6.10. The former distribution spanned a range of 100 basis points (from 6.00% to 7.00%). This one spans 160 basis points (8.10% – 6.50%). It also differs from the first example in that it has a skewed probability distribution, with less probability on the lowest value, and greater weightings on the others.

The procedure is once again to run the Monte Carlo simulations to obtain a table of results and graph similar to Table 6.12 and Figure 6.4. Table 6.13 presents the simulation results for various futures hedge ratios. Figure 6.5 depicts a simulated hedge analysis.

Table 6.13
Simulation Results for Various Futures Hedge Ratios—
Forecasted Rates Higher Than Implied Forward Rates
(Values Are $ Thousands and Represent Net Interest Income for Six Months)

Number of Futures Contracts Shorted	April 1 90-Day CD Rates: 15% @ 6.50%	55% @ 7.25%	30% @ 8.10%	Weighted Average	Standard Deviation
0	17.31	15.78	14.06	15.49	1.08
2	17.10	15.96	14.67	15.74	0.81

cont.

Number of Futures Contracts Shorted	April 1 90-Day CD Rates:			Weighted Average	Standard Deviation
	15% @ 6.50%	55% @ 7.25%	30% @ 8.10%		
4	16.90	16.14	15.28	16.00	0.54
6	16.70	16.32	15.89	16.25	0.27
8	16.49	16.50	16.51	16.50	0.01
10	16.29	16.67	17.12	16.75	0.28
12	16.09	16.85	17.73	17.00	0.55
14	15.88	17.03	18.34	17.25	0.82
16	15.68	17.21	18.95	17.50	1.09
18	15.48	17.39	19.57	17.75	1.36
20	15.27	17.56	20.18	18.00	1.63

Figure 6.5
Simulated Hedge Analysis—
Forecasted Rates Higher than Implied Forward Rates

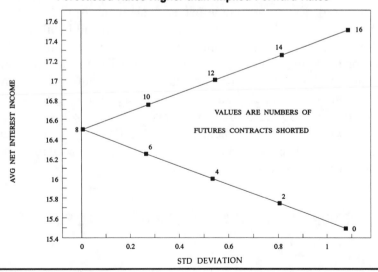

Notice that the results in Figure 6.5 appear just the opposite of those in Figure 6.4. That is, the unhedged position is now in the lower right-hand region of the risk/return profile. This is due to the forecast of interest rates now being higher than the implied forward rate of 6.90%. Therefore, remaining unhedged and very liability-sensitive results in the poorest expected earnings. Hedging in this situation is a "win-win" proposition in that risk is reduced and expected profitability improves!

As in Section 6.8, the ALCO should first and foremost decide to get back to its safety zone. Therefore, it should hedge with at least eight futures contracts. But, in contrast to the previous situation, in this situation, there are positive expected returns from hedging with more than eight contracts. The question is now one of how much further beyond the minimum risk position of eight contracts sold should the bank consider?

The safety zone again extends from eight to 12 contracts sold, where 12 contracts would effectively achieve the "hedge market equity" position equivalent to using a 7.5 month CD (strategy four in Table 5.7). We believe that it would be prudent for this bank to set operating limits that extend in Figure 6.5 from the positions achieved with from eight to 10 futures contracts sold. Within this region, there is only a very slight asset-sensitivity. Therefore, we recommend that the ALCO consider using perhaps nine contracts sold. This reflects the forecast by this ALCO that rates will be higher than the implied forward rates, but it is well within the operating limits set by the bank. An "aggressive" mismatch position would be one that took the bank to its operating limit of 10 contracts sold.

In our experience, it is a simple matter to show the ALCO graphs similar to Figures 6.4 or 6.5. From such graphs, the asset and liability manager should explain that the bank's safety zone is the region bordered by the points labeled eight through 12. If the ALCO believes that rates will be lower than the implied forward rates, then a graph similar to Figure 6.4 will be shown and the ALCO should probably adopt a hedged (eight contract) position. If the ALCO strongly believes that rates will rise above the implied forward rates, then a picture similar to Figure 6.5 will be generated, and a slight asset sensitivity (such as the point associated with nine contracts) may be selected.

6.11 HISTORICAL SIMULATION USING ACTUAL FUTURES AND SPOT RATES

Thus far, all of our discussions have involved purely hypothetical yield curves and rate shifts. Graphs such as Figures 6.4 and 6.5 are highly idealized in that "perfect" hedges are almost never possible. By a perfect hedge, we refer to a hedge where all risk is eliminated, which is to say that the

Table 6.14
Data Used for Historical Simulation

	Three Month LIBOR	Six Month LIBOR	Futures Rates by Delivery Month-Year:					
Date			June 90	September 90	December 90	March 91	June 91	September 91
01/15/90	8.19	8.25	8.11					
02/15/90	8.25	8.33	8.40					
03/15/90	8.50	8.69	8.76					
04/16/90	8.38	8.57	8.51	8.56				
05/15/90	8.33	8.44	8.39	8.46				
06/15/90	8.25	8.30	8.33	8.27				
07/16/90	8.12	8.20		8.06	8.03			
08/15/90	7.93	7.93		7.89	7.76			
09/14/90	8.06	8.06		8.10	7.91			
10/15/90	8.13	8.13			8.00	7.85		
11/15/90	8.00	7.93			7.90	7.56		
12/14/90	7.75	7.66			7.90	7.37		
01/15/91	7.50	7.50				7.37	7.27	
02/15/91	6.56	6.50				6.67	6.58	
03/15/91	6.25	6.37				6.38	6.56	
04/15/91	6.00	6.18					6.31	6.55
05/15/91	6.00	6.13					6.11	6.33
06/14/91	6.19	6.43					6.19	6.53
07/15/91	6.19	6.37						6.30
08/15/91	5.62	5.82						5.73
09/16/91	5.43	5.37						5.50

standard deviation is zero. Therefore, in real hedge situations, it is usually not possible to achieve a zero risk position. To provide the reader with a more realistic perspective, we have conducted a simple historical simulation using actual spot and futures rates.

This simulation utilizes mid-month LIBOR spot and Eurodollar futures rates for hypothetical hedges identical to the case study situation where a "new bank" is set up on or about the 15th of each month starting in January 1990, and continuing with a new set of positions once each mid-month until May 1991. Hence, there are 18 "new banks" set up and analyzed. The interest rate data used in this study are shown in Table 6.14. (We have used LIBOR and Eurodollar rates because CD futures contracts no longer exist. The concepts are exactly the same.)

We will present the detailed calculations for one of the 18 analyses in Table 6.15. For this particular example, assume that our bank is starting on May 15, 1990. The loan will mature on November 15, and the CD will mature on August 15. The CD must be rolled over on August 15 for another three-month period, and it is the forward period from August 15 through November 15 that we wish to hedge using the Eurodollar futures contract due to deliver in September 1990. This is the closest alignment we can achieve to our target rollover date of August 15. As in the case study example, assume that we may purchase or sell futures contracts in $100 increments. (*Note*: This is unrealistic since contracts are actually transacted in $1,000,000 increments. However, the calculations and principles presented are still accurate.) The details are presented in Table 6.15.

Table 6.15
Calculations for One Futures Hedge Historical Analysis
(Beginning on May 15, 1990, and Selling Eight Futures Contracts)

Results with Futures Hedge:

On May 15, 1990:

- Lend $1,000 for six months at LIBOR + 2%, or 8.44% + 2.00% = 10.44%.

- Issue $800 CD for three months at LIBOR, or 8.33%.

- Sell eight $100 contracts at 8.46% for September delivery.

On August 15, 1990:

- First CD matures and pays $816.66 interest and principal.

- Futures contracts are closed out at 7.89% for a loss of eight contracts × $0.25 × (8.46 − 7.89) = −1.14.

- Issue new CD for $816.66 + 1.14, or $817.80, at a rate of 7.93%, the current three-month LIBOR rate.

On November 15, 1990:

- Loan matures, returning $1,052.20 in interest and principal.   *cont.*

- Second CD matures, paying $834.01 interest and principal.

- Net Interest Income (Hedged) = $52.20 – $34.01 = $18.19

Results without Futures Hedge:

On May 15, 1990:

- Lend $1,000 for six months at LIBOR + 2%, or 8.44% + 2.00% = 10.44%.

- Issue $800 CD for three months at LIBOR, or 8.33%.

On August 15, 1990:

- First CD matures and pays $816.66 interest and principal.

- Issue new CD for $816.66 at a rate of 7.93%, the current three-month LIBOR rate.

On November 15, 1990:

- Loan matures, returning $1,052.20 in interest and principal.

- Second CD matures, paying $832.85 interest and principal.

- Net Interest Income (Unhedged) = $52.20 – $32.85 = $19.35.

The results may not look too promising yet. The hedge "lost" $1.14, and leaving the bank unhedged would have resulted in greater earnings over this particular six-month period. As always, hindsight is perfect. It is also one more very practical reason why the asset and liability manager using approach 1 in Section 6.9 is likely to have a limited future with the bank. Indeed, it is premature to jump to conclusions. We have not yet calculated our target results if the hedge had worked perfectly. After all, our objective was to eliminate the mismatch between the six-month loan and the three-month CD. As we have learned, this is equivalent to having the futures hedge "locking in" the implied forward rate in the yield curve as it existed on May 15, 1990. From the "spot" rates of 8.33% for three months and 8.44% for six months, we know how to calculate the implied forward three-month rate for August 15, 1990. We leave this as an exercise for the reader. The answer is 8.376%.

Therefore, a "perfect" hedge would allow us to issue the second CD at the equivalent cost of 8.376% on August 15. Table 6.16 will calculate the net interest income that we are implicitly targeting in this hedge.

Table 6.16
Calculation of the Hypothetical "Perfect Hedge"
for the May 15, 1990, Historical Example

On May 15, 1990:

- Lend $1,000 for six months at $10.44%.

- Issue $800 CD for $800 at 8.33%.

On August 15, 1990:

- First CD matures, paying $816.66 principal and interest.

- Issue new CD for $816.66 at implied forward rate of 8.376%.

On November 15, 1990:

- Loan matures, returning $1,052.20 interest and principal.

- Second CD matures, bank pays $833.76 interest and principal.

- Net Interest Income (Target) = $52.20 – $33.76 = $18.44.

We are now in a proper position to evaluate the effectiveness of the hedge in reducing the balance sheet mismatch. The relevant results are presented in Table 6.17.

Table 6.17
Hedge Performance Evaluation for the May 15, 1990, Historical Example
(All Values Are Six-Month Net Interest Incomes)

Unhedged	$19.35
Hedged	$18.19
Target ("Perfect Hedge")	$18.44

In this example, the hedge worked well, but not perfectly. The bank certainly came closer to achieving its objective of a "stable" earnings of $18.44 with the hedge rather than without it. The "extra" profits of the unhedged balance sheet are associated with extremely high risk. In this particular case, the unhedged bank won, but it could just have easily lost.

Using the methods just described, we may calculate the same three results for each starting date listed in Table 6.14. The results are shown graphically in Figure 6.6.

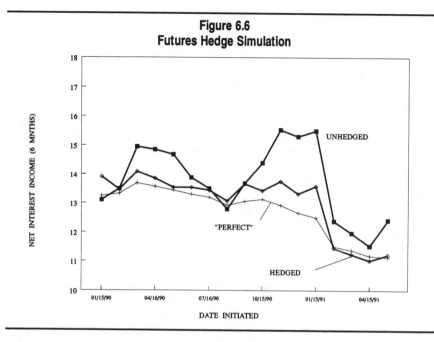

Figure 6.6
Futures Hedge Simulation

Keep in mind that the results in Figure 6.6 pertain to futures hedges where eight contracts were sold. We may also analyze the results for various hedge ratios in a risk/return profile. To do so, calculate a hedge "efficiency" by dividing the target ("perfect") hedge results into the actual hedge results for a variety of hedge contracts from 0 to 20. Next, the efficiency percentages for each hedge ratio (or number of contracts used) are plotted according to their averages and standard deviations. The detailed results are displayed in Appendix 6A. The risk/return plot obtained by this procedure is shown in Figure 6.7.

Notice that the lowest risk positions achievable with such a futures strategy is a reduction from about 5.6% volatility to about 1.7%. This residual volatility is due to several factors which include the following:

- Intraday rate movements. (The spot and futures rates were not recorded at exactly the same moment on each of the respective dates.)

- Modest futures/forward rate inconsistencies. (The implied forward rates often are a little different from the futures rates, principally because of the impact of mark-to-market margins and their impact on the economics of a futures contract compared to a forward contract.)

- Misalignment of the delivery date of the futures contracts with the desired closeout dates of our experimental positions.

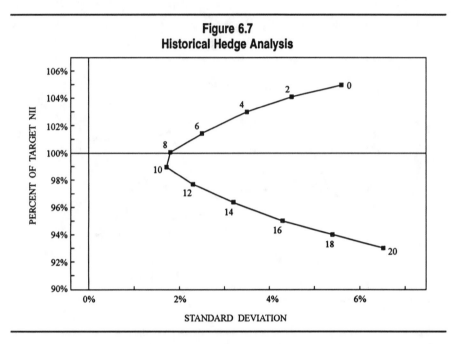

Figure 6.7
Historical Hedge Analysis

In examining the results shown in Figure 6.7, it appears that using eight contracts would be a very acceptable decision. It nearly minimizes the volatility of returns compared to the targets, but it does not give up profitability as would the use of any larger number of contracts.

In our experience, Monte Carlo simulations would yield results very similar to the empirical results portrayed in Figure 6.7. The maximum amount of risk reduction achievable is usually in the range of 60% to 70% for such simple hedge strategies. It is beyond the scope of this book to deal with more sophisticated strategies.

6.12   A COMMENT ON EVALUATING HEDGE PERFORMANCE AND "BACK SEAT" DRIVERS

There will always be a natural tendency to view the world through the "speculator" perspective. That is, the ALCO will always try to second-guess their hedge decision by seeing if they increased or decreased earnings because of their futures positions. This is NOT the point. The point is how much the ALCO succeeded in reducing the risk due to mismatching. In Figures 6.6 and 6.7, the eight contract positions were effective at reducing (but not eliminating) the risk of mismatching. In this critical respect, the hedges were successful. The fact that they also resulted in lower average earnings only means that the bank decided not to accept those incremental gains with their associated risks, which could just as easily have been incremental losses.

We suggest always focusing the ALCO's attention on the risk dimension. In Figure 6.7, the ALCO, had it experienced such results, could take great pride in having achieved results that were within 1% of "perfect" performance, as indicated by the average efficiency being 99%. At the same time, it decreased risk from 5.6% to 1.7%, or 70%. **NOT BAD!**

Naysayers will point out the bank "gave up" average earnings of $18.49 and settled for average earnings of $17.68 (as displayed in Table 6A.1 in Appendix 6A). That extra $0.81 represents high risk mismatch gains. Over the long run, 50% of the time they will be gains, and 50% of the time they will be losses. The expected, long-run shareholder value in accepting that extra risk will always be negative because such gains will generally not provide returns in excess of the hurdle ROE.

6.13 SUMMARY

This chapter introduced all of the "top-down" issues in interest rate risk management. It asserts (once again) that banks cannot expect to profitably and consistently mismatch their balance sheet based on their forecasts of interest rates. Therefore, banks should not attempt any large scale "bet the bank" mismatching. However, modest positioning can be very healthy when properly controlled and when precautions are taken against inadvertent speculation.

Any consideration of intentional positioning or mismatching should be based on the ALCO's expectations for interest rates relative to the implied forward rates calculated from the current yield curve, or from the rates available in the futures exchanges.

Futures contracts provide an effective means of correcting balance sheet mismatches. The principles presented in considering their use apply just as well to interest rate swaps and forward rate agreements, although the credit risk involved may be higher.

Chapters 7 and 8 will present a discussion of interest rate risk analytical techniques and pitfalls.

APPENDIX 6A: DETAILED RESULTS OF HISTORICAL FUTURES ANALYSES

For reference, the detailed results of all of the historical futures analyses in the next two tables are provided. Table 6A.1 displays the net interest income figures for the unhedged, "perfect" target results, and the actual results for various numbers of futures contracts sold.

Figure 6.6 shows the results for three of the columns from this table. They are the "target" results for the "perfect hedge" situation; the unhedged results, which are equivalent to the "0" column, indicating that no futures contracts were sold; and the column where eight contracts were sold.

Because these targets vary for different starting dates, we calculate hedge efficiency ratios by simply dividing the actual result by the target result, and express the ratio in percentage terms. If the actual hedge achieved perfection, the ratio would be 100%. For each column in Table 6A.2, we take the average and standard deviation of the efficiency ratios. They are displayed in the last two rows of the table, and they are the values used to generate Figure 6.7 in the text.

Table 6A.1
Summary of Historical Hedge Analyses for Selected Numbers of Futures Contracts

Start Date	Target	Numbers of Futures Contracts Sold								
		0	2	4	6	8	10	12	16	20
01/15/90	18.25	17.77	17.97	18.18	18.38	18.58	18.79	18.99	19.40	19.81
02/15/90	18.33	18.15	18.14	18.14	18.13	18.13	18.12	18.12	18.11	18.10
03/15/90	18.69	19.60	19.38	19.16	18.94	18.72	18.50	18.28	17.84	17.41
04/16/90	18.57	19.51	19.25	19.00	18.74	18.49	18.23	17.98	17.47	16.96
05/15/90	18.44	19.35	19.06	18.77	18.48	18.19	17.90	17.61	17.02	16.44
06/15/90	18.30	18.55	18.46	18.37	18.29	18.20	18.11	18.03	17.85	17.68
07/16/90	18.20	18.17	18.15	18.14	18.12	18.11	18.09	18.08	18.05	18.02
08/15/90	17.93	17.47	17.54	17.62	17.69	17.76	17.83	17.90	18.04	18.19
09/14/90	18.06	18.37	18.36	18.36	18.35	18.35	18.34	18.34	18.33	18.32
10/15/90	18.13	19.09	18.84	18.60	18.35	18.11	17.86	17.62	17.13	16.64
11/15/90	17.93	20.27	19.82	19.36	18.91	18.46	18.01	17.55	16.65	15.74
12/14/90	17.66	20.06	19.56	19.05	18.55	18.05	17.54	17.04	16.04	15.03
01/15/91	17.50	20.28	19.79	19.30	18.81	18.33	17.84	17.35	16.38	15.40
02/15/91	16.50	17.18	16.94	16.71	16.47	16.23	15.99	15.75	15.28	14.80
03/15/91	16.37	16.78	16.59	16.40	16.21	16.03	15.84	15.65	15.27	14.90
04/15/91	16.18	16.33	16.21	16.08	15.95	15.83	15.70	15.57	15.32	15.06
05/15/91	16.13	17.24	16.94	16.63	16.33	16.02	15.72	15.42	14.81	14.20
06/14/91	16.43	18.74	18.22	17.70	17.18	16.65	16.13	15.61	14.57	13.52
Average	17.64	18.49	18.29	18.09	17.88	17.68	17.48	17.27	16.86	16.46

Table 6A.2

Summary of Efficiency Ratios for Historical Hedge Analyses

Start Date					Numbers of Futures Contracts Sold						
	0	2	4	6	8	10	12	14	16	18	20
01/15/90	97%	98%	100%	101%	102%	103%	104%	105%	106%	107%	109%
02/15/90	99%	99%	99%	99%	99%	99%	99%	99%	99%	99%	99%
03/15/90	105%	104%	103%	101%	100%	99%	98%	97%	95%	94%	93%
04/16/90	105%	104%	102%	101%	100%	98%	97%	95%	94%	93%	91%
05/15/90	105%	103%	102%	100%	99%	97%	95%	94%	92%	91%	89%
06/15/90	101%	101%	100%	100%	99%	99%	99%	98%	98%	97%	97%
07/16/90	100%	100%	100%	100%	99%	99%	99%	99%	99%	99%	99%
08/15/90	97%	98%	98%	99%	99%	99%	100%	100%	101%	101%	101%
09/14/90	102%	102%	102%	102%	102%	102%	102%	102%	101%	101%	101%
10/15/90	105%	104%	103%	101%	100%	99%	97%	96%	94%	93%	92%
11/15/90	113%	111%	108%	105%	103%	100%	98%	95%	93%	90%	88%
12/14/90	114%	111%	108%	105%	102%	99%	96%	94%	91%	88%	85%
01/15/91	116%	113%	110%	108%	105%	102%	99%	96%	94%	91%	88%
02/15/91	104%	103%	101%	100%	98%	97%	95%	94%	93%	91%	90%
03/15/91	102%	101%	100%	99%	98%	97%	96%	94%	93%	92%	91%
04/15/91	101%	100%	99%	99%	98%	97%	96%	95%	95%	94%	93%
05/15/91	107%	105%	103%	101%	99%	97%	96%	94%	92%	90%	88%
06/14/91	114%	111%	108%	105%	101%	98%	95%	92%	89%	85%	82%
Standard Deviation	5.6%	4.5%	3.5%	2.5%	1.8%	1.7%	2.3%	3.2%	4.3%	5.4%	6.5%
Average	105%	104%	103%	101%	100%	99%	98%	97%	95%	94%	93%

The last two lines are the data plotted in Figure 6.7.

CHAPTER 7

Interest Rate Risk Analyses: Gap Analysis and Simulation Models

Thus far, this book has discussed many of the overall balance sheet policy and positioning issues that a bank's ALCO must address. However, everything up to this point presumes that the interest rate risk characteristics of the entire bank balance sheet are known with some accuracy. Chapters 7 and 8 will discuss the various analytical techniques that may be employed to conduct interest rate risk assessments. Chapter 9 will present the interest rate risk characteristics of specific bank products and the special problems they present.

Chapters 5 and 6 presented interest rate risk management using the generalized risk and return framework presented in Chapters 1 and 2. We believe that the concepts are straightforward. Risk and return should always be measured from the cash flows of the business unit. Risk is the volatility of cash flows, which is quantified in the form of the standard deviation. From this brief review, it should be clear that any analytical technique that purports to measure risk must deal with ALL of the net cash flows of a bank. Indeed, this is a daunting task. Banks routinely experience massive daily cash flows as they clear large volumes of personal and corporate transactions.

As we discuss the various analytical techniques available to the asset and liability manager in this chapter and the next, and as we present the special pitfalls associated with some important bank products in Chapter 9, we will emphasize where others have tended to either oversimplify these issues or have gotten caught up in too much detail. We are strong supporters of the "80/20 rule" in asset and liability management. That is, one can obtain 80% accuracy with only 20% of the maximum effort expended. As with the risk and return dilemma, we do not want too much or too little detail. We strive to be on the "efficient frontier," maximizing our understanding of the fundamental risk relationships, but expending as little effort as possible in doing so. As stated in earlier chapters, no one makes money for the shareholders analyzing interest rate risk once the bank is firmly planted in the safety zone!

7.1   OBJECTIVES OF INTEREST RATE RISK ANALYTICAL TECHNIQUES

There are two main questions one should always be able to answer in dealing with interest rate risk analyses. They are:

- What is the AMOUNT of equity at risk for a given shift in interest rates?

■ What is the TIMING of the cash flow changes that will be experienced for a given interest rate shift?

To put this simply, it is important to know HOW LARGE the effects will be in present value terms, and WHEN the effects will be felt by the bank. We emphasize that these effects should be understood first and foremost in terms of cash flows, and only secondarily for their accounting magnitude and timing.

To gauge the amount of equity at risk, we rely on the use of duration (or interest rate elasticity) concepts. These will be presented in Chapter 8. For the timing of the cash flow shifts, there are two types of techniques that have dominated the ALM landscape over the past 12 to 15 years. They are gap analysis and simulation modeling, which will be the topics of this chapter.

7.2   GAP ANALYSIS

Gap analysis is by far and away the most commonplace and universally understood ALM technique of all. For many years, all U.S. banks were required to submit gap reports in their quarterly "Call Reports of Condition." It seems that virtually every bank executive in the United States and in most other industrialized countries feels quite comfortable discussing his or her bank's gap structure and gap strategies. It is ironic, then, that gap analyses are no longer relied upon as a primary risk management tool by most large banks. Despite this fact, most large banking organizations persist in presenting gap analyses in their discussion of interest rate risk in their annual reports. Why has this best-known technique been so seriously discredited in managing bank balance sheets, while it has persisted in shareholder and regulatory presentations? This will be the focus of the next several sections.

The concept of gap analysis is relatively simple. Each of the bank's asset and liability categories are classified according to when they will be repriced and when they will be placed in groupings called time buckets. Typically, banks have selected time buckets such as those presented in Table 7.1, which show the gap results for the case study bank from Chapter 5 where the CD has a 4.5-month maturity. As was shown, this maturity will hedge the net interest income target account over a 12-month period.

In Table 7.1, both the loan and the CD happen to fall into the same bucket. That bucket includes all items with repricing dates that are greater than (>) three months and less than or equal to six months from January 1.

Table 7.1
Gap Analysis for Case Study Bank
Using 4.5-Month CD Funding
(As of January 1)

	O/N to 3 Months	>3 to 6 Months	>6 to 12 Months	>1 to 2 Years	>2 to 5 Years	>5 Years or N/S	Total
Earning Assets:							
Loan	-	1,000	-	-	-	-	1,000
Funding Sources:							
CD	-	800	-	-	-	-	800
Net Capital	-	-	-	-	-	200	200
Gaps:							
Incremental	0	200	0	0	0	(200)	0
Cumulative	0	200	200	200	200	0	

Notes:"O/N" is overnight or 1 day.
  "N/S" means "not stated."

(*Note*: We hypothesized that our case study bank was created on January 1. However, it is more conventional to display a gap analysis as of the last day of the year or quarter.)

In most real situations, the line labeled "Net Capital" is usually a "plug" value to ensure that total earnings assets equals the sum of all of the funding sources. (An alternative, although rarer, approach would be to display total assets and total liabilities.) The classification of net capital in the longest term, "not stated" bucket is commonplace since equity has no stated maturity. However, an alternative approach will be presented in Chapter 14 on "Transfer Pricing."

The final two lines in Table 7.1 display the incremental and cumulative gap results. The incremental gaps are simply the differences between earning assets and funding sources for each individual time bucket. The cumulative gaps are cumulative subtotals of the incremental gaps. By definition, the incremental gaps must always total to zero, since we specified that total earning assets always equal total funding sources. This also means that the last cumulative gap must be zero.

Unfortunately, the specific gap results shown in Table 7.1 are not especially informative. They show that the only mismatch relates to $200 of the loan being funded by equity or net capital. Most analysts would focus on the cumulative gaps for the three-month, six-month, and one-year timeframes. In this case, the cumulative gaps for the three-month through one-year buckets are all +$200, giving a false impression that this bank is somewhat asset sensitive during the second, third, and fourth quarters. (A positive incremental gap suggests that more assets are repricing than liabilities, and thus, earnings should tend to increase if rates rise during that particular period. A string of positive cumulative gaps as seen in Table 7.1 strongly suggests that the bank is asset sensitive over a one-year time horizon.) However, we know from Chapter 5 that if the bank uses a 4.5-month CD, net interest income is hedged for the year.

It is helpful to determine the forecast of earnings for this bank with and without a 1% rate increase on January 2. This is shown in Table 7.2. (*Note*: For simplicity, we are going back to the assumption made in Chapter 5 that the yield curve is flat at 6% on January 1 when the bank is created, and that it happens to shift up to 7% on January 2.)

Table 7.2
Case Study Net Interest Income by Quarter
Using 4.5-Month CD

No Rate Change on January 2:	1st Quarter	2nd Quarter	3rd Quarter	4th Quarter	Total Year
Loan Yield	8.00%	8.00%	8.00%	8.00%	8.00%
Average CD Rate	6.00%	6.00%	6.00%	6.00%	6.00%
Net Interest Margin	3.20%	3.20%	3.20%	3.20%	3.20%
Interest Income	20.0	20.0	20.0	20.0	80.0
Interest Expense	12.0	12.0	12.0	12.0	48.0
Net Interest Income	8.0	8.0	8.0	8.0	32.0

cont.

Rates Rise 1% on January 2:	1st Quarter	2nd Quarter	3rd Quarter	4th Quarter	Total Year
Loan Yield	8.00%	8.00%	9.00%	9.00%	8.50%
Average CD Rate	6.00%	6.50%	7.00%	7.00%	6.63%
Net Interest Margin	3.20%	2.80%	3.40%	3.40%	3.20%
Interest Income	20.0	20.0	22.5	22.5	85.0
Interest Expense	12.0	13.0	14.0	14.0	53.0
Net Interest Income	8.0	7.0	8.5	8.5	32.0

Table 7.2 illustrates the quarterly net interest income figures with a 4.5-month CD both with and without a rate shift on January 2. Notice that net interest incomes are the same for the total year, and this would be true for any rate change, rising or falling, of any magnitude. Even more important is the effect of the rate increase on the pattern of quarterly earnings. Notice that earnings actually decline in the second quarter compared to the first in the rising rate scenario. This was not evident from the gap analysis at all. In fact, the result for the second quarter is exactly the opposite from the gap profile, which indicated an asset-sensitive situation in the second quarter!

This illustrates one of the fundamental shortfalls of gap analysis. It ignores the mismatches that exist **within** each time bucket. The second quarter time bucket is actually liability sensitive, not asset sensitive! This liability sensitivity is due to the CD repricing after 4.5 months, whereas the loan will not reprice until six months, at the very end of the time period.

This shortfall is further substantiated when we consider that had we funded with a 3.5-month CD, the bank would actually be liability sensitive over the course of the entire year. However, the gap analysis would still appear EXACTLY the same as that shown in Table 7.1, which indicates only asset sensitivity!

7.3 SHORTFALLS OF GAP ANALYSIS

We have now documented one serious shortcoming of gap analysis: It ignores mismatches that exist within the various time buckets. There are other potential problems, including nonmaturity accounts, administered or nonmarket rate accounts, balance fluctuations and embedded option features, which will be briefly described here. Detailed discussions of these characteristics and how to treat them for analytical purposes will be presented in Chapter 9.

Nonmaturity accounts. Several product types do not have stated maturities or repricing dates. The best examples include demand deposits, the savings account, credit card receivables and the equity account. Should these balances be spread among certain time buckets, or should they all be summarily thrown into the catch-all "not stated" longest-term bucket? There are arguments for and against either approach.

Administered or nonmarket rate accounts. Certain products show repricing behavior that generally reflects short-term market rate shifts, but not exactly. The best examples are prime-rate loans and the money market deposit account. Technically, the rates for these products could change on any day, but they have a tendency to move infrequently but in relatively large (50 basis point) increments. How should they be classified for gap purposes? Fortunately, a methodology has been developed to deal with these balances. This will be presented in Chapter 9.

Balance fluctuations. Demand deposit accounts show striking seasonal balance fluctuations. They also demonstrate modest balance sensitivity to the general level of interest rates. Finally, they legally may be withdrawn completely on any given day. Numerous debates exist regarding the proper gap treatment of these balances.

Embedded option features. Many bank products have option characteristics whereby the cash flows differ significantly depending on whether rates rise or fall. Mortgage loan prepayments are the best-known example of this phenomenon. If rates increase, prepayments will decline and the average life of a mortgage portfolio will extend. If rates drop, prepayment rates rise and the average life shrinks. How can this be portrayed in the gap analysis? Another example is the charge card account, where both the maturity (prepayable at the customer's convenience) and the rate characteristics (which in many jurisdictions cannot be increased without giving the borrower the option to pay off all outstanding balances at the current rate) present difficulties.

From this listing, it appears that there are numerous potential problems with gap analysis. Indeed, many of the larger banks no longer rely on this technique as their primary tool in assessing interest rate risk. However, we hasten to add that banks have not ignored this technique. It still can provide some utility.

7.4   USES FOR GAP ANALYSIS

Despite its shortcomings, gap analysis remains the best understood analytical technique in all of asset and liability management. The pitfalls notwithstanding, there is still useful general information about the bank's mismatches that are well portrayed by this method. Therefore, it is likely that gap presentations will persist for some time as the simplest vehicle to convey a "picture" of interest rate risk in annual reports. That is, it will still play a role in conveying risk information outside of the organization. Hopefully, reliance on this technique will decline for internal risk measurement and decision-making purposes, particularly in the context of ALCO meetings.

Another popular application of gap analysis is in the area of policy setting and risk-limit definition. The technique is relatively straightforward, simple to implement, and well understood by virtually all bank analytical staff. Therefore, interest rate policy limits may be stated in terms of a cumulative six- or 12-month gap as a percentage of earning assets. This could be useful in large, multibank holding companies where a variety of different risk assessment tools coupled with a wide array of dissimilar product assumptions have been employed. In such circumstances, a gap limit may well be the lowest common denominator to ensure general compliance among all of the bank affiliates without forcing distortions in the detailed analyses being conducted within each bank.

Our major caution to any bank considering the continued use of gap analysis for any purpose today is to recognize its serious limitations. A large number of examples are known to the authors where a bank's actual earnings sensitivity turned out to be exactly the opposite of the cumulative gap figure! All in all, it is probably the best single portrayal of the balance sheet mismatches, but it overlooks many sources and categories of interest rate risk. No asset and liability manager should mistake gap analysis for the microscope of asset and liability management; think of gap analysis as a pair of dark glasses. It can help an asset and liability manager look sophisticated but sometimes makes it harder to see.

7.5   SIMULATION MODELING: THE BRUTE FORCE APPROACH

If gap analysis is elegant (and sometimes deceptive) in its simplicity, then simulation analysis is the bulldozer of risk analysis methods. Models exist that can literally analyze every individual loan and deposit account in a large bank! The volume of detailed results that can be generated has become so large that it has become one of the main obstacles to its effective implementation. The authors firmly believe that effective simulation modeling is one of the most important activities in all of bank financial management. Unfortunately, relatively few banks have succeeded in implementing truly effective modeling disciplines. The next several sections will present our views on the keys to modeling success.

A computer simulation model starts with a current balance sheet, including detailed maturity or repricing schedules and the associated rates and yields of those balances, and forecasts of income statements, balance sheets, and cash flow schedules for a series of future time periods, typically 12 to 36 months. This is accomplished by literally simulating the repricings, maturities, rollovers, and new business originations for all balance sheet activities of the bank! To generate a plausible set of financial statements, assumptions must be made about a number of important issues, including target balances, maturity schedules for new business, yield curve behavior, nonyield curve rate assumptions, and pricing assumptions for new business.

Target balances. Will the balances for each balance sheet account grow or decline in coming months? How will seasonality factors affect balance patterns? Which items are being targeted for special marketing emphasis? Will maturing balances in one category be channeled into another for strategic or risk management reasons, such as maturing municipal bond balances being reinvested in taxable securities because of changes in tax law or tax planning?

Maturity schedule for new business. For any new balances generated during the forecast period, what distribution of maturities will these "newly added" balances display? For example, the bank may be reinvesting maturing balances from its investment portfolio by purchasing Treasury bills, where half of the purchases are new three-month bills and half are 12-month. This "new add" maturity schedule would be specified as: 50% three-month and 50% 12-month.

Yield curve behavior. How will the current yield curve change over the course of the forecast period? Usually, the model will have a single yield curve that serves as a reference standard for most, if not all, of the yield/repricing assumptions used in the model. It is commonplace to use a CD or LIBOR yield curve, although a Treasury yield curve is acceptable. The advantage of a CD or LIBOR yield curve is that more bank product pricing strategies are based on these rates than any other type of rate, for the following good reason: They are most representative of the bank's marginal cost of funds.

Nonyield curve rate assumptions. There are several important interest rates that are not derived directly from the CD or LIBOR yield curve. These include the federal funds rate, prime rate, money market deposit rate, savings rate, credit card rate, and mortgage rate. Proper treatment of these rates is essential.

Pricing assumptions for new business. This refers to the yields or rates that will be associated with the new transactions which will be booked during the forecast period. The yield curve and the nonyield curve rate assumptions provide some important pricing indices, such as the prime rate or the federal funds rate. However, these are not sufficient in many instances. For example, new commercial loans will show a characteristic spread above the prime rate. If the yield curve being used in the model is the national secondary CD rate for large banks, then retail CDs under $100,000 will usually be set at some average spread below the yield curve. Therefore, this set of assumptions is often viewed as "pricing spreads" above or below the reference rates generated by the yield curve or nonyield curve rates.

7.6   A SIMULATION MODEL SPECIFICATION FOR THE CASE STUDY EXAMPLE

To illustrate the specifications that must be made just to set up a new simulation model, Table 7.3 will provide a description of a model for the case study example from Chapter 5. This will also allow us to describe some of the chart of account characteristics that must be considered, as well as some of the cash flow considerations that should be incorporated.

Inspection of Table 7.3 should lead to an immediate question: Why are the "Federal Funds Sold" and "Federal Funds Purchased" categories neces-

Table 7.3
Chart of Accounts for Case Study Example

Code	Description
LOAN_COMM	Commercial Loans
FED_F_SOLD	Federal Funds Sold
DEP_CD	CDs
FED_F_PRCH	Federal Funds Purchased
EQUITY	Equity

sary? Recall that risks and returns must be based on tracking ALL cash flows experienced by the bank. These accounts are necessary to realistically track interim cash flows and accruals for accounting and cash management purposes. A description of how all are used will follow later in the chapter.

7.7   THE CONCEPT OF "SECURITIES" IN SIMULATION MODELS

Most computer models base their simulations on the concept of "securities." The term "security" is used here in a generic sense, referring to a single or similar set of transactions. This is most easily illustrated by specifying the starting balance sheet for the case study. There are two securities as of January 1, a loan "security" and a CD "security." In the context of simulation models, a security is a single or accumulated set of transactions that can be summarized in terms of a common origination date, maturity date, aggregate balance, and associated rate (which could be a floating rate). Other features that may be have to be delineated are the accrual periods or coupon intervals and whether the transaction is amortizing or not.

The two securities for the case study are presented in Table 7.4. Assume that the bank wishes to hedge net interest income for the year and has selected a 4.5-month CD for its funding. This exhibit lists only those attributes that are operative for the case study. To simplify this analysis, we will continue to assume that the "year" is composed of 12 months, each of which has only 30 days. Therefore, our "year" will be 360 days

Table 7.4
Initial Securities for Case Study Simulation Model

Code	Origination Date	Maturity Date	Balance	Rate	Type
LOAN_COMM	92/01/01	92/07/01	1000.00	8.00	Bullet
DEP_CD	92/01/01	92/05/16	800.00	6.00	Bullet

long. (Calendar features such as uneven numbers of days in the months can become a major complication in simulation models. This simplified year will ignore those problems without sacrificing any essential concepts.) Furthermore, we will specify that our forecast horizon will be the next 12 monthly time periods.

With this detail about each security, the model can generate new securities during the forecast period with great accuracy. Of course, each individual security in the model may represent an aggregation of a larger grouping of actual loans or deposits. The most common approach is to combine all long-term loans with the same origination month and year and maturity month and year into a single security. ALM analysts must decide the level of detail they need for their specific circumstances. For instance, the investment portfolio is composed of a small number of large transactions. Therefore, many banks place every investment security separately into their simulation models. However, the auto loan portfolio is made up of large numbers of smaller transactions. Aggregation by origination month/year makes perfect sense in that case.

These two securities are not sufficient to specify the starting balance sheet as of January 1. We have not yet specified the bank's equity of $200. To do so, we must first specify that the equity balance sheet account is not a "security" type. That is, there will be no securities in this account since equity has no maturity date. We will refer to this category of account as a "nonsecurity" account. A "point-in-time" balance for equity of $200 is specified as of January 1.

For simplicity, we will specify that the two other detailed balance sheet categories are nonsecurity as well. These are "Federal Funds Sold" (FED_F_SOLD) and "Federal Funds Purchased" (FED_F_PRCH). These two accounts have no balance on January 1.

7.8   SPECIFICATIONS FOR FORECAST ASSUMPTIONS

Now that the starting balance sheet is determined, it is important to examine the assumptions that will drive the forecasts. Some of these include target balances, maturity schedule for new transactions, yield curve assumptions, nonyield curve rate assumptions, and pricing assumptions for new transactions.

Target balances. This is where any anticipated balance sheet growth or shrinkage would be specified. For the case study example, there are no anticipated changes in balances. Therefore, the target balances would be $1,000 across all 12 months for "Commercial Loans" (LOAN_COMM) and $800 for all 12 months for CDs (DEP_CD).

The remaining accounts, two for fed funds and one for equity, are special accounts needed in every model. The equity account (EQUITY) will be the repository for all earnings net of dividend payments. The fed funds accounts (FED_F_SOLD and FED_F_PRCH) are normally designated as "balancing accounts." That is, whenever the bank finds it has excess cash to invest, the model will deploy those funds in whichever account has been designated as the asset balancing account. In this simple model, that will be the "Federal Funds Sold" (FED_F_SOLD) account.

Alternatively, if the bank must borrow in the current period, the incremental borrowings would appear in the liability balancing account. In this case, that would be "Federal Funds Purchased" (FED_F_PRCH). No formal targets are needed for these last three special accounts. They will be used as determined by the simulation software during the "solve" routine.

Finally, if it is assumed that dividends are only paid at the end of the year, then the dividend account will be zero for every month until the December period. It will then be targeted as the total net income for the year.

Maturity schedule for new transactions. Since we have already specified that the loan and CD will each roll over at their same original maturities, we may specify that all maturing loan balances will roll over into a new loan with a maturity of six months. Likewise, any maturing balances in the CD account will roll over into another CD with a 4.5-month maturity.

Yield curve assumptions. Here is where the interest rate forecast is input into the model. There should be a minimum of three yield curve forecasts analyzed: rates remain unchanged, rising rates, and falling rates. However, as indicated in Chapter 6, an analysis of hundreds or even thousands of yield curve forecasts using the Monte Carlo simulation would be better. For this model, we will select three simple scenarios:

- Scenario 1: All CD maturities are 6% from January 2 through year-end;

- Scenario 2: All CD maturities are 7% from January 2 through year-end;

- Scenario 3: All CD maturities are 5% from January 2 through year-end.

(*Note*: A sudden 1% rate jump or fall is not out of the question. However, most banks would use other patterns for their models. Many use a gradual increase or decrease over an extended period, such as a 200-basis point increase spread ratably over 12 months, 16.67 basis points per month, thus averaging a 100-basis point rate difference compared to the stable rate scenario.)

Nonyield curve rate assumptions. Finally, rates must be specified for the two fed funds accounts. This is done using an "exogenous" account. Other examples of exogenous or nonyield curve accounts include the prime rate and money market deposit account rate. Whenever possible, exogenous rates should be based on the yield curve in some manner. Then, in generating alternative rate scenarios, the analyst need only change the yield curve itself, and all other ancillary rates will be automatically adjusted. A common fed funds specification is something like: "Assume that the federal funds rate in each forecast period is equal to the 90-day CD rate."

Pricing assumptions for new transactions. For each balance sheet category, some type of rate-setting assumption must be created. The following list includes typical specifications for the case study accounts in this example.

- The rate associated with new loan (LOAN_COMM) "securities" is equal to the six-month CD yield curve rate plus a "pricing spread" of 200 basis points.

- The rate associated with any new CD (DEP_CD) "securities" is set at the appropriate yield curve rate (4.5-month CD rate) plus 0 "pricing spread."

- The rate associated with any "Federal Funds Sold" (FED_F_SOLD) or "Purchased" (FED_F_PRCH) balances will be equal to the exogenous federal funds rate plus 0 "pricing spread." (This is needed because the exogenous variable only supplies the base pricing index. There may well be a pricing spread adjustment that should be applied against the reference index.)

This completes the forecast assumptions needed.

7.9   SOLVING THE MODEL

At last, the model is ready to be solved. The financial statements generated by the model for the scenario where CD rates are 7% for the forecast periods are shown in Table 7.5.

Recall from Table 7.2 that net interest income (and net income) for the year was $32—the difference between interest income of $85 and interest expense of $53. In examining the income statement portion of Table 7.5, net income is $33.02. While the interest income from the loan and the interest expense from the CD are the same as in Table 7.2, there is a new source of earnings here: interest income from "Federal Funds Sold" of $1.02.

The simulation model makes the plausible assumption that each month's earnings are available to be invested in whichever asset is designated the asset balancing account, which is "Federal Funds Sold" (FED_F_SOLD) here. For example, net income for January is $2.67. This amount is added to the equity account for February, bringing it to $202.67. It also appears on the asset side of the balance sheet in the balancing account, explaining the $2.67 balance in February for "Funds Sold." For the full year, the earnings from these accumulating federal funds balances add up to $1.02.

Astute readers will question why the model does not understand that these "earnings" and federal funds balances during the first six months of the year cannot exist. The loan is a bullet loan and will not generate any actual cash flow until July 1. Therefore, the earnings are only accounting accruals; there will be no investible cash until July when the first loan matures. Indeed, if the bank wants to keep the May 16 CD rollover balance at exactly $800, it will have to borrow funds to pay the $18 interest expense at the first CD maturity on May 16!

However, we point out that this treatment by the model, assuming that earnings represent real cash flow that can be invested, is the most reasonable assumption to make in real life models. Most of the time, a loan or CD account have somewhat even increments that mature each month because the current balances were generated ratably over prior months and

Table 7.5
Summary Reports for Case Study Simulation Model
Scenario 2: CD Yield Curve at 7%

	Quarter 1			Quarter 2					Total
	Jan	Feb	Mar	Apr	May	Jun	Qtr 3	Qtr 4	Year
BALANCE SHEET:									
Assets:									
Loan	1000.0	1000.0	1000.0	1000.0	1000.0	1000.0	1000.0	1000.0	1000.0
Federal Funds Sold	0.0	2.7	5.3	8.0	10.8	13.2	18.2	27.0	14.6
Total	1000.0	1002.7	1005.3	1008.0	1010.8	1013.2	1018.2	1027.0	1014.6
Liabilities:									
CD	800.0	800.0	800.0	800.0	800.0	800.0	800.0	800.0	800.0
Federal Funds Purchased	0.0	0.0	0.0	0.0	0.0	0.0	0.0	0.0	0.0
Equity	200.0	202.7	205.3	208.0	210.8	213.2	218.2	227.0	214.6
Total	1000.0	1002.7	1005.3	1008.0	1010.8	1013.2	1018.2	1027.0	1014.6
INCOME STATEMENT:									
Interest Income:									
Loan	6.67	6.67	6.67	6.67	6.67	6.67	22.50	22.50	85.00
Federal Funds Sold	0.00	0.02	0.03	0.05	0.06	0.08	0.32	0.47	1.02
Interest Expense:									
CD	4.00	4.00	4.00	4.00	4.33	4.67	14.00	14.00	53.00
Federal Funds Purchased	0.00	0.00	0.00	0.00	0.00	0.00	0.00	0.00	0.00
Net Income	2.67	2.68	2.70	2.71	2.40	2.08	8.82	8.97	33.02
RATES:									
Assets:									
Loan	8.00%	8.00%	8.00%	8.00%	8.00%	8.00%	9.00%	9.00%	8.50%
Federal Funds Sold	7.00%	7.00%	7.00%	7.00%	7.00%	7.00%	7.00%	7.00%	7.00%
Liabilities:									
CD	6.00%	6.00%	6.00%	6.00%	6.50%	7.00%	7.00%	7.00%	6.63%
Federal Funds Purchased	7.00%	7.00%	7.00%	7.00%	7.00%	7.00%	7.00%	7.00%	7.00%

years. Thus, balances usually show a "ladder" or "tractor" type of behavior.

7.10 PORTFOLIOS AS "TRACTORS"

To illustrate the tractor, consider a portfolio of retail CDs (each transaction is under $100,000) where the current balance is $3 million and customers are only borrowing for three-month original maturities. In all likelihood, about one-third of the balances were generated in the past 30 days, about one-third were booked in the period from 31 to 60 days ago, and the final one-third were derived from 61 to 90 days ago.

The concept of the treads of a tractor (or bulldozer) is appropriate. The portfolio may be visualized in "batches" (referred to as "tranches") grouped by month of origination. In a stabilized ("steady state") situation, as each month passes, one tranche will mature and roll over into a similar amount of new three-month CDs. This happens month after month, as shown in Figure 7.1.

Figure 7.1
The "Tractor" Analogy
($3 Million 90-Day CD Portfolio Has Three Tranches

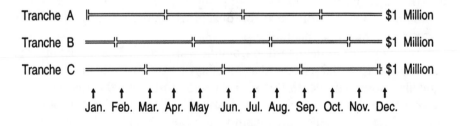

In Figure 7.1, each tranche represents a $1 million grouping of 90-day CDs, all of which were originated in the same month. Tranche A includes CDs originated in January and maturing in April. In April, a similar amount rolls over for maturity in the month of July, and so on. Tranche B CDs originate on a February, May, August, November cycle. Each tranche becomes a segment of the tracks of a tractor, going through its aging cycle and renewing or rolling over in its proper sequence.

Tractors are convenient and important assumptions in ALM. They represent a true "steady state" condition. For example, one could display a maturity or gap profile for this CD portfolio as of the first or last day of any month, and that profile would be essentially the same across all months. That is, $1 million would have 1-30 days to maturity, $1 million would have 31-60 days to go, and the final $1 million would fall in the 61-90 day category.

The tractor assumption is still valid, even if there are a mixture of different original maturities in the portfolio, so long as the mix of maturities is not changing rapidly. In such cases, it is convenient to divide the portfolio into its component maturities and treat each maturity grouping as a separate tractor. Even in a retail CD portfolio, banks characteristically set pricing such that customers cluster their choices around certain popular points. For example, suppose a bank offered the following CD pricing schedule:

Maturity Range	Rate
30–89 Days	5.00%
90–179 Days	5.25%
180–359 Days	5.50%
360 Days or More	6.00%

It would be common to find that greater than 90% of the balances are booked for exactly 30, 90, 180, or 360 days. Customers will tend to place their funds in the minimum maturity point of each maturity pricing range. In this case, the portfolio may be treated as four tractors of those four corresponding original maturities.

We now return to the question from the last section: Is it acceptable that the simulation model assume that monthly net interest income values are equivalent to monthly cash flows? For tractor portfolios, the answer is yes. Consider the example depicted in Figure 7.1. Here are the equations for monthly accrued expense and monthly cash flow expense. (Assume that all CDs were booked at a 6% rate.)

$$Accrued\ Expense = \frac{Portfolio\ Volume \times Portfolio\ Rate \times 1\ Month}{12\ Months}$$

$$= \frac{\$3\ Million \times 6.00\% * 1}{12}$$

$$= \$15,000$$

$$Cash\ Flow\ Expense = \frac{Maturing\ Balances \times Rate\ on\ Maturing\ Balance \times Original\ Maturity}{12\ Months}$$

$$= \frac{\$1\ Million \times 6.00\% \times 3 Months}{12\ Months}$$

$$= \$15,000$$

From these equations, accrued income or expense will be a reasonable approximation for the cash flow income or expense as long as the portfolio rate is in line with the rate associated with the balances maturing. The reason that this works is explained by the property for tractors that states the following:

$$Monthly\ Maturing\ Balance = \frac{Portfolio\ Volume}{Original Maturity\ (Months)}$$

Of course, the reason that there is a significant error for our case study simulation is that there are no tractors. If an analyst understands that any forecasted account will seriously deviate from the tractor assumption, then it is possible to enhance the model to accommodate the specific circumstances and prevent errors. For the case study situation, the problem can be corrected easily by including two more accounts, "Loan Interest Receivable" and "CD Interest Payable," both of which are noninterest bearing. Then, in February, the equity account would increase as before by the accrued earnings of $2.67. However, the interest receivable account would increase by the $6.67 and the payable account would show a $4.00 balance. There would be no fed funds sold or purchased since there were no actual cash flows to invest or fund at that time.

In May, when the first CD matures, the payment of $18 in interest expense would deplete the payable account and force $18 in the "Federal Funds Purchased" category. Hence, the model would exactly reflect the cash invested/borrowed positions of the bank for every month of the forecast period.

The advantage of simulation models is that they may always be enhanced to reflect whatever specific circumstances the bank encounters. The better commercially available models can simulate virtually any realistic situation. Indeed, it has become a game to try to imagine situations that simulation models cannot handle!

7.11 Displaying the Simulation Results

Even without the receivables and payables accounts, the model produces quite satisfactory results. Assuming that all three interest rate scenarios have been solved, it is typical that a graph of the monthly earnings be generated. This is presented in Figure 7.2 for the stable and high rate scenarios. (The low rate scenario pattern is a mirror image of the high rate scenario.)

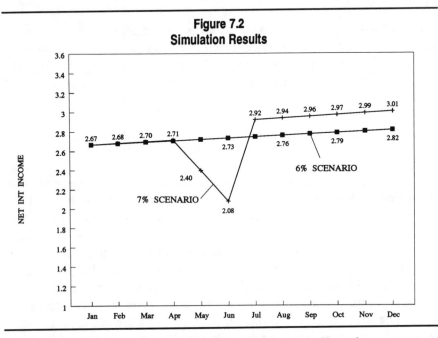

Figure 7.2
Simulation Results

Although annual earnings in Figure 7.2 are similar, the patterns of monthly earnings are quite different. This is the first accurate "picture" of the monthly earnings volatility of the case study bank presented in this book. This picture is one that any manager can understand.

Again, the multidimensionality of ALM manifests itself. Although the bank is fairly well hedged for the calendar year's earnings, there is still risk on a monthly or quarterly basis. It is not possible to hedge earnings across all conceivable time horizons. But at least the ALCO for this bank would obtain a full understanding of the subtleties of its adopted strategy from this simulation model. No other technique better elucidates the timing pattern shifts of cash flows and earnings than this one. It should be undertaken by all banks.

7.12   A LOOK INSIDE THE SOLVED MODEL

To probe the benefits of simulation modeling further, it is informative to ask what other types of information and results have been generated by the simulation software system. A critical issue involves the securities that were described in Section 7.7. After solving the model in the 7% rate scenario, a listing of the securities would appear as shown in Table 7.6.

Table 7.6
Initial Securities for Case Study Simulation Model

Code	Origination Date	Maturity Date	Balance	Rate	Type
LOAN_COMM	92/01/01	92/07/01	1000.00	8.00	Bullet
LOAN_COMM	92/07/01	93/01/01	1000.00	9.00	Bullet
DEP_CD	92/01/01	92/05/16	800.00	6.00	Bullet
DEP_CD	92/05/16	92/10/01	800.00	7.00	Bullet
DEP_CD	92/10/01	93/02/15	800.00	7.00	Bullet

Notice that the two original securities are still present. However, there are now three new securities generated by the model during the solve routine. These represent the new transactions created as based on the forecast maturity, spread, and yield curve assumptions supplied to the system. The second loan (LOAN_COMM) security is the rollover loan created from the maturity of the first loan on July 1. Its new maturity is January 1 of the following year, based on the six-month new-add/rollover maturity assumption. Its balance is $1,000 from the target balance specification that $1,000 be maintained for all time periods. Its rate of 9.00% is taken from the CD yield curve (at 7% in this scenario) plus the spread of 2%.

Similarly, each of the two new CD (DEP_CD) securities have characteristics consistent with the appropriate set of assumptions for that account. With these securities, it is possible to conduct virtually any type of risk analysis desired by the bank, including gap analysis and duration calculations. Indeed, it is possible to generate a gap or duration analysis for the balance sheet as of any day in the year.

7.13   SOME COMMENTS ON DATA FEEDS AND INTERFACES

Time and again, banks have purchased commercially available simulation software, thinking that it would solve all of their ALM analytical problems. While it is true that there are excellent systems on the market that can perform virtually all of the interest rate risk analyses a bank would need, purchasing the software is only the first step in the proverbial thousand-mile journey. Once the software and hardware are installed, there is a substantial learning curve that must be tackled. Appendix 7A provides some hard-learned suggestions for undertaking the task.

One aspect of implementing any ALM technique deserves special attention: developing data feeds and automating interfaces between applications systems and the analytical software. This area has been the Waterloo for numerous banks and has become a focus of several vendors who sell ALM software. And rightly so, for it is a critical area.

There is no excuse for banks not developing extracts for each of their major applications systems and making them available to all areas of the bank through some type of database management system or report writer capability. The extracts should contain all of the data needed for analytical purposes, but no confidential information, such as customer names, social security numbers, or phone numbers should be included. However, census tracts or zip codes may be important for marketing or Community Reinvestment Act (CRA) purposes. Certainly, data fields such as balance, rate, origination date, and maturity date should be in every extract file. Ideally, every loan and deposit account will have a separate record in the extract file, although aggregations of data by origination month and year and by branch are certainly reasonable.

A centralized support unit should have responsibility for creating and maintaining these files. The advantage of this approach is that it ensures the following: the highest quality database in terms of all rates being specified on the same calculation basis; erroneous records are purged in a timely manner; and product realignments or groupings are reflected properly. It will also ensure that updates are conducted on a regular schedule.

The ALM staff then becomes just one of many bank units that will develop interfaces between the database and the ALM simulation software. Realistically, relatively few banks have such a resource. What should the ALM staff do then? The worst case would be that they must manually input the maturity schedules for each product account every month. This is, of course, tedious and error-prone.

More enterprising ALM staffs will campaign for the development of automated extracts to flow from the applications systems to the ALM simulation software. This is not as difficult as it may sound. ALM software vendors routinely provide the capability to read "flat files" directly into their systems. If so, then the ALM staff need only send the vendor's documentation on these files along with a "systems request" to the appropriate data processing department. Then, it is a matter of getting into the project queues for each major application system.

The burden this approach creates for the ALM staff is that they will be responsible for any needed enhancements or modifications to the extracts. Also, there are numerous horror stories where an ALM analyst attempts to specify the particular fields to place in the extract, only to find out that the wrong field was requested. This is an extremely common occurrence, especially if the application system was developed in-house and its documentation is either not current or nonexistent. Despite these problems, the benefits are well worth the efforts.

7.14   ON DEVELOPING IN-HOUSE SIMULATION SOFTWARE

In the early 1980s, many larger banking organizations were actively developing their own in-house simulation systems, often using general financial modeling or statistical languages. In those years, the quality of vendor-created software left much to be desired. Banks were correct in thinking that they could produce similar quality software but without having to conform to the vendor's conventions. That is, if a bank had to live with mediocre software, it may as well have mediocre software tailored to its own specific needs and conventions.

The 1990s are a different matter entirely. Software is available that is reliable, user-friendly, and well maintained. Software is available on mainframes, minicomputers, and microcomputers. Virtually any level of sophistication and any degree of detail may be had. We know of no rationale or justification for any bank attempting to develop its own simulation software today. Nevertheless, we still learn of major organizations in the throws of major development projects for their own ALM system. In our opinion, the cost of purchasing commercially available software and its associated hardware will be the smallest long-term cost associated with ALM work. It is one of the best investments any bank can ever make.

7.15   SUMMARY

This concludes our brief introduction to gap analysis and simulation modeling. Once again, those techniques are used to understand how interest rate shifts will affect the timing pattern of cash flows and earnings. We concluded that simulation models provide the only accurate measures of such risks. Chapter 8 turns the attention to the issue of measuring the risk to the market value of equity (and the economic equity ratio). The technique that will be presented in this context is a form of duration known as modified duration or interest rate elasticity.

APPENDIX 7A: SOME THOUGHTS ON IMPLEMENTING AND USING SIMULATION SOFTWARE

This appendix gives some suggestions that may help a bank scale the simulation software learning curve. It is one of the most important learning curves any banking organization can undertake. Only with well-run models can banks truly understand their risk profiles.

The 80/20 rule. Our number one suggestion is to always observe the 80/20 rule. This rule asserts that one can get 80% of the way to a complete solution by expending only 20% of the total possible effort. This rule pops up in innumerable situations. One example is that for many deposit categories, more than 80% of the balances will be from the largest 20% of accounts. Put another way, go after the largest benefit when faced with a choice of approaches. Make sure that the results of the analytical effort will make a material improvement in assessing the bank's risk profiles.

Start simple, add detail only as needed. For example, in creating the chart of accounts for a bank's first simulation model, use only the detail that will be routinely reported to the ALCO and senior management. A typical situation for the loan portfolio would be to establish five categories: commercial, construction, direct installment, indirect installment, and mortgage. Surprisingly good forecasts may be obtained with this summary level of detail. Add more detailed subcategories to the model only if the improvement in forecasting accuracy is significant.

Understand historical trends and relationships. Most initial runs of simulation models give very unsatisfactory results in terms of the product yields in the forecast periods. A simple, informative approach is to analyze the historical yields. For example, commercial loan portfolios usually show a very stable spread relationship to the prime rate. Simply calculate the historical commercial loan portfolio yield spread over the prime rate. Input that spread as the pricing above the forecasted prime rate. Often, extrapolating historical relationships for the total bank provides more accurate forecasts than the summation of departmental forecasts. That is, simple top-down estimates are often better than detailed bottom-up forecasts. The ALCO staff should always analyze straightforward extrapolations of current trends, since there is a reasonable chance that such trends will persist. Always question a department that suddenly believes that the pricing on its new loans will be significantly higher than historical trends support, or a loan unit that believes that its charge-offs will suddenly drop in half from its charge-off rate over the past several years. In some multibank holding companies, the holding company staff can sometimes generate better forecasts than the banks themselves submit just by extrapolating current trends, whereas the bank management often believes it can dramatically reverse all of its adverse trends!

Use the report writer. Most simulation software comes with powerful report writers. This is as important a feature as the simulation "engine" itself. Learn and use the report writer. It can become a powerful analytical tool in its own right. More importantly, it should be used to reproduce the bank's financial accounting reports and budget reports. Now, why should these reports be regenerated by the simulation model? In our experience, there is a tendency for the simulation results to be discredited if they do not tie (or "foot") to other internal information systems. Also, this exercise will uncover numerous discrepancies between the three main systems: financial reporting, budgeting, and ALM. Common discrepancies arise from chart of account classifications and totals, the accrual bases of interest rates, and the treatments of discounts or accruals. Such discrepancies must be hunted down and rooted out . . . relentlessly!

Reconcile, reconcile, reconcile. This, along with the 80/20 rule, is the most important advice offered for consideration. Periodically (at least once per quarter), the ALM staff should retrieve their forecast from three or six months ago and check its accuracy against the bank's actual financial results. Suppose it is April and the analysts wish to reconcile the forecast created the prior December. What should be checked is the reasonableness of the forecast assumptions. To do this, the December model should be updated for actual target balances for January, February, and March. The old yield curve forecast should also be updated with the actual yield curves for the same months. (Note that errors in the target balances and yield curves are to be expected. These are not considered inaccuracies in this discussion. However, if the pricing spreads or new-add maturity distributions are off, these errors would be difficult to identify without this approach.)

Now, resolve the model for January, February, and March and compare the model's results with the actuals for those months. Check each detailed product account for accurate yields in each month. Run a gap report for the end of March as generated by the December model and compare it with the current gap in the April model. Any discrepancies in yield or gap structure indicate poor forecast assumptions. Here is another application of the 80/20 rule: Focus attention on the errors that are causing the most error in net income or gap structure. In all likelihood, fewer than 20% of the errors are causing more than 80% of the aggregate error! Focus on that 20%.

Reconciling forecasts to actuals in this manner on a regular basis is the best way to improve the quality of the simulations. It is by far the simplest method for identifying inaccurate forecast assumptions. The two accounts that should be very accurate at all times are the investment securities portfolio and retail CDs. If a bank's models are showing much error in these two accounts, then something is fundamentally wrong with how the model is being used and immediate attention is required.

CHAPTER 8

Interest Rate Risk Analyses: Duration

For all its significance as a risk measurement tool, duration has been one of the most poorly marketed concepts in all of banking! Many bankers feel that they have been badgered, tormented, intimidated, and berated for not knowing the theory and applications of duration. In reaction, they have developed a large set of defenses and rationalizations as to the inadequacies and dangers of duration. More attention has been paid to disparaging duration than to understanding it!

Fortunately, this situation is slowly changing for the better. Duration is one of the most important concepts in the practice of financial risk management. It is a tragedy that the banking industry has spent so much energy criticizing it and fighting against its use. We believe that this happened because the technique was initially presented as "the one and only" correct risk management tool and as the ultimate in theoretical sophistication. Neither could be further from the truth. It is a basic concept that can be abused and oversold just as any other risk measure can. In reading these sections, put aside whatever rhetoric you may have heard and give the concept a chance. We think you will find the effort rewarding!

8.1   INTRODUCING INTEREST RATE ELASTICITY: DURATION INCOGNITO

For analysts who do understand duration and agree with its importance, it is a great mistake to charge forward in ALCO or board meetings with technical discussions about its associated equations, calculations, and theoretical strengths and shortcomings. In fact, we recommend that the term "duration" never be used in presenting the concept to an ALCO or board of directors!

Instead, we suggest that an approach similar to the following be employed:

> "Today, we will present a new approach to supplement our current interest rate risk analytical techniques. The focus of this analysis is one we think you will all agree is critical to the long-term success of the bank: our market capitalization and stock price. By this analysis, we will explain to you how much and in what direction our stock price will change with any shift in interest rates. More importantly, we will explain to you why this risk exists and ask you if you are comfortable with it or wish to decrease it."

Every senior executive and board member is receptive to understanding the behavior of their stock price. Indeed, they should probably ask the bank why it has not bothered to address this area sooner!

The authors adopted the term "interest rate elasticity" (or "IRE") as the name of this mysterious "new" technique. This was our alternative to the more conventional term: modified duration. Every bank should decide for itself how to present this idea. The name is not important, but the concept is. A definition of interest rate elasticity (IRE) follows:

> *Interest Rate Elasticity (IRE)*: **The percentage change in the market value of an asset or liability (or equity) for a 1% increase in interest rates.**

We will now present the concept of duration and IRE in a simple theoretical framework with mathematics no more complicated than the net present value equation. Our goal is to leave the reader with an intuitive grasp of the concept: what it is and how to use it in the context of bank ALM.

8.2   DURATION CALCULATIONS MADE EASY

Any reader with math anxiety may wish to skip this section. It is not necessary to be able to do long-hand duration calculations to use it properly in ALM. However, if the reader is at all curious about the math behind them, then read on!

This section will present an intuitive derivation of the duration equation. The next will discuss how this equation is modified for the IRE concept and its relationship to actual bond valuation. This derivation will be discussed as a three-step process:

Step 1: Duration of a Zero Coupon Bond

Step 2: Duration of a Portfolio of Two Zero Coupon Bonds

Step 3: Coupon Bonds as Portfolios of Zero Coupon Bonds

Step 1: Duration of a zero coupon bond. The simplest transaction to analyze is a bullet CD or zero coupon bond. In either case, there will be one and only one future cash flow that encompasses both principal and interest. For example, consider a five-year zero coupon bond whose market value today is $2,000. **For any zero-coupon or bullet transaction, the remaining time until its maturity is equal to its duration.** Therefore, the duration of a new five-year zero coupon bond is simply five years.

Step 2: Duration of a portfolio of two zero coupon bonds. Suppose that, in addition to the five-year bond in Step 1, there is a second zero coupon bond. Its maturity is two years and its current market value is $1,000. The duration of this second bond is two years. But what is the overall duration of the portfolio containing these two bonds? **The duration of a portfolio of zero coupon bonds is the weighted average duration of the individual bonds, where the weighting factors are the market values of the bonds.** The calculations for this example are shown in Table 8.1.

Table 8.1
Duration Calculation for Two Zero Coupon Bonds

Step (i): List the bonds by duration and market value (or price).

Bond	Duration	Price
A	2 Years	$1,000
B	5 Years	$2,000

Step (ii): Multiply durations by prices.

Bond	Duration	X	Price	=	Product
A	2 Years		$1,000		2,000
B	5 Years		$2,000		10,000

Step (iii): Sum the prices and products.

Bond	Duration	X	Price	=	Product
A	2 Years		$1,000		2,000
B	5 Years		$2,000		10,000
			$3,000		12,000

Step (iv): Divide the sum of the products by the total market value.

$12,000-Years / $3,000 = 4 Years = Duration of Portfolio

Hence, the weighted-average duration of this two-bond portfolio is four years. Believe it or not, these two steps are all one needs to know to calculate the duration for almost any financial transaction! The next step is just a generalization of the first two.

Step 3: Coupon bonds as portfolios of zero coupon bonds. For more complicated transactions, such as coupon bonds, you need only to apply the principles learned in Steps 1 and 2. Consider a three-year, 8% annual coupon bond as shown in Table 8.2. This table shows both the market value of the bond and its yield-to-maturity.

Table 8.2
Duration of a Coupon Bond

Assumptions:
Principal:	$1,000
Coupon:	$80, or 8%
Maturity:	3 Years

Year (a)	Yield Curve (b)	Cash Flow (c)	Present Values (d)	Product (e)
1	7.00%	80	74.77	74.77
2	8.00%	80	68.59	137.17
3	9.00%	1080	833.96	2501.87
	8.78%		977.31	2713.82

Market Value of Bond:
=   Sum of Column (d)
= $977.31

Yield to Maturity:
=   Weighted Average Yield (Weighted by Present Values)
=   8.78%

Duration of Bond:
=   Sum of Column (e) / Sum of Column (d)
= $2,713.82-Years / $977.31
=   2.78 Years

The essence of the procedure is to list out each cash flow to be paid by the bond (shown in Column (c)), calculate the present value of each cash flow (Column (d)) by discounting by the appropriate yield from the yield curve (Column (b)), then proceeding with the weighted averaging as described in Step 2. The new element here is the calculation of the present values, where each value in Column (d) was obtained from the following equation:

$$Present\ Value = \frac{CF_t}{(1 + r_t)^t}$$

where

$$CF_t = Cash\ Flow \text{ for } Year\ t$$
$$r_t = Yield \text{ for } Year\ t$$

The duration of this bond is 2.78 years. This procedure may be applied to any security or transaction that has fixed cash flows.

The formal equation for the duration of a bond is as follows:

$$Duration = D = \frac{\displaystyle\sum_{t=1}^{N} \frac{t \times CF_t}{(1 + r_t)^t}}{MV}$$

where

$$MV = \sum_{t=1}^{N} \frac{CF_t}{(1 + r_t)^t}$$

which is the standard equation for the market value or net present value. As imposing as these equations appear, their use is no more complicated than the simple steps just presented. It is left as an exercise for the mathematically inclined reader to prove that the duration of a zero coupon bond (where there is only one future cash flow) is equal to its maturity.

At this point, the reader should be wondering just why anyone would bother with calculating duration. Just what is the significance of "2.78 years" for this three-year bond? For an explanation, the reader is referred to Appendix 8A. This appendix explains the intuition behind the duration value of a bond and how it is used in the process known as bond immunization. The material is placed in an appendix because it is not essential to the development of the IRE concept.

8.3   FROM DURATION TO INTEREST RATE ELASTICITY

Now that the duration calculation is understood, and now that some readers have ventured through Appendix 8A and the world of bond immunization, the concept is still not very satisfying in the context of asset and liability management. Duration is measured in units of years, which is difficult to relate to risk profiles. If anyone ever wanted to immunize a bank, perhaps it would be of some use.

Enter the term interest rate elasticity. The definition of interest rate elasticity (IRE) was presented in Section 8.1. It is the percentage change in the market value of any financial security given a 1% rise in interest rates. How is this related to duration? The equation to convert duration into IRE (or modified duration) is shown here:

$$IRE = \frac{-D}{(1 + r)}$$

where r is the bond's yield-to-maturity as explained in Table 8.2. This equation is derived in Appendix 8B. This section demonstrates the use of IRE and this equation with the simple three-year annual coupon bond.

From Section 8.2, the duration of the three-year bond was found to be 2.78 years. The yield-to-maturity was 8.78%. Placing these values into the last equation gives the following equation:

$$IRE = \frac{-2.78}{(1.0878)} = -2.56\%$$

This value of –2.56% is the percentage change in the bond's price "for a 1% change in rates." What this phrase means is the rate at which the bond price changes for very small changes in rate. This is best shown by an example. For a simple bond such as this, it is a simple matter to calculate the market value changes with 1% shifts in the yield curve. This is shown in Table 8.3.

From Table 8.3, the average change in market value for the 1% rise and 1% fall in rates is $25.0. This is 25.0/977.3 = 2.56% in magnitude. Of course, when rates rise, the market value declines, indicating that the IRE

Table 8.3
Market Value of a Three-Year Annual Coupon Bond
(Effect of 1% Rate Shifts)

Year	Cash Flow	Original Yield Curve	Original Present Values	1% Higher Rates: Yield Curve	1% Higher Rates: Present Values	1% Lower Rates: Yield Curve	1% Lower Rates: Present Values
1	80	7.00%	74.8	8.00%	74.1	6.00%	75.5
2	80	8.00%	68.6	9.00%	67.3	7.00%	69.9
3	1080	9.00%	834.0	10.00%	811.4	8.00%	857.3
		8.89%	977.3	9.89%	952.8	7.90%	1002.7

Changes in Market Value (from 977.3):	(24.5)	25.4
Percentage Change in Value:	–2.51%	2.60%

will have a negative sign associated with it. Therefore, the IRE value of –2.56% is confirmed.

However, notice from Table 8.3 that the individual percentage changes in market values differ somewhat from the IRE value of 2.56%. This is because the market value of a fixed-rate bond is not a linear function of yield curve shifts. It is actually a curved function as depicted in Figure 8.1.

To accentuate the curvature, Figure 8.1 portrays the market values for a 30-year, 8% annual coupon bond for a wide range of yields-to-maturity. For reference, the IRE prediction based upon the duration at the 8% point is also plotted. The IRE line is the tangent to the price curve, reflecting the slope of the curve at the point where it was calculated (in this case at 8%). Therefore, the IRE technically refers to very small changes in interest rates.

The curvature in the price behavior is related to a phenomenon called "convexity." There has been much attention drawn to measuring and hedging convexity. That attention is certainly warranted if one is attempting to arbitrage small discrepancies in the bond and/or futures markets. However, it is not nearly so important in asset and liability management for financial institutions, as will be explained in later sections.

Nevertheless, IRE does have a bias in that it underestimates the price changes for bonds when rates drop, and it overestimates them when rates rise. The authors do not view this as much of a concern. The average error

Figure 8.1
Bond Price Behavior

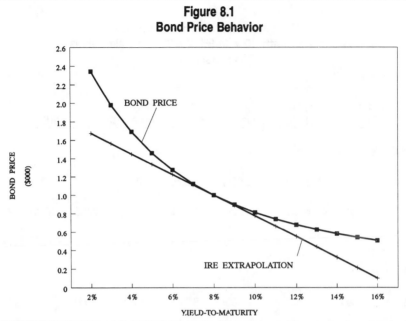

is very small, and it is the average sensitivity against rate increases and declines that will be assessed. As will be discussed in Chapter 9, there are much larger sources of error to be handled than this one. As always, the 80/20 rule applies: in ALM, 80% of the risk comes from 20% of the sources of risk.

8.4   APPLICATION OF IRE ANALYSIS TO CASE STUDY EXAMPLE

We return now to the case study example of Chapter 5 to illustrate the application of IRE analysis. Keep in mind that duration values and IREs are additive, but they must always be weighted by their respective market values. Therefore, the IRE of equity for a bank balance sheet will be the overall weighted average IRE of all assets and liabilities. A full analysis for the case study bank using a 4.5-month CD is shown in Table 8.4.

Table 8.4 displays two sets of results, one pertaining to the original situation where the yield curve is at 6%. There is also a set of results for a shifted yield curve at 7%. This is included to demonstrate a more common

Table 8.4
IRE Analysis for Case Study Example
Using 4.5-Month CD with 6% and 7% CD Yield Curves
(As of January 1)

	Book Balance	Original Maturity	Original Coupon	Current Yield	Market Value	Duration	IRE	$ Change
Yield Curve at 6%:								
Loan	1000	6 months	8.00%	8.00%	1000.0	0.500	–.47%	(4.72)
CD	800	4.5 months	6.00%	6.00%	800.0	0.375	–.35%	(2.83)
Equity	200	n/a	n/a	n/a	200.0	1.000	–.95%	(1.89)
Yield Curve at 7%:								
Loan	1000	6 months	8.00%	9.00%	995.2	0.500	–.47%	(4.65)
CD	800	4.5 months	6.00%	7.00%	797.1	0.375	–.35%	(2.79)
Equity	200	n/a	n/a	n/a	198.1	1.003	–.95%	(1.86)

situation in real life, where book values and market values are not equal to one another.

The duration values are included for reference. Recall that we recommend that durations not be shown or discussed, especially if the senior management is negatively disposed to the concept. There are three important columns in this table: Market Value, IRE, and $ Change. While IRE is the percentage change in the market value for a 1% rate change, the last column labeled "$ Change" is the dollar amount of the change, obtained simply by multiplying the market value by the IRE. The market value of equity is always the net residual when the market value subtotal of liabilities is subtracted from the market value subtotal of assets.

The dollar changes are also directly additive. That is, the dollar change in equity for a 1% rate rise is simply the difference between the asset dollar change and liability dollar change. The durations and IREs for the loan and CD are calculated with the procedures just described. The IRE (and duration) of equity are the weighted averages of the asset and liability values using their market values as the weighting factors. Keep in mind that in doing the weighted average calculations, asset values are positive numbers and liability market values are negatives.

The 7% yield curve section (lower half) of Table 8.4 permits a double check on the dollar change predictions from the 6% yield curve section (upper half). For example, the dollar change of the loan when CD rates are 6% is –$4.72 (upper half). This is consistent with a loan market value of $995.27. In the lower half of the table, the loan value is seen to be $995.2 (rounded). There will be a small error due to the curved nature of prices discussed in the preceding section. The equity dollar change prediction of –$1.89, or $198.11, is extremely close to the actual value after the rate shift of $198.1.

There are three results from Table 8.4 that are worth emphasizing to an ALCO or board of directors. The first is the market value of equity. This figure is an estimated mark-to-market value of the entire bank. Particular attention should be paid to whether this value is greater than or less than the book value of the bank. For publicly traded entities, this value should be consistent with the total market capitalization of the bank. If it is not, further work is needed to sort out the discrepancy.

The second and third important results are the IRE of equity and the predicted dollar change in equity for every 100 basis rate change in rates. These are, after all, the goal of the analysis. The IRE is literally the percentage change in stock price that should be expected if interest rates shift. Note that the IRE of equity shown in the upper half of Table 8.4 is the same value originally discussed when the case study was first presented in Chapter 5.

Recalling the initial sections of Chapter 7, these last two results represent the estimates of the magnitude of the equity risk faced by the bank with interest rate changes. Table 8.5 summarizes the IRE results for some other CD maturities.

From prior discussions, recall that the use of the six-month CD hedges the economic equity ratio. Table 8.5 now shows why this happens. Note that with a liability duration that is the same as the asset duration, the IREs for the asset, the liability, and for equity are all the same at –0.47%. Therefore, however interest rates shift, all of the market values will fall or rise by the same percentage, leaving a constant ratio of equity to assets.

Recall also that the 7.5-month CD hedged the market value of equity. From Table 8.5, we see why. With this maturity, the dollar change for the CD equals the dollar change for the loan. If the change in asset value is exactly offset by an equal change in liability value, then the value of equity must remain unchanged!

Table 8.5
IRE Analyses for Various CD Maturities
(Case Study Situation—6% Yield Curve)

	Book Balance	Original Maturity	Original Coupon	Current Yield	Market Value	Duration	IRE	$ Change
Loan	1000	6 months	8.00%	8.00%	1000.0	0.500	–.47%	(4.72)
4.5-Month CD:								
CD	800	4.5 months	6.00%	6.00%	800.0	0.375	–.35%	(2.83)
Equity	200	n/a	n/a	n/a	200.0	1.000	–.95%	(1.89)
6-Month CD:								
CD	800	6 months	6.00%	6.00%	800.0	0.500	–.47%	(3.77)
Equity	200	n/a	n/a	n/a	200.0	0.500	–.47%	(0.94)
7.5-Month CD:								
CD	800	7.5 months	6.00%	6.00%	800.0	0.625	–.59%	(4.72)
Equity	200	n/a	n/a	n/a	200.0	0.000	–.00%	0.00

8.5   "HELP! I DIDN'T UNDERSTAND THE DURATION/IRE EQUATIONS!"

If this thought is floating through the mind of any reader, we say, "Relax." Even if none of the calculations are understood, there is no need to worry. What matters is that the reader understand the interpretation of the results, not how to reproduce the calculations. Therefore, if the discussion of the tables in Section 8.4 was understood, that is all that counts. There is absolutely no reason to abandon or reject the use of IRE just because the equations look intimidating. After all, senior executives and bank directors could care less what equations are programmed into simulation model software systems. They only care about understanding the output. The same applies to IRE.

Today, many of the simulation model software packages include IRE and duration capabilities. This is the ideal situation. Let the model do the number crunching. The analyst and the executive should focus on interpreting and using the results. We are convinced that the critical results discussed from Tables 8.4 and 8.5 should always be of primary importance to any ALCO and to every board of directors—that is, if they wish to understand interest rate risk.

8.6   SUMMARY

This concludes the overview of the major interest rate risk analytical techniques. IRE (and duration) are critical components of any assessment of interest rate risk. After all, this is the best method for measuring the overall effect of an interest rate shift on the present value of all future cash flows. Therefore, it is the best gauge of the riskiness to the market value of equity.

We emphasize that IRE/duration are not replacements for gap analysis or simulation modeling. Those techniques only determine the timing pattern of cash flow changes, not the net present value of those changes over all time periods. In this sense, IRE complements simulation modeling. It does not replace it.

APPENDIX 8A: DURATION INTUITION AND BOND IMMUNIZATION

The objective of bond immunization is to achieve a total rate of return on investment for a specific time horizon. Keep in mind that total returns represent the true economic returns on a cash flow basis, reflecting the effects of principal losses or gains as well as reinvestment returns on coupons. It is identical to the internal rate of return concept from corporate financial theory. This is not as simple a task as it may seem at first glance. The only simple guarantee of a total rate of return for a specific time horizon is to find a zero coupon bond that matures at the desired final point in time. Short of this, the technique of bond immunization provides a realistic alternative.

The difficulty in achieving a known rate of return is that the reinvestment rates on the coupon payments associated with most bonds will vary as interest rates fluctuate during the course of the investment period. These fluctuations will have an impact on the total returns experienced by a portfolio.

As an example, consider a situation where a portfolio manager is confronted with the task of investing $1,000 today for exactly seven years. Suppose further that the yield curve today is flat at 8%, and there are only two maturities available: seven years and 10 years. Both have 8% annual coupons. The objective is to achieve an 8% total rate of return over the seven-year investment horizon.

This is not possible with either of the individual bonds! For example, if the manager purchases $1,000 worth of the seven-year bonds, and interest rates decline during the investment period, the 8% objective will not be achieved. This is illustrated in Table 8A.1 for rate shifts at two different times: (1) the day after the bond is purchased, and (2) halfway through the seven-year investment period. In either case, rates shift once and stay at the new level for the remainder of the seven-year period.

From this table, the adverse effect is larger for rate decreases that occur earlier in the investment holding period. This is because the shortfall is related to reinvestment returns below the critical 8% level. If coupons cannot be reinvested to earn at least 8%, then the overall rate of return will fall short of that target. Naturally, the longer the period of the reinvestment shortfall, the larger the total return shortfall will be.

What about investing in the ten-year bond? A similar set of total returns are displayed in Table 8A.2.

Table 8A.1
Total Returns Over Seven-Year Horizon
Purchase of Seven-Year 8% Coupon Bond

Rate Shift	New Rate	Rate Change on Day After Purchase	Rate Change Occurs after 3.5 Years
−2.00%	6.00%	7.61%	7.88%
−1.00%	7.00%	7.81%	7.94%
0.00%	8.00%	8.00%	8.00%
+1.00%	9.00%	8.20%	8.06%
+2.00%	10.00%	8.40%	8.12%

Table 8A.2
Total Returns Over Seven-Year Horizon
Purchase of 10-Year 8% Coupon Bond

Rate Shift	New Rate	Rate Change on Day After Purchase	Rate Change Occurs after 3.5 Years
−2.00%	6.00%	8.10%	8.48%
−1.00%	7.00%	8.04%	8.24%
0.00%	8.00%	8.00%	8.00%
+1.00%	9.00%	7.97%	7.77%
+2.00%	10.00%	7.96%	7.55%

Notice that the total returns are at 8% or better if rates remain un-changed or if they decline. The shortfall exists when rates rise! Moreover, the shortfall is worse if the rate rise occurs later rather than earlier! In this situation, the portfolio manager will be obligated to sell the bond with three years of remaining cash flows in the open market at the end of the seven-year holding period. Hence, the total return is affected more by the principal (or market value) risk of that sale transaction than with coupon reinvestment risk. This risk increases as the close-out time draws nearer.

All of this may be explained by separating the two sources of risk in this situation: principal (or price) risk and reinvestment risk. Price risk refers to the market value gain or loss caused by a rate shift that would be incurred by selling the remaining portion of the bond before maturity. Reinvestment risk refers to the change in the coupon reinvestment earnings due to the rate shift, including compounding. Whenever interest rates rise, the prices of bonds fall, but the reinvestment income from the coupons rises. Therefore, these two risks tend to offset one another.

To illustrate, consider the 10-year bond in more detail. The two risks for a 1% rate increase are measured and shown separately over a wide variety of investment holding periods in Table 8A.3.

Table 8A.3
Price Risk Versus Reinvestment Risk
(10-Year 8% Annual Coupon Bond—
Effects of a 1% Rise in Interest Rates on Day 2)

Holding	Bond Price			Reinvestment Income			Total
Period	@9%	@8%	Diff	@9%	@8%	Diff	Return
1	940.0	1000	(60.0)	0.0	0.0	0.0	2.00%
2	944.7	1000	(55.3)	7.2	6.4	0.8	5.44%
3	949.7	1000	(50.3)	22.2	19.7	2.5	6.62%
4	955.1	1000	(44.9)	45.9	40.5	5.4	7.21%
5	961.1	1000	(38.9)	78.8	69.3	9.4	7.56%
6	967.6	1000	(32.4)	121.9	106.9	15.0	7.80%
7	974.7	1000	(25.3)	176.0	153.8	22.2	7.97%
8	982.4	1000	(17.6)	242.3	210.9	31.3	8.10%
9	990.8	1000	(9.2)	321.7	279.0	42.7	8.20%
10	1000.0	1000	0.0	415.4	358.9	56.5	8.28%

Note: All figures have been rounded to nearest $ .10.

The first line of Table 8A.3 pertains to a one-year holding period. If the yield curve shifts to 9% for all maturities on the day after the 8% bond is purchased at par, its market value at the end of the holding period will be $940.00. This is the present value of a nine-year (remaining) maturity 8%

coupon bond priced to yield 9%. If rates had not changed, the nine-year bond could have been sold at par, or $1,000. The difference is the loss of $60.00 shown in the first line. There is no reinvestment income in the first line because the coupon payment of $80 is received on the day the position is closed out (after one year), and there is no time to reinvest it. The total return in line one is simple to understand. Total cash received upon sale of the remaining bond for $940 and the coupon of $80 is $1,020. Compared to the $1,000 invested, this is a 2% rate of return for the one-year holding period.

The second line shows the effects of the rate rise if the investment period is two years. In this case, the remaining bond will have eight years remaining and will be sold after the second year for $944.70, a loss of $55.30. The reinvestment income columns show that there will be earnings from reinvesting the first year's coupon of $80. The reinvestment earnings will be $7.20 if the $80 can be reinvested at the higher rate of 9%, but only $6.40 if rates remain unchanged and the reinvestment yield is 8%. The difference of $.80 is shown in line 2.

There is an important significance to the relative magnitudes of the two columns labeled "Diff" in Table 8A.3. Their absolute values are plotted in Figure 8A.1.

Notice that the magnitudes of these two offsetting risks are equal to one another at 7.25 years. This is also the duration value of this 10-year bond.

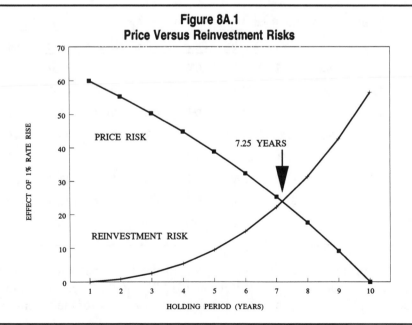

Figure 8A.1
Price Versus Reinvestment Risks

Therefore, the first intuitive definition of duration is now at hand: **The duration is the point at which price risk and reinvestment risk cancel each other out.**

Recall that the reason why no single coupon bond can assure a total return is that either coupon reinvestment risk or price risk skewed the total return. Duration provides a method of ensuring that the two cancel each other out. The task of "hedging" or "immunizing" a target rate of return then becomes one of finding a combination of bonds whose weighted average duration equals the investment horizon. This duration-matching condition must then be maintained throughout the holding period.

As an example, we will return to the seven-year and 10-year bonds discussed above. The objective is to guarantee a total rate of return for a seven-year time horizon. Table 8A.4 shows the portfolio characteristics for a rate scenario where rates rise dramatically during the holding period.

The objective of the immunization is to achieve at least an 8% total return over the seven-year period. Starting with $1,000 to invest, this requires a final portfolio value of $1,714 or more. Notice that this example ends with a portfolio value of $1,721, achieving the objective.

Table 8A.4
Example of Bond Immunization
(Seven-Year Investment Horizon—8% Total Return Desired)

	Market	10-Year Bond			7-Year Bond			Portfolio	
Year	Yield	Price	Duration	Number	Price	Duration	Number	Value	Duration
0	8%	1000	7.25	0.848	1000	5.62	0.152	1000	7.0
1	10%	885	6.59	0.703	913	4.94	0.380	969	6.0
2	12%	801	5.97	0.530	856	4.25	0.644	975	5.0
3	14%	743	5.38	0.349	825	3.53	0.920	1018	4.0
4	16%	705	4.78	0.186	820	2.76	1.184	1102	3.0
5	18%	687	4.15	0.065	843	1.92	1.413	1236	2.0
6	18%	731	3.50	0.000	915	1.00	1.594	1458	1.0
7	18%	783	2.75	—	1000	0.00	—	1721	

At the outset of the positions (shown in the line designated Year 0), note that both bonds are valued at par ($1,000 each). Also, the duration values of 7.25 years for the 10-year bond and 5.62 years for the seven-year bond are calculated exactly as explained in Section 8.2. The manager should purchase enough of each bond so that the weighted average duration of the combined portfolio is 7.0. This may be calculated from the following equation:

$$N_{10\,yr} \times P_{10\,yr} \times D_{10\,yr} + N_{7\,yr} \times P_{7\,yr} \times D_{7\,yr} = 7.0\ years$$

where

$$N = Number\ of\ Bonds\ Needed$$
$$P = Price\ of\ Each\ Bond$$
$$D = Duration\ of\ Each\ Bond$$

This equation must be combined with another equation that defines the total value of the initial portfolio:

$$N_{10\,yr} \times P_{10\,yr} + N_{7\,yr} \times P_{7\,yr} = \$1,000$$

These two simultaneous equations may be solved for the numbers of each bond needed to achieve immunization: 0.848 units of the 10-year bond and 0.152 units of the seven-year bond.

After one year (the second line of values in the table), interest rates have risen by 200 basis points. Hence, the market value of the portfolio has declined to $969 (including collected coupons). As just explained for the initial purchases, one then sets up analogous equations as the last set, only now there are six years remaining in the investment horizon. Therefore, a combination of the two bonds must end up with a weighted average duration of six years. Solving the equations, it is found that 0.703 of the longer term bond and 0.380 of the other bond are needed. To implement this, the manager must sell 0.145 (which is 0.848 minus 0.703) of the current nine-year (which was originally a 10-year) bond, generating $128 in cash. This is combined with the coupons received of $80 from the two original purchases for a total amount of $208. With this, 0.228 of the shorter term bond valued at $913 each is purchased. The portfolio is now "rebalanced."

This process is repeated at the end of each year so that the weighted average duration always matches the remaining investment period. The table summarizes all of the positions needed given the pattern of rising rates shown in the "Market Yield" column. This procedure works because however rates shift, the price risk is offset by the reinvestment risk.

The particular proportions of each bond needed to rebalance the portfolio at the end of each year is very much a function of the market yields at

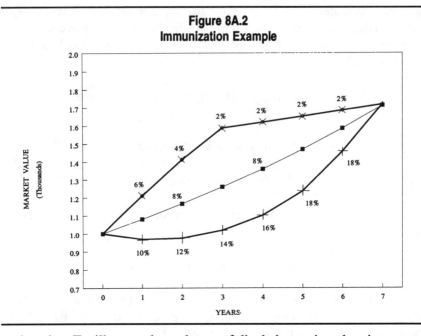

Figure 8A.2
Immunization Example

each point. To illustrate how the portfolio behaves in other interest rate scenarios, consider Figure 8A.2.

This figure shows the portfolio values at the end of each year from Table 8A.4 for the rising rate scenario. For comparison, the portfolio values for a constant rate and a falling rate scenario are displayed. In the latter, rates fall to 2%. Notice that whatever happens to interest rates, the investment objective of $1,714 is achieved at the seven-year horizon.

This brings us to the second intuitive definition of duration: **Duration indicates the time point where total return is immunized, or hedged, against any shifts in the yield curve.**

APPENDIX 8B: MATHEMATICAL DERIVATION OF THE IRE EQUATION

The net present value equation is used to calculate the market value of an asset or liability. It may be written as follows:

$$MV = \sum_{t=1}^{N} \frac{CF_t}{(1 + r_t)^t}$$

This equation may be differentiated with respect to r:

$$\frac{\Delta MV}{\Delta r} = \sum_{t=1}^{N} \frac{-t \times CF_t}{(1+r_t)^{t+1}}$$

$$= \frac{-1}{1+r_{ytm}} \times \left[\sum_{t=1}^{N} \frac{t \times CF_t}{(1+r_t)^t} \right]$$

where r_{ytm} is the yield-to-maturity for the bond. The terms within brackets in the last equation are equal to the duration of the bond multiplied by its market value (from the duration equation from page 158), giving the following equation:

$$\frac{\Delta MV}{\Delta r} = \frac{-D \times MV}{1+r_{ytm}}$$

which may be divided by the market value for:

$$IRE = \frac{\Delta MV}{MV \times \Delta r} = \frac{-D}{1+r}$$

This is the formal equation for IRE. The middle set of terms corresponds to the percentage change in the market value of an asset or liability for a 1% increase in rates.

CHAPTER 9

Interest Rate Risk Characteristics of Bank Products

Thus far, all of the discussions on interest rate risk have been in the context of the simplistic case study example from Chapter 5 of a single six-month loan being funded by one CD of any maturity. Each balance sheet item was assumed to be priced directly off of the CD yield curve. In reality, bank activities and products show a wide range of behavior and responses to shifts in the yield curve. To facilitate our discussion, we will categorize these effects into the four main "sources" of interest rate risk shown in Table 9.1: yield curve repricing risk, spread risk, balance fluctuation risk, and options risk.

Table 9.1
Sources of Interest Rate Risk in Bank Activities

Source of Risk:	Example Products
Yield Curve Repricing Risk	CDs, Money Market Assets
Spread Risk:	
Short-Term Rate	Prime-Based Loans
Quasi-Fixed Rate	Savings Account
Balance Fluctuation Risk	Demand Deposit Account
Options Features:	
Balance-Oriented Options	Mortgage Prepayments
Rate-Oriented Options	Capped-Rate Loans

We reiterate that risk arises from any volatility in cash flows due to an unexpected change in interest rates. It does not refer to fluctuations due to expected rate changes that were anticipated by the implied forward rates in the yield curve. Many bank products display more than one source of interest rate risk.

Yield curve repricing risk. This refers to the straightforward effects of shifts in the yield curve on the direct pricing of many balance sheet items, such as Treasury bills or notes purchased for the investment portfolio, CDs issued to fund the bank, federal funds or repurchase agreement transactions, and loans that are directly indexed to an open market rate such as LIBOR or commercial paper. There are two ways that the yield curve affects these items. First, the yield curve will affect the yield or coupon associated with the product when it is first issued or purchased. Second, a shift in the yield curve after issuance will change the product's current market value, as well as the reinvestment yields that can be obtained with any interim cash flows.

Spread risk. The interest rate or yield associated with many bank products are not directly or completely linked to a market yield curve. Examples include prime-based loans, the money market deposit account, credit card receivables, and the savings account. The first two show interest rate/yield behaviors that approximately fluctuate with short-term market interest rates (such as federal funds, Treasury bills, or LIBOR), but not exactly. The latter two are examples of quasi-fixed rate products. That is, their rate or yield is invariant over long periods of time, but they do change under conditions of extreme market rate moves or shifts in competitive circumstances. (This source of rate risk is sometimes referred to as "basis" risk. This term will not be used because basis risk is used broadly to include many other types of mismatch, such as a mismatch between the delivery date of a futures contract and the expected transaction date of the underlying item being hedged, even if both are based on the same index rate, such as the Eurodollar rate.)

Balance fluctuation risk. Some products display volume fluctuations that are related to shifts in the level of interest rates. A good example would be the noninterest-bearing demand deposit account (DDA). Depositors have a tendency to allow their checking account balances to increase in periods of low interest rates. However, as rates rise and the "opportunity cost" of holding nonearning balances increases, they will be more conscientious in minimizing those balances. A more direct relationship is seen with corporate DDA balances because banks often calculate an "earnings credit" for collected balances that are used to pay for cash management services. As the earnings credit rises, lower balances are needed to pay for a set amount of services. As rates fall, higher balances are needed. Such balance fluctuations will also cause cash flow and earnings volatility for a bank. Hence, they cannot be ignored in analyzing interest rate risk.

Options risk. There are many types and examples of options risks in bank activities. It is one of the more difficult sources of risk to incorporate into interest rate risk analytical techniques. Also, it is usually hidden as an embedded feature in a wide array of bank product offerings. Nevertheless, it is a major source of risk and should never be ignored. This risk displays the major characteristic that it is asymmetric, or one-sided, in nature. That is, the behavior of a product with an embedded option feature will differ if interest rates rise compared to its behavior if rates were to fall. The best example is the prepayment option on fixed-rate mortgage loans. As rates rise, mortgage prepayments decline and the expected life of the portfolio will increase. However, as rates fall, prepayments increase and the average life will fall.

This chapter will now discuss some of the overall interest rate risk features of several important bank products. These examples provide a broad foundation for the wide variety of challenges any asset and liability analyst must address. The products covered are those listed in Table 9.1. Of course, we have already covered the yield curve repricing risk of CDs and loans indexed to money market rates in great detail in Chapters 5 and 6.

9.1   PRIME-BASED LOANS: AN EXAMPLE OF SHORT-TERM SPREAD RISK

The prime rate has played an important role in bank balance sheets over the past several decades. Many types of commercial, construction, and personal line-of-credit facilities use the prime rate as the base pricing index. Figure 9.1 displays a graph of the prime rate, along with the 90-day LIBOR rate as a reference. Notice that, in contrast to the volatility of the

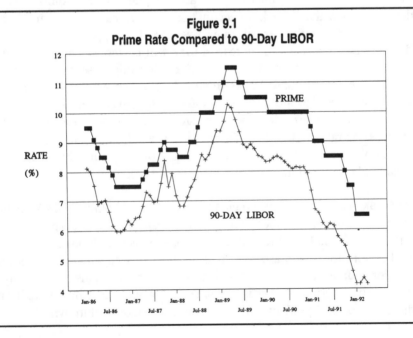

Figure 9.1
Prime Rate Compared to 90-Day LIBOR

LIBOR rate, the prime rate shows fewer rate changes, and whenever the rate does change, it tends to move in 50-basis point increments.

Many asset and liability analysts complain about the difficulty of handling the prime rate. They perplex themselves into thinking they must predict precisely when the next movement in the prime will occur, and by what magnitude. Their reasoning is that prime-based loan balances in gap reports should be placed in whichever time bucket contains the predicted date of the next prime rate change. Such predictions are not necessary and such categorizations in gap analyses are rarely correct.

What is important is to capture the general features of prime rate movements relative to market rates without getting caught up in the details. Fortunately, an analysis by Rodney Jacobs unlocked the key to incorporating the prime rate in interest rate risk analyses. His method posed the question: What is the interest rate risk-minimizing funding portfolio for a group of prime-based loans? Regression analyses were run for a variety of hypothetical portfolios and found that the most stable funding was a combination of 90-day CDs and overnight federal funds.

Keep in mind that these test portfolios were all "tractors" in the sense they were described in Chapter 7. A re-creation of this analysis for 90-day LIBOR and federal funds is shown in Figure 9.2. The point labeled 100% 90-day LIBOR is based on a three-month moving average of the 90-day LIBOR rate. (*Note*: The authors used the LIBOR rate because it was read-

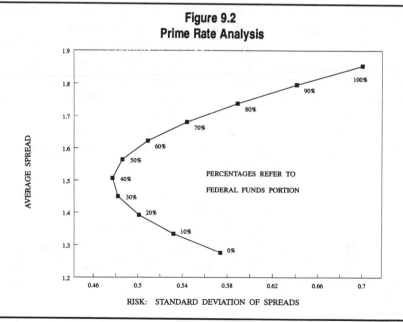

Figure 9.2
Prime Rate Analysis

ily available. The results for CD rates should be about the same as these.) This is the purest "tractor" of all, one where 1/90th of the portfolio matures and rolls over every day within a 90-day rotation pattern.

Note that the risk-minimizing ratio of LIBOR (or CDs) to overnight federal funds is about 60% LIBOR and 40% fed funds. This analysis, at the time it was published, had a profound effect on the management of prime-based loan portfolios. Many banks literally applied these results in their transfer pricing and cost of funds calculations. Of course, with more and more banks explicitly adopting these results, there was a tendency for the analysis to become a self-fulfilling prophecy. That is, as more banks actually funded their prime loans using this combination of maturities, the closer the actual prime rate tended to move with that portfolio, since many banks attempted to maintain a close spread relationship between the hypothetical funding portfolio and their prime-based loans.

While all of this seems fine for the interest rate risk management problem of prime-based loans, it totally ignores another important risk element. Suppose a hypothetical bank had nothing but prime-based loans as assets and wanted to pick an appropriate cost of funds. Should it literally apply the 60:40 mix of 90-day CDs and federal funds? We think not. The reason is that this strategy would result in massive liquidity risk for the bank. Most prime-based loans are not short-term loans but multi-year commitments. Granted, their yield is relatively short-term in price sensitivity, but their maturities could easily be five or seven years.

Liquidity risk will be discussed in detail in Chapter 10. For now, we will assert that the market price of this type of liquidity risk is in the range of 20 to 40 basis points on top of the cost of funding using the optimal short-term funding mixture. This "liquidity premium" must be added into the transfer price or cost of funds to reflect the liquidity risk inherent in using short-term funds to support long-term loan commitments. This issue will be revisited in Chapter 14 on "Transfer Pricing."

For gap analyses then, prime-based loans balances should be spread identically to its optimal funding mixture, showing the following type of distribution among the time buckets in Table 9.2.

Table 9.2
Interest Rate Gap Analysis for Prime-Based Loans

	O/N to 1 Month	>1 to 2 Months	>2 to 3 Months	>3 to 6 Months	>6 to 12 Months	>12 Months or N/S	Total
Prime Loans	600	200	200	-	-	-	1,000

This display most accurately reflects the interest rate sensitivity repricing behavior of this portfolio. The 1- to 30-day bucket consists of the 40% federal funds equivalent and one-third of the 90-day CD tractor. The 31-60 day bucket shows the second one-third of the CD tractor, and the 61-90 day bucket shows the final one-third tractor segment.

For simulation models, it is only important that the average prime rate behavior be captured. This should, again, be based on these results. That is, the exogenous variable for the prime rate should be calculated as 60% of the 90-day moving average of the 90-day CD rate plus 40% of the average federal funds rate for the month being forecasted. This approach will show a prime-rate forecast that rises and falls smoothly over time, rather than the discrete "steps" or "jumps" displayed in real life. This should not detract from the results obtained in the simulation runs. However, if the bank truly wants to simulate a more "realistic" prime-rate, it is a simple matter to build an equation for the prime rate exogenous variable that is rounded to the nearest 0.5%. This will accomplish the desired effect.

For duration or IRE analyses, the prime-based portfolio should be treated as if its duration were identical to that of the hypothetical funding portfolio. The 90-day CD tractor will have a weighted average duration of about 45 days, or 0.125 of a year. The federal funds portion will have a duration of 1/360th of a year, or 0.00278 of a year. The weighted average combination of these will be $0.60 \times 0.125 + 0.40 \times 0.00278$, or 0.075 year. This is equivalent to about a 27-day average duration. It represents an IRE of about -0.07% if CD rates are about 8%.

9.2   THE MONEY MARKET DEPOSIT ACCOUNT

The product that is conceptually closest to prime-based loans in terms of ALM analysis is the money market deposit account (MMDA). Indeed, exactly the same type of analysis as described in the prior section for the prime rate would be entirely appropriate for the MMDA rate.

There is one additional complication that can arise, however. That has to do with the MMDA not showing 100% of a change in short-term market rates. That is, in some markets, if the 90-day CD and federal funds rates were instantly to rise 1%, the MMDA rate might only rise 50% to 70% of the full 100 basis points over some extended lagged period.

In such cases, it is important to reflect this partial sensitivity in all interest rate risk analyses. For example, assume that a regression study for the MMDA rate of a particular bank reveals that the best fit portfolio is 45%

90-day CDs and 15% federal funds—and that is all. What is peculiar about
this result is that the coefficients only add up to 60%, not the 100% found
in the prime rate analysis. What happened to the remaining 40%? It simply
does not exist! That is, the MMDA rate in many regions of the country
never reflects all of any particular shift in market rates.

The sensitivity assumption we recommend for such a hypothetical situation would be as follows:

15%   Federal funds

45%   90-day moving average of 90-day CD rate (a 90-day
      tractor)

40%   "Long-term" tractor

This "long-term" tractor is a critical concept in ALM. There are numerous balance sheet categories that depend, to one degree or another, on it.
These include the savings account, credit card, demand deposits, fixed-rate
mortgages, and equity, to name a few.

In a sense, 40% of the MMDA balances behave as rate-insensitive balances. They show no sensitivity to the level of market rates. We believe
that a specific "generic" assumption should be assigned to such balances,
despite their apparent rate insensitivity. This will be essential if transfer
pricing is to be attempted. (For more information, refer to Chapter 14 on
Transfer Pricing.)

At this point, this chapter will embark upon a discussion of pragmatic,
as opposed to theoretical, asset and liability management.

9.3   THE NEED FOR A "GENERIC" LONG-TERM TRACTOR IN ALM

As mentioned, numerous important bank products show some degree of
"rate insensitivity." Some, such as demand deposits and equity, have no
interest rate directly associated with their balances. Some, such as credit
card receivables and savings accounts, have what may be termed a "quasi-
fixed rate" behavior. That is, they show no rate sensitivity to shifts in
market rates unless, perhaps, rates move by unusually large magnitudes.
Some, such as MMDA in some regional markets, show that on average,
they only reflect a portion of any market rate move. The portion that does
not respond would also be considered rate "insensitive."

How should rate insensitive balances be treated for interest rate risk
measurement purposes? We believe that a default "generic" maturity as-

sumption should be assigned. This is because not to do so would subvert any attempt at formal product or departmental profitability measurement, or would lead to inconsistencies among interest rate risk analyses.

Perhaps this position will be more palatable if presented in a different way: How should "rate-insensitive" balances be treated for IRE and duration purposes if no maturity assumption is assigned? Without any such assumption, there would be large "holes" in any bank's IRE analysis. No IRE for net equity would be possible. We have thought about this question for many years and have yet to come up with a satisfactory alternative to this approach. Some suggest simply assigning a fixed interest rate as a kind of perpetuity or consol bond concept as a possible alternative. Using an arbitrary perpetual rate such as 10% would inevitably lead to destructive pricing or marketing decisions.

In our opinion, relying on the generic long-term tractor yields very satisfactory and usable results. Whatever generic maturity is used, it should have the following characteristics:

- It should reflect the volatility behavior of the long-term portion of the yield curve.

- It should pick up most of the positive slope in the "standard" yield curve.

- It should not "lock in" any particular rate level for excessively long periods of time.

For example, if one arbitrarily selected a 30-year effective "tractor" maturity for any insensitive balances, and the level of the yield curve were to change abruptly by 500 basis points, it would be many, many years before this shift in the general level of interest rates would be reflected in a 30-year tractor (which is a 30-year moving average of 30-year rates). Indeed, less than 100 basis points of the 500 basis point rate shift would be reflected in the tractor rate after five years! This would be almost as bad as declaring 10% as the permanent long-term transfer rate. It would work some of the time, but there would be many extended periods where all decision-making would be severely distorted.

If such an excessively long-term rate is bad because it is not responsive enough when treated as a tractor, what about using a shorter-term point on the yield curve? This is exactly the logic many banks have settled upon. Indeed, many banks have settled upon the three- to five-year points on the yield curve simply because those points capture most of the positive slope in a "standard" yield curve, yet they do not "lock in" current rates for very extended periods of time. In a real sense, these are satisfactory compromises that meet the needs of most banks. (Again, this approach is symbolic of the 80/20 Rule.)

How much of a distortion could such an arbitrary assumption cause to overall interest rate risk assessments? We think the answer is surprisingly little. First, many "insensitive" balances appear on both sides of the balance sheet, so they tend to cancel one another out from a total bank perspective. Second, most bankers severely underestimate rate volatility in their interest rate scenarios anyway. Selecting a shorter term sensitivity for insensitive balances will tend to counter this tendency. Finally, the results work! Using such assumptions in real life, we have found that fairly reasonable IREs for bank equity are generated. By this, we mean that IREs calculated with three- to five-year tractor assumptions for all insensitive balances are quite consistent with empirical IREs found from regression analyses of bank stock prices against interest rate changes.

For the more skeptical reader, we offer the following query. Suppose there were a bank that consisted of nothing but demand deposits and equity on the liability side of the balance sheet. If the ALCO were forced to invest all of these "insensitive" funding sources in a single maturity "tractor" of investments, what maturity do you think an ALCO might favor: a 30-year tractor, a 10-year tractor, or a four-year tractor? We suspect that most bankers would opt for the shorter, four-year tractor. Picking the 30-year or 10-year investments could "lock in" a specific asset yield structure that is too insensitive to large interest rate moves. Some responsiveness in asset yield would be desirable from two perspectives: It would capture most of the yield curve slope so the yield improvement is not great going beyond the four- or five-year range; but it would not "lock in" portfolio yields for too long. If rates were unexpectedly to rise, a substantial portion of the rate rise would be reflected in the bank's spreads during the first year or two.

We are not claiming that the rationale presented in this section is airtight. We only present what we have perceived in our collective experience. These arguments will become even more important when internal profitability concepts are presented in Chapters 13 and 14. Our recommendation is that a three-, four-, or five-year tractor should be adopted as a default assumption for all insensitive balances in the bank. We are aware of some banks that have opted for 30-month or even two-year tractors. For the remainder of this book, we will assume that the bank has opted for the three-year assumption. Therefore, for the MMDA sensitivity assumption presented in Section 9.2, assume that the bank adopted a three-year tractor for insensitive balances. The following sensitivity profile would then apply:

15%   federal funds;

45%   90-day moving average of 90-day CD rate (a 90-day tractor); and

40%   three-year tractor.

This would imply the gap distribution shown in Table 9.3.

Table 9.3
Hypothetical Gap Profile for MMDA Balances

	O/N to 3 Months	>3 to 6 Months	>6 to 12 Months	>1 to 2 Years	>2 to 5 Years	>5 Years or N/S	Total
MMDA Sensitivity Components:							
Overnight	150	-	-	-	-	-	150
90-day	450	-	-	-	-	-	450
3-year	33	33	67	133	133	-	400
Total MMDA	633	33	67	133	133	-	1,000

In this profile, the first bucket consists of $150 of the fed funds equivalent portion, $450 of the 90-day tractor portion, and $33.33 of the three-year tractor. The $400 in the three-year tractor must be spread evenly over the buckets equal to or less than three years. This means that $33.33 will be placed in each quarterly period contained in each bucket under three years. The alternative to this approach for gap analyses would be to place the insensitive balances in the "not stated" bucket. We believe that this gives a deceptive appearance to the gap analysis.

For simulation modeling, the simplest approach would be to establish an exogenous variable for the MMDA rate and have its rate change by 15% of the change in the federal funds rate plus 45% of the change in the 90-day tractor rate. The insensitive portion of the balances need not be considered at all over short (less than 18-month) forecast horizons.

For IRE analyses, one would calculate the IRE of each of the sensitivity segments and accumulate them according to the percentage weightings given above. This is summarized for a 6% flat yield curve in Table 9.4.

Notice that the weighted average IRE of 0.567% is virtually entirely determined by the long-term tractor assumption. Almost no IRE is contributed by the short-term components of the sensitivity assumption, as evi-

Table 9.4
Example IRE Calculation for MMDA Balances
Based on Hypothetical Regression Results

Sensitivity Component	Weighting	Average Duration	Average IRE	Weighting x IRE
Federal Funds	15%	0.0028	0.0026%	0.0004%
90-day Tractor	45%	0.1250	0.1180%	0.0005%
3-year Tractor	40%	1.5000	1.4150%	0.5660%
Total MMDA	100%			0.5670%

Note: The total MMDA IRE is the sum of the last column of values, which is the weighting multiplied by the average IRE of each sensitivity component.

dent in the far right-hand column of Table 9.4 where 99+% of the final IRE is derived from the three-year tractor line.

9.4   DEMAND DEPOSITS

This has historically been one of the most controversial topics in asset and liability management. Arguments such as the following have been voiced in ALCO meetings:

■ "Demand deposits have no interest rate, so all balances should be treated as long-term, rate insensitive."

■ "All demand deposits may be withdrawn at any time, so all balances should be considered overnight, rate sensitive."

■ "Corporate demand deposits are subject to the short-term earnings credit rate, so all corporate DDA balances are short-term, rate sensitive. But all personal demand balances should be considered long-term, rate insensitive."

As should be evident, virtually every possible attitude has been expressed, from all balances being treated as totally rate insensitive, to all balances being treated as being completely sensitive on an overnight basis. Is there any way to approach this difficult issue?

The most common approach to dealing with demand deposits comes from a direct examination of the pattern of monthly balances. Figure 9.3 shows the monthly balances for an actual bank over a three-year period. Although not readily apparent, there are strong annual seasonality patterns present. These patterns become apparent if the data are presented in a different manner. Figure 9.4 shows the balances by month for the three years displayed as layers on one 12-month x-axis.

Figure 9.3
Demand Deposit Balances

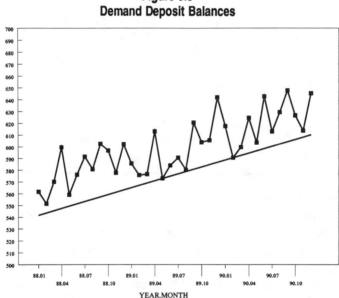

Notice that there are strong seasonal patterns in the balances. These are quite predictable and do impart some shorter-term characteristic to the product. Indeed, the simplest approach is to draw a line connecting the seasonal bottoms for each year (the straight line in Figure 9.3). The portion of balances below the line are considered "core" balances and are viewed as being rate-insensitive. The balances above the line are called "volatile" and are considered short-term, rate sensitive in nature. Hopefully, there will be some growth displayed by the core balances, which will represent the long-term growth trend of the portfolio.

Our recommendation is that the volatile balances be assigned a short term (30- or 90-day) sensitivity, and that the core balances be assigned the generic long-term tractor assumption as discussed in the previous section.

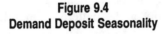

Figure 9.4
Demand Deposit Seasonality

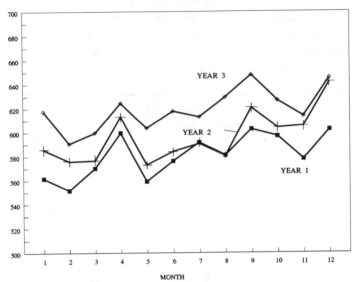

For simulation modeling, what is important is to reflect the monthly seasonality patterns and the long-term growth trends. The seasonality factors may be estimated directly from data such as shown in Figure 9.4. Some banks go to great lengths to generate precise forecasts of DDA and float balances for liquidity planning purposes, even to the extent of forecasting daily balances for forecast horizons of up to six months or more. Of course, if such models are available, they should be incorporated into the simulations.

For gap analyses, the core balances should be accorded the long-term tractor assumption. The residual between the period-end actual balance and the core balance should be deemed "volatile" and assigned to a 30-day or 90-day tractor.

For IRE purposes, calculations similar to those displayed in Table 9.4 are appropriate using the two components assigned to volatile and core balances.

9.5   CASH AND DUE FROM BANK BALANCES

For retail-oriented regional banks, this entry will be of considerable importance. The balances are composed of vault cash, required reserve account balances, and float. It is interesting how often this item is either virtually ignored or totally misallocated for risk-management purposes. So often, these balances are treated as short-term and liquid in nature. We disagree. These balances are required for the continuing operations of any bank, so the majority of the balances will be long-term and illiquid in the sense that they cannot be run off.

Cash and due from bank balances should be treated identically to demand deposit balances, as presented in Section 9.4. Again, balances may be divided between "core" and "volatile" in the same graphical manner shown above. As with demand deposits, the majority of the balances will normally be assigned to the "core" category and should be imputed with the long-term tractor assumption. This approach is also effective in dealing with credit card receivables.

9.6 MORTGAGE LOANS

Mortgage loan prepayments are the clearest example of option-type risk in a bank balance sheet. It is important that this risk be estimated and incorporated into any interest rate risk analysis conducted for the total bank. As will be shown, prepayment risk can drastically alter the financial performance of banks or thrifts in ways quite different from the more straightforward mismatch or spread risks discussed thus far.

There have been several conventions used to depict prepayment rates for mortgage loans. The most popular approach used for pricing mortgage-backed securities is the Public Securities Association (PSA) model. This model assumes that prepayment rates start at 0.2% (annualized) in a new portfolio's first month, then increases another 0.2% each month until the rate reaches an annualized 6% rate after 30 months. The prepayment rate then stays at 6% for the remaining life of the portfolio. (An annualized 6% prepayment rate is equivalent to 0.5% of the remaining loans prepaying in each month.)

We will adopt the constant prepayment rate approach for its conceptual simplicity. By this approach, the prepayment rate is assumed to be constant for the life of a mortgage loan portfolio. This is adequate for bank ALM purposes where the mortgage portfolio is well seasoned and consists of a wide range of origination dates and coupon rates. (This assumption is quite inappropriate for mortgage-backed securities which usually consist of loans generated over a short period of time with quite uniform coupons.)

Prepayment rates can vary widely, depending upon the direction and magnitude of interest rate shifts. The Office of Thrift Supervision (OTS) has sponsored the development of extensive analytical models to analyze the interest rate risk of thrift institutions. Table 9.5 shows the prepayment assumptions commonly used by the OTS for various shifts in the mortgage coupon rate. The "Coupon Differential" column represents the difference between the current mortgage rate available in the marketplace and the mortgage coupon on the loan being considered. If the current rate is 10% and the loan bears a coupon or note rate of 9%, then the coupon differential would be +1.0%.

Table 9.5
OTS Mortgage Prepayment Assumptions

Coupon Differential	PSA Model	Annual Equivalent Rate
+2.00%	117%	7.0%
+1.50%	117%	7.0%
+1.00%	117%	7.0%
+0.50%	133%	8.0%
0.00%	150%	9.0%
−0.50%	167%	10.0%
−1.00%	200%	12.0%
−1.50%	267%	16.0%
−2.00%	383%	23.0%
−2.50%	567%	34.0%
−3.00%	750%	45.0%
−3.50%	833%	50.0%
−4.00%	883%	53.0%
−4.50%	917%	55.0%
−5.00%	933%	56.0%

Notice that as the current mortgage rate in the marketplace declines, creating very large negative coupon differentials, prepayment rates sky-rocket to over 50% per annum. This can become a very serious issue for any financial institution that retains any significant balance sheet percentage in mortgage loans.

Before considering how to incorporate prepayment risk into ALM analyses, it is helpful to consider why prepayments occur. Mortgage prepayments may occur for a variety of reasons. For convenience, we will classify the reasons into two main categories: demographic and economic. They are listed in Table 9.6.

Table 9.6
Some Reasons for Mortgage Prepayments

Demographic Prepayments:

The house is sold because:

Occupants purchase a new home (trading up).

Occupants move to a new locale.

Occupants get divorced, settlement requires sale.

Owner dies, estate is liquidated, or mortgage insurance pays off.

The house is destroyed due to fire or other disaster and insurance pays off mortgage.

Economic Prepayments:

Interest rates decline enough to justify refinancing.

Notice that interest rate shifts only affect the rate of economic prepayments. They have little or no effect on demographic prepayments. Over many decades, the rate of demographic prepayments have hovered around 6% per annum. This is the reason for the 6% prepayment assumption dominating the PSA and other standard models. Therefore, a 6% base level of prepayments should always be assumed for any bank portfolio of mortgage loans. (From Table 9.5, the OTS is assuming that the base prepayment rate is currently about 7%.)

To illustrate the effect of prepayments of mortgage loans on the risk profile of a bank or thrift, consider another hypothetical case study situation. In this example, a thrift has the balance sheet shown in Table 9.7.

Table 9.7
Case Study Situation for
Analysis of Mortgage Prepayments

Balance Sheet on January 1:

   Assets:

      $100 Million 30-year, 10.0% Mortgage Loans

   Liabilities and Equity:

      $ 60 Million Five-year, 8.5% Long-Term Debt

      $ 30 Million 90-day, 7.0% CDs

      $ 10 Million Equity

Assumptions:

- All balance sheet rates and coupons are at current market.

- All book values equal market values at January 1.

- Any cash received from loan prepayments is reinvested in 90-day CDs.

- All market rates will shift once, on January 2, by the same amount.

To simplify the analysis, also assume that the mortgages will behave like a fully seasoned portfolio. Table 9.8 summarizes the prepayment rates and their effects on the weighted average life of the loans for three rate scenarios.

Table 9.8
Effects of Rate Shifts on Prepayment Rates
and Weighted Average Lives of Mortgages

Rate Shift	Seasoned Annual Equivalent Rate	Weighted Average Life
+3.00%	6.0%	11.6 Years
0.00%	9.0%	9.1 Years
−3.00%	45.0%	2.2 Years

We illustrate shifts of 300 basis points up and down because prepayment effects are much more prominent with larger interest rate shifts. Based on the discussions in Chapter 5, we must now at least examine the effects of these types of rate shifts on expected earnings and the market value of portfolio equity. These are summarized in Table 9.9.

Table 9.9
Effects of Prepayments on Case Study Bank
Earnings and Market Value of Equity

Rate Shift	Net Interest Income					Market Value of Equity
	Quarter 1	Quarter 2	Quarter 3	Quarter 4	Year	
+3.00%	700	475	475	475	2,125	7,652
None	694	677	659	642	2,672	10,000
−3.00%	644	711	570	444	2,368	2,066

Note: The Market Value of Equity is measured as of January 2.

From these results, the risks of prepayments emerge in concrete form. The major conclusion to be drawn from this case study is that prepayments create the potential for the bank or thrift to lose with any type of large rate shift, either up or down, in both critical target account dimensions: earnings and equity. That is, earnings for the year are lower in both the up 300 basis point and down 300 bp scenarios. Likewise, the market value of equity declines in both rate shift environments. Why is this?

In a rapidly rising rate situation, the fall in equity value and earnings are attributable to the mismatch of the long-term fixed rate assets being funded by some short-term CDs. Another factor that lowers returns is that as rates rise, prepayment rates will decline. This means that some incremental funding, at much higher rates, will be needed.

When rates fall significantly, borrowers will find that it is in their interest to refinance their existing fixed rate mortgages. Experiences from 1986 and 1992 prove that prepayment rates can increase to the range of 50% per annum. Whether new loans are originated to replace the older, higher yielding loans or the cash inflow due to prepayments is used to pay down borrowings or reinvested in eligible securities, overall net interest margins will decline, as will the market value of equity.

Embedded option features of bank products usually behave in a manner that adversely affects the bank's performance. They also increase the volatility of the bank's cash flows whenever large shifts in interest rates occur. The quarterly net interest income figures from Table 9.9 attest to this point. Therefore, embedded options cause expected return levels to decrease and risk levels to increase for large rate movements in either direction: up or down.

This "lose, lose" conclusion does NOT lead us to conclude that mortgages should never be held on a bank's balance sheet. However, as we have advocated throughout this book, we do believe that the ALCO and board of directors should understand the general risk and return implications of holding any significant percentage of the balance sheet in fixed-rate mortgages. Ideally, ALM analysts can use option pricing models to determine if the implicit price being paid for the option features are adequate to compensate the bank for the additional risk it is undertaking. While this particular topic goes well beyond the scope of this book, we affirm once again that modeling, analyzing, and communicating the risk and return implications of mortgage prepayments on the bank's overall interest rate risk profile is essential.

9.7 INCORPORATING PREPAYMENT RISK INTO ALM ANALYSES

This is the one product type that banks should consider treating in somewhat greater analytical detail by stratifying existing balances into coupon ranges of 100 or 200 basis points. Each coupon range can then be modeled separately as to prepayment expectation using tables such as Table 9.5. The prepayment rate assumption should reflect the coupon differential between the average coupon rate in the range being analyzed and the current or forecasted mortgage rate. Alternatively, rather than using general national prepayment tables, the data needed to generate such a table can be obtained from a historical analysis of the bank's own portfolio.

For simulation models, this approach would require having a separate account for each coupon range of mortgages. If mortgages are a significant balance sheet item (greater than about 10% of total assets), we recommend that this effort be made. As is evident from Table 9.5, if the difference between the coupon range and current mortgage rates becomes large (greater than 100 basis points), then prepayment rates increase dramatically. Fortunately, computer simulation software has advanced to the point where prepayment assumptions can simply be input for each mortgage coupon range and the software system will adjust the cash flow patterns accordingly.

For both gap and duration analyses, a stratification-by-coupon approach is also recommended if mortgages are a significant balance sheet percentage. The duration or IRE for each coupon range will be a function of the weighted average coupon as well as the assumed prepayment rate. Once again, simulation software systems are available that will perform the duration calculations based on an assumed prepayment rate.

9.8   OTHER OPTION FEATURES OF BANK PRODUCTS

Banking products are replete with embedded option features, most of which increase the interest rate risk of the bank. One of the most important recent developments in finance is the derivation of option pricing models and the development of markets for a variety of derivative securities that may be used to hedge or alter the features of more conventional transactions. For an introduction to some simple option pricing theory, refer to Appendix 9A.

The following paragraphs present only a few representative examples of option-like features embedded in some common bank products. Some of these include commercial loan prepayments, loan caps and collars, multiple index lending facilities, adjustable rate mortgages, passbook or add-on CDs, and savings account rate.

Commercial loan prepayments. Whenever interest rates decline significantly, many corporate borrowers will request a reset of the interest rate on their fixed-rate borrowings. How many times has this been accommodated to "preserve a good relationship?" Our only point is that a prepayment option has significant value that increases as interest rates decline. Prepayment penalties should be stipulated in all fixed-rate facilities. They should reflect the "economic" or "mark-to-market" value of the prepayment and should be charged by the bank in such circumstances. We advise that lending units should be charged a prepayment premium as a portion of their cost of funding in any transfer funding system. This will be covered in detail in Chapter 14 on "Transfer Pricing."

Loan caps and collars. The development of the markets in "derivative" products has facilitated tremendous advances in various forms of financial engineering. This includes the use of "caps" and "collars" as adjuncts to conventional floating rate facilities. Without such features, floating rate loan rates may rise without limit. Including a cap feature places an upper limit on the interest rate that may be charged. The lower the upper limit, the more expensive the upfront cost of the cap feature will be. As a mechanism to defray the expense of caps, a collar concept has evolved. With a collar, there is both an upper and a lower limit to the range of potential interest rates the borrower will pay. The authors view the development of such facilities as quite beneficial to the banking industry in that they force bankers and corporate borrowers alike to deal with the true economic value of such features. Most banks, if they sell any such products to their customers, exactly offset the derivative product's features by purchasing an identical product from a securities firm or another large bank. In this way, the borrower obtains protection from rising interest rates, while the bank preserves its desired floating-rate loans.

Multiple index lending facilities. Oftentimes, corporate borrowers are offered facilities where drawdowns are for limited periods (up to six months) with yields that are computed based upon two, three, or four pricing indices. For example, a borrower may select a 45-day drawdown period with pricing based upon the lower of CDs+1.5%, LIBOR+1.7%, or current prime fixed. All this accomplishes is to offer the borrower the opportunity to benefit from short-term fluctuations in the spread relationships between whichever pricing indices are specified. (The indices could also be based upon commercial paper or federal funds or other market rates.) Regardless of the options allowed, this should not change the transfer pricing or cost of funds methodologies under any circumstances. This will also be covered in Chapter 14 on "Transfer Pricing." In our experience, it is not worthwhile dealing with these options in any detailed manner. Simply find the historical average spread between the entire portfolio of these types of loans and whatever market index rate is convenient for simulation modeling purposes, such as 90-day CDs, Eurodollars, or federal funds rates. (From the loan pricing perspective, another corollary of the 80/20 rule is: If your bank does not understand the value of the product features it is offering, maybe the bank should think twice about offering them in the first place.)

Adjustable rate mortgages. ARMs normally have annual and lifetime caps that limit how much the interest rate may change over a single year or over its entire life. This should not be overlooked in running simulations or IRE calculations over wide interest rate movements. Recent advances in "option-adjusted spread" (OAS) technology have facilitated such analyses. The OAS is the incremental increase in short-term discount rates needed to make the present value of Monte Carlo simulated mortgage cash flows equal to its market price. In theory then, it represents a prepayment risk premium over Treasury rates that is analogous to the credit risk premium (or "credit spread") over Treasuries that are commonplace for corporate bonds. (Refer to Chapters 10 and 11 for a discussion of credit risk and liquidity risk premia.)

"Passbook" or "add-on" CDs. These accounts allow depositors to add to their CD balance at the original interest rate at some future date. If interest rates fall, they will deposit new dollars into the old CD account. If rates rise, customers simply take out a new CD at the higher rate. This product simply proves that bankers can find ways to give away options on the liability side of the balance sheet as well as the asset side. If the branch system is offering this product, the ALM staff should attempt to determine the value of the options and assess the value against whatever earnings credit is given to the funds raised. (The OAS approach works well here.)

Savings account rate. This is one of the few option features that works to the benefit of the bank. The savings account rate was capped for years at 5% (5.25% for thrifts) by Regulation Q. Since it was deregulated, it has tended to hold steady at about 5% in most regional markets. However, with the significant decline in interest rates in late 1991, many regional banks have started lowering the savings account rate well below 5%. It remains to be seen whether this is a truly "capped" rate if and when interest rates rise well above 5% again. If so, then this will be one example of an option feature with substantial value to the banking industry. Simulation models can easily accommodate such a capped rate feature over any interest rate scenario. For IRE purposes, a long-term tractor equivalent IRE may be used if the rate is "capped" at 5%, or a short-term equivalent IRE may be used if the rate is floating below the cap.

9.9   SUMMARY

This chapter completes our overview of interest rate risk management. It presented a broad spectrum of product features that all result in interest rate risk to the bank. These include repricing sensitivity (or maturity), balance fluctuation risk, spread risk, and embedded options risks. Virtually all bank loan and deposit products contain one or more of these risk-generating characteristics. For example, credit card receivables contain balance fluctuation, spread, and options risks.

Practical approaches to incorporating these behavioral features into all ALM analyses were presented. These features must also be reflected in any transfer pricing system any bank may choose to adopt. This topic will be presented in Chapter 14.

APPENDIX 9A: A PRIMER ON OPTION PRICING

There are a wide variety of options pricing models in use today. For an in-depth treatment of option pricing theory, the reader is referred to *Options, Futures, and Other Derivative Securities* by Hull and *Options Markets* by Cox and Rubenstein.

The key to option pricing is to examine whether there exists an equivalent portfolio of the underlying security and a risk-free security that mimics the future market value characteristics of the option. If there is such a hypothetical portfolio, then that equivalent portfolio must have the same current market value or price as the original option being analyzed. Otherwise, there would be an arbitrage opportunity.

To illustrate the concept, we will hypothesize a simplified world in which for each time period, rates must either go up an increment or down an increment. This is diagrammed in Figure 9A.1. We will create an option to purchase a four-year 7% annual coupon bond in 12 months. The bond trades at par, or $1,000, today. In three months, the bond's yield will either be 9% with a probability of 60%, or 6% with a 40% probability. (It is not necessary that the amount of the rate increase equal the magnitude of the rate fall or that the probabilities be equal.) The current 12-month risk-free interest rate is assumed to be 7%.

Figure 9A.1
Diagram of Assumed Interest Rate Movements

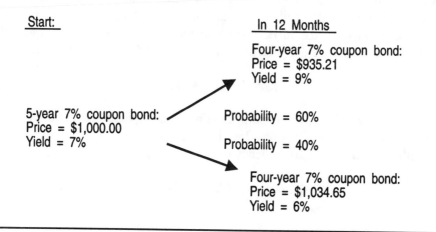

Start:

In 12 Months

5-year 7% coupon bond:
Price = $1,000.00
Yield = 7%

Four-year 7% coupon bond:
Price = $935.21
Yield = 9%

Probability = 60%

Probability = 40%

Four-year 7% coupon bond:
Price = $1,034.65
Yield = 6%

Clearly, these are not very realistic assumptions. Nevertheless, if the concept works, then the time periods may be decreased, and the rate shifts likewise decreased to very small intervals. The procedure would then be conducted over these smaller intervals to cover realistic timeframes and interest rate movements. The large intervals and rate movements used in this presentation are for illustrative purposes only. (For more detail, see the paper Ho, Thomas S.Y. and Lee, Sang-Bin, "Term Structure Movements and Pricing Interest Rate Contingent Claims," *Journal of Finance* 41: 1011-1028, 1986.)

We assume that the option in question stipulates that in 12 months, one four-year, 7% coupon bond may be purchased for $1,000. The objective is to determine the value of the option today, assuming that there is some equivalent portfolio of the bond and a risk-free, one-year investment.

We now forge ahead with the assumption that the equivalent portfolio exists. If it does, then we may notate the equivalent portfolio as consisting of x units of the bond and y dollars of the risk-free investment at time zero. The equivalency condition may be formed into the following equation, which applies to the starting time:

$$MV_{option} = x \times MV_{bond} + y \qquad [1]$$

where x is the number of bonds and y is the dollar amount of risk-free investment. There is insufficient information from this first equation to determine the value of the option. However, there is sufficient information to determine the value of the option and the equivalent portfolio at the end of one year.

At that time, either the option is worthless if rates have risen and the value of the bond is less than the exercise price of $1,000, or the option is worth $34.65 if rates fall to 6% and the market value of the bond is $1,034.65. That is, the market value of the option must be the larger of zero or the difference between the bond's value and the exercise price:

$$MV_{option} = MAX [0 , MV_{bond} - X] \qquad [2]$$

where X is the option exercise price. From this equation, it is possible to write out two new equations for the two possible outcomes. After 12 months, the following equivalency equation is expected:

$$MV_{option} = x \times (MV_{bond} + 70) + y \times 1.07 \qquad [3]$$

Notice that the value of the risk-free investment has now increased by 7%, the one-year risk-free rate of return. Also, notice that the bond has paid its $70 coupon, which must be included in the overall value of the portfolio. This equation may be used with either of the two possible outcomes. If rates fall and the bond value rises, then Equation 3 becomes as shown:

$$34.65 = x \times (1034.65 + 70) + y \times 1.07 \qquad [4]$$

However, if rates rise and the bond value declines, then Equation 3 is as follows:

$$0 = x \times (935.21 + 70) + y \times 1.07 \qquad [5]$$

Equations 4 and 5 for the 12-month outcomes are consistent. That is, they may be solved for x and y. This means that the original assumption that an equivalent portfolio could be constructed was true. This equivalency assumption was one of the major breakthroughs in all of corporate financial theory.

It is now a simple matter to solve Equations 4 and 5 for the values of x and y. From Equation 5, calculate the following:

$$y = \frac{-1005.21 \times x}{1.07} \qquad [6]$$

This expression for y may be substituted back into Equation 4, yielding the following:

$$34.65 = 1104.65 \times x + 1.07 \times \left[\frac{-1005.21 \times x}{1.07} \right]$$

$$34.65 = 1104.65 \times x - 1005.21 \times x$$

$$34.65 = 99.44 \times x$$

$$x = 0.34844 \qquad [7]$$

Hence, 0.34844 bonds valued at $1,000 each are a part of the equivalent portfolio. The amount of risk-free investment is determined by placing x = 0.34844 into Equation 6.

$$y = \frac{-1005.21 \times 0.34844}{1.07}$$

$$y = \quad -327.34 \qquad\qquad [8]$$

Now that both x and y are solved, these values may be substituted back into Equation 1 to determine the value of the option at the starting point.

$$MV_{option} = 0.34844 \times 1000 + (-327.34)$$

$$= \quad 348.44 - 327.34$$

$$= \quad 21.10 \qquad\qquad [9]$$

This completes the analysis. To generalize this procedure, one would use much shorter time intervals and smaller rate shifts and iterate through the steps starting from the final time period and working backwards to the starting point.

There are several remarkable and important conclusions that may be drawn.

1. The equivalent portfolio exists and can be managed as to mimic the price behavior of the option. Therefore, the option contract is actually redundant. It only exists because it is operationally simpler to execute than the equivalent portfolio.

2. The value of the option is not dependent on the relative probabilities of rates rising or falling. The value will be the same regardless of whether 90% of the market participants believe rates will rise, or 90% believe that rates will fall. It is the volatility of interest rates and not the direction of interest rates that determines the option's value.

3. The derivation of the option value does not depend on whether market participants care about risk or not. That is, even if everyone in the markets felt that high risk banks should earn the same returns as low risk banks (a situation referred to as risk-neutrality), they would still derive the same market value for the option.

CHAPTER 10

Credit Risk and Other Risk Factors

The previous chapters have discussed interest rate risk in great detail. Interest rate risk has long been the central focus of asset and liability management, but it is certainly not the only risk of concern to bankers. The 1980s in the United States were years when credit risk was the dominant risk which separated the best performing banks from the rest of the pack. In Japan, the principal causes for concern were credit risk and the risk of fluctuations in the large equity portfolios held by banks. In many European countries, Indonesia, and the Philippines, foreign exchange risk was a very important element of risk management for bankers.

This chapter offers a commonsense framework (that is nonetheless consistent with financial theory) for looking at how any financial risk impacts a company, whether the company is a financial institution or any other type of corporate business entity. This risk could be credit risk, foreign exchange risk, interest rate risk, or stock market risk. After setting this theoretical framework, we can examine the impact of different levels of risk on the bank's cost of funds and capital structure.

With this framework in mind, we can use the techniques of previous chapters to discuss credit risk, foreign exchange risk, and stock market risk. The next several sections will focus on the ramifications of loan portfolio credit risk on the overall funding costs of the bank.

10.1 THE EFFECTS OF ASSET QUALITY ON BANK BORROWING SPREADS

One of the hardest things for bank management to deal with in a practical way is the very real fact that their bank is not as good a credit as the U.S. Treasury. Intuitively, no one should have trouble accepting that basic fact, but dealing with it and its implications escapes many bankers. One of the reasons the concept of the bank's own risk level is so hard to deal with is the correct perception that, for most banks, the probability of default is very, very small. Another complication is the use of FDIC insurance to protect large depositors in "too big to fail" banks.

This chapter will present a framework that shows how the overall asset risk profile from any type of risk affects the cost of funding the bank. It will then discuss the implications of this framework for the management of credit risk, stock market risk, and foreign exchange risk within a bank setting.

The key question that is being addressed here is: How does asset risk affect the bank's funding spread over that of the Treasury? Specifically, if the bank were using only one zero coupon bond (or large certificate of deposit) of a specific maturity (and, hence, duration) as its sole source of debt funding, how much higher would the interest rate on that debt be over the identical maturity zero coupon Treasury security? Appendices 10A, 10B, and 10C present the theoretical frameworks for this discussion. They demonstrate that options theory can be used to evaluate a bank's aggregate debt and equity characteristics for any assumed balance sheet situation.

Some of the major conclusions from that framework are summarized below. All results will pertain to the risk-adjusted pricing of bank debt, expressed as the spread over Treasuries concept. They include the following:

- The pricing of the bond is always based on a spread over and above the riskless rate (Treasury rate) for the same maturity.

- The spread over the riskless rate of interest increases as the volatility of assets increases.

- The spread increases as the leverage of the firm increases.

- The spread is a function of the maturity of the loan.

These conclusions are demonstrated in graphical form in the next three figures. Figure 10.1 shows the direct link between an increase in volatility

Figure 10.1
Asset Volatility Effect

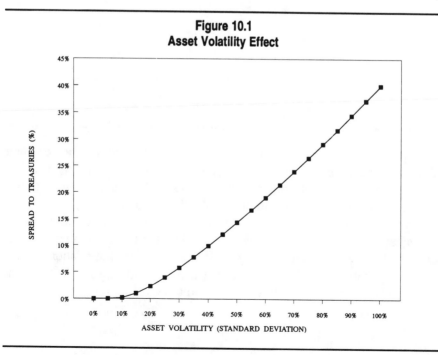

ASSET VOLATILITY (STANDARD DEVIATION)

of assets and the cost of the bank's certificates of deposit. Assuming that
the bank's leverage is 10% at the maturity of the certificate of deposit and
that the risk-free rate is now 7%, Figure 10.1 shows the steady increase in
borrowing costs that results as the bank takes more risk.

Figure 10.2 shows the dramatic increase in funding costs that results
once the bank increases its leverage beyond approximately 75% of total
assets, or lowers its equity ratio below about 0.25. (This figure assumes a
0.15 volatility for assets and the same 7% risk-free Treasury rate.)

Figure 10.2
Leverage Effect

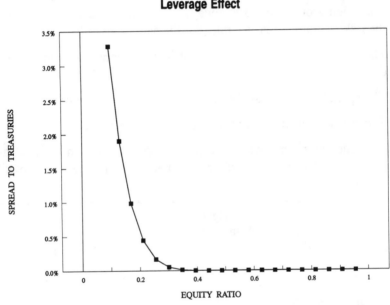

Capital adequacy is not just a regulatory concept, as this example
shows. It has a very precise impact on the cost of borrowing money. Just
like in more traditional options analysis, the bank's market funding costs
can be used to calculate the "implied volatility of assets."

Another phenomenon that is easy to illustrate using this framework is
the generally upward sloping "spread over Treasuries" premium as the maturity of borrowings increases. Figure 10.3 summarizes the relationship between the maturity of the asset and the bank's funding spread. As in the
last figure, the asset volatility was assumed to be 0.15.

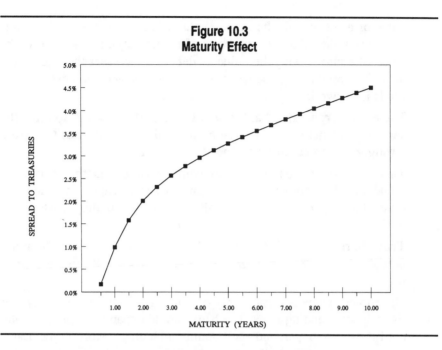

Figure 10.3
Maturity Effect

10.2   CREDIT RISK AND SHAREHOLDER VALUE

In previous chapters, we have repeatedly emphasized that there is no free lunch when it comes to taking interest rate risk. At best, interest rate risk taken by bank management can be offset by shareholders with transactions for the shareholders' own account. At worst, taking so much interest rate risk that the bank is pushed out of the safety zone reduces shareholder value by increasing the probability that shareholders will suffer the dead-weight losses associated with the cost of bankruptcy.

A similar set of principals is true for credit risk. In the theoretical discussion above, the "borrower" could be a corporate client of the bank or the bank itself. From Section 10.1, the following conclusions can be drawn:

1. **Taking more credit risk increases the volatility of the bank's assets and increases the cost of debt and equity capital to the bank.**

   If the volatility of assets increases, two things happen. The first impact of higher risk is, ironically, a rise in the value of equity. This comes about because the greater "upside" potential on the asset portfolio makes a call option on the value of assets worth more money—and equity is a call option on the value of assets. Since the market value of assets equals the market value of debt plus the market value of equity (when there are no costs of bankruptcy), an increase in the value of equity lowers the value of debt and increases the rate on the debt. The relationship between asset volatility and the cost of bank funds is shown in Figure 10.1.

2. **For a high credit risk bank and a low credit risk bank to have the same cost of debt funding, the high credit risk bank has to have a stronger equity capital position (lower leverage).**

This proposition combines both commonsense and the theoretical foundation laid above. Up to a point, a strong capital position can offset the impact of higher credit risk on the funding cost of the bank.

3. **True shareholder value is created by lending only when the price paid by the borrower is greater than correct risk-adjusted pricing.**

Shareholder value is earned only by lending at rates above the proper risk-adjusted lending rates. The bank should expand its loan portfolio until it can no longer find such premium lending opportunities. Earning a "credit spread" above the bank's cost of funds can destroy shareholder value if the pricing is not sufficient for the level of risk involved. A simple guide on this issue would be to compare the spread to Treasuries on any loan to the spread to Treasuries on similar credit quality corporate bonds. (This is similar to the discussion in Chapter 4, Section 4.1.)

4. **The bank creates more shareholder value than competitors by being better than competitors at four activities:**

- **Finding loan opportunities with pricing better than risk-adjusted loan rates;**
- **Evaluating the risk of lending opportunities, therefore pricing more accurately;**
- **Evaluating the true current value of the borrower's assets, therefore pricing more accurately; and**
- **Adjusting pricing as risk changes.**

Creating shareholder value in lending means knowing when to make loans and learning when to forgo loan business that is not priced correctly. An underpriced loan is a loan that destroys shareholder value.

5. **The bank has to maintain an optimal capital structure or else high risk levels will cause the bank shareholders to lose value as the probability of incurring bankruptcy costs from excess credit risk increases.**

Like the case of interest rate risk, it is possible for the bank to take too much credit risk. If the bank goes beyond the credit risk safety zone, the shareholder value created by taking on more credit risk at rates above risk-adjusted loan rates can be offset by a higher probability of bankruptcy and bankruptcy costs. **The bank's best protection against going beyond the credit risk safety zone is more equity capital.** This fundamental truth is based on rock solid practical and theoretical foundations. Nonetheless, it flies in the face of the common observation that "high capital ratios have not prevented many banks from going under." Comments like that rest upon a fundamental fallacy: that book value capital ratios are proper capital ratios for risk measurement. When we say "optimal capital structure," we mean one measured by the relationship between the market value of equity and the market value of assets. The formula in Appendix 10A explains how equity can be negative on a mark-to-market basis when the market value of traded common stock is positive. The mark-to-market calculation assumes immediate liquidation. The publicly traded common stock with a price above zero recognizes the option on the firm's assets. There is still time for a rise in assets to "bail out" equity holders prior to the initiation of bankruptcy proceedings.

Going back to the discussion in Section 10.1, the simplest indicator that the bank's capital structure is out of line is the cost of debt to the bank. If the cost of the bank's debt is high relative to its peers, either its credit risk is too high or its capital position is too weak. The bank is outside the credit risk safety zone if there is no way of increasing capital to reduce credit risk. How can it be impossible to reach the safety zone? If the true market value of the bank's equity capital is already zero, no rational investor will contribute equity. Why not? Why invest prior to bankruptcy to own a part of the bank when the investor can wait until after bankruptcy to own the entire institution for much less cash!

6. **Diversification of credit risk can be a substitute for more capital.**

When a bank gets outside the credit risk safety zone, there is an alternative to more capital. That alternative is a simple one: lower credit risk. This can be achieved in two ways. The first method is through asset sales, which will be discussed in Chapter 12. The other alternative is to diversify the credit risk taken by the bank to lower the volatility of its assets. This reduces the cost of bank debt and reduces the need for capital, as shown in Section 10.1. How does diversification reduce volatility? This is discussed in the next section, "Diversification of Credit Risk."

10.3   DIVERSIFICATION OF CREDIT RISK

The principles laid out above are very straightforward. The bank should keep making risky loans as long as it receives a premium above the risk-adjusted lending rate. It offsets this additional volatility either by maintaining a stronger capital position or by finding new lending markets that offer "diversification" compared to the existing loans in the bank's portfolio. What does diversification really mean?

Before answering that question, we must be more precise about what we really mean by volatility. When we talk about volatility, we mean volatility in the sense that has become common when talking about options. In the options case, the focus is on the volatility (standard deviation, to be precise) in the rate of return (on a market value basis) on the underlying asset. What does this mean when we are thinking about a real estate construction loan that was at the prime rate plus 2% for a year before the bank put the loan on nonaccrual status?

In the case of the construction loan, its true return is not the nominal interest rate alone. As vacancy rates for commercial buildings rise and the builder's other buildings go unleased, the risk of the loan and the proper risk-adjusted pricing increase. If the bank does not (or cannot) increase the pricing on the loan or "price to lose" the business, the return on the loan declines and may turn negative. This process is normally unrecognized by most banks' accounting practices and, sadly, credit review practices. The loan may not be truly "marked-to-market" until it is written off. The proper volatility calculation is one that is based on the true economic rate of return on the loan, as if it were marked-to-market on a frequent basis.

With this in mind, we will examine the case of Bank A and Bank B. Bank A only makes loans to the Rainy Day Umbrella Factory. The bank has 100% of its loan portfolio in loans to Rainy Day and has properly calculated the volatility of loans to the firm at 0.15 (an annual volatility of 15 percent). Therefore, the volatility for the full portfolio is also 0.15. Bank B also makes loans to Rainy Day. Bank B understands loan pricing better than Bank A, however. Bank A will not consider loans to the Sunshine Sun Tan Company because loans to Sunshine have a volatility of 0.25 even though Sunshine will pay a loan rate in excess of the proper risk-adjusted pricing. Bank B notices, however, that loans to Rainy Day and loans to Sunshine have perfect negative correlation. Loans to Rainy Day go bad when Sunshine's business is good and vice versa. Negative correlation means a correlation of −1.

What is the overall volatility of the loan portfolio at Bank B? We refer the mathematically inclined readers to Appendix 10D. For those who are not interested in the details, all that really matters is that Bank B can reduce the risk of its loan portfolio to zero if it puts 62.5% of its loan portfolio in loans to Rainy Day and 37.5% of the portfolio in Sunshine. This is illustrated in Figure 10.4.

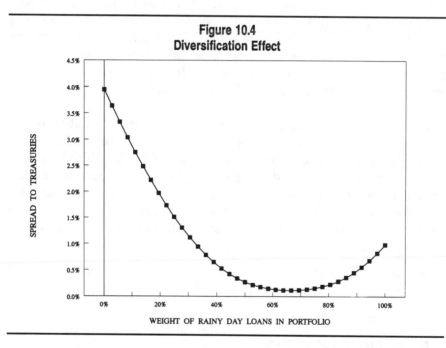

Figure 10.4
Diversification Effect

This loan mix reduces the aggregate risk of the loan portfolio to virtually nothing, but does that mean Bank B should be willing to lend to Rainy Day and Sunshine without charging either any risk premium (that is, any spread over Treasuries)? The short answer is of course not! Both loans would destroy shareholder value unless they were each priced in excess of the risk-adjusted loan rate. By careful structuring of its loan portfolio, however, Bank B can take more risk than Bank A on an individual loan and still reduce its aggregate loan risk in the process. This in turn lowers the cost of both debt and equity to Bank B.

10.4   CREDIT RISK PORTFOLIO MANAGEMENT

What does the example of Rainy Day and Sunshine mean for credit risk and loan portfolio management? There are a number of lessons. Perhaps the most fundamental aspect of credit risk management is deceptively simple: Even if you know exactly how big the risk is and price for it correctly, you still have risk! In the example of Rainy Day and Sunshine, it was fairly obvious that lending to both was a risk-reducing strategy. It is less obvious but even more important to note that it is better to lend to both companies (assuming both loans are above the risk-adjusted loan rate) even if the returns on the loans are not negatively correlated. By spreading the risk over more loan categories, the bank still can reduce aggregate risk. In the language of modern finance that is often applied to the stock market, the bank can diversify away all "nonsystematic" risk. Only systematic risk remains after such diversification.

Both aggregate risk of an individual loan and the correlation of the loan's return with other credits (and other risks) are important. In order to analyze these factors correctly, the bank's Chief Credit Officer needs to have a detailed credit understanding of the principal economic factors that drive loan portfolio performance and the correlations between those factors. While there could be a large number of factors on such a list, most bankers would want to analyze the following factors' impact on loan portfolio performance:

- The aggregate level of economic activity (on a national level, gross national product)

- Inflation

- The level of interest rates

- The vacancy rate for commercial real estate

- The market value of the most important types of collateral used in the region

These factors are consistent with the arbitrage pricing theory of Stephen Ross, which is perhaps the most directly applicable to loan portfolio management. (For more information, refer to Ross, Stephen A., "The Arbitrage Theory of Capital Asset Pricing," *Journal of Economic Theory* 13: 341-

360, December 1976.) The arbitrage pricing theory expresses the risky return on securities (normally thought of as equities) as a linear function of a number of economic variables and a random error term. The predecessor of arbitrage pricing theory, the capital asset pricing model, relied on one factor (the "return on the market") to explain differences in securities returns.

Like many techniques in equity portfolio management, risk of an individual loan or a loan category can be measured by the dependence of the loan's return on the factors above. If the principal factors above explain almost all of the loan loss experience of a particular class of loans, diversification can be very effective in reducing total risk. In the example of Rainy Day and Sunshine, the factor that determined 100% of the return on loans to Rainy Day and Sunshine was the weather. Even though the weather itself is unpredictable, risk in the loan portfolio in aggregate can be eliminated in this simple example.

In the real world, no set of economic factors can explain the performance of one loan or a class of loans so perfectly. The remaining risk in each category can only be managed (and, with luck, "diversified away") by holding a very large number of loan types in the portfolio. This basic tenet of commonsense lending is the counterpart of the capital asset pricing model, which suggests a rational investor will only hold the "market portfolio," a portfolio made up of every stock in the stock market, weighted in the same way as that stock's share of total market capitalization. There is only one risk that remains in such a portfolio—the risk of the market portfolio itself. All other risks have been diversified away. The power of this theory in the equity markets has spurred the rise of hundreds of billions of dollars invested via "indexing" or in index funds that try to duplicate the performance of the total market perfectly.

The lack of lending diversification—or the correlation of every class of asset with one or two major risks—helps explain the downfall of many savings and loan associations in the United States in the late 1980s. The United States Congress required a very high percentage of assets be invested in home mortgage loans and mortgage-related securities. For diversification, savings and loans concentrated on commercial real estate financing and, in some cases, real estate development through affiliated development companies. Almost all of the risk and return in these narrowly defined portfolios could be explained by three factors: the level of interest rates, the level of property prices, and commercial office vacancy rates. Diversification beyond this limited degree was sharply restricted by law. As a result, the volatility of savings and loan asset values was unnecessarily high. Risk that could have been fairly easily "diversified away" remained on the balance sheet. The price that was paid for this is well-known to every taxpayer in the United States.

Another lesson from the example of Rainy Day and Sunshine discussed earlier is the tight link between credit risk and what is more traditionally thought of as asset and liability management. Increases in credit risk increase the marginal cost of debt and equity and increase the need for capital to remain in the credit risk safety zone. No asset and liability manager can afford to ignore this important link. Just as important, no Chief Credit Officer can ignore the fact that his or her own actions play a very large (some would say dominant) role in determining the cost of funds for the bank.

10.5   MEASURING THE DIVERSIFICATION OF THE LOAN PORTFOLIO

The efficient measurement of credit risk requires a long-term perspective on the amount of credit risk inherent in any individual type of loan. A credit officer who has never experienced 25% commercial building vacancy rates will not have an easy time correctly estimating the credit risk of commercial real estate construction projects unless he or she has done a good job of analyzing the true return on the bank's construction loans over a long period of time.

There is an important difference in lending that makes it harder to "diversify away" risk. In the stock market, investors have both upside risk and downside risk. In lending, bankers face a large amount of downside risk and not very much upside potential. As explained in Section 10.1, the risk of a loan is like the risk of an option, not the risk of common stock. That makes it harder to offset the chance of a loss in both a statistical and a practical sense. It is also a key reason why a skillful Chief Credit Officer is much more valuable than he or she is popular with lending officers in the field.

In practice, the Chief Credit Officer has to rigorously enforce the maximum possible diversification that is consistent with the need to generate only those loans with a real return at or above the proper risk-adjusted loan rate. While the topic is too lengthy to be covered here in detail, the bank should have management limits on geographical concentration, industrial diversification, maturity, and acceptable types of collateral. These limits must be adjusted as perceived risk changes. The same is true for loan pricing and the amount of collateral required on a particular type of credit.

The economic factors affecting loan portfolio performance listed in Section 10.4 are just a small subset of a complete list of independent economic factors that affect loan performance. The primary responsibilities of the Chief Credit Officer can be reduced to five principal duties:

1. To ensure that the performance of the bank's loan portfolio depends on a balance of these independent risk variables, rather than a concentration on a few of them.

2. Within broad loan classes, to ensure that the portfolio is very highly diversified according to the four areas: geographical concentration, industrial diversification, maturity, and acceptable types of collateral.

3. To ensure that no loans are added to the portfolio unless they create shareholder value by virtue of pricing in excess of the risk-adjusted loan rate.

4. To ensure all legal and procedural aspects of lending are followed to the letter.

5. To ensure that the bank's lending officers are better than the competition in those areas that create shareholder value:

   ■ Finding loan opportunities with pricing better than risk-adjusted loan rates;

   ■ Evaluating the risk of lending opportunities, therefore pricing more accurately;

   ■ Evaluating the true current value of the borrower's assets, therefore pricing more accurately; and,

   ■ Adjusting pricing as risk changes.

The next to last role is the subject of Section 10.6, "Collateral and Credit Risk."

10.6 COLLATERAL AND CREDIT RISK

Loans that require collateral are the easiest to analyze in a framework like that covered in Section 10.1. Take the example of home mortgage loans. When housing prices become more volatile, banks must require more collateral (a lower loan to value ratio) in order to be able to offer the same lending rate to clients. This is because a higher degree of volatility in the underlying asset increases the probability of loss on the credit even if the bank seizes the collateral. While the single period nature of the approach in Section 10.1 cannot be applied very precisely to a complex security like a home mortgage, it provides an intuitive justification for changes in loan to value ratios.

Another example of the same phenomenon is the stock market crash of October 1987, which made it obvious to all market participants that market volatility was higher than expectations. In addition to margin calls needed for existing credits, financial institutions who were lending with equity securities as collateral should have either increased lending rates to reflect the higher level of market volatility or should have required a greater degree of collateral coverage on loans backed by equity securities.

10.7   STOCK MARKET RISK

Many of the world's largest banking markets are dominated by commercial banks with large holdings of equity securities. Japan and Germany are among the two most notable examples. In the United States, not much attention is given to equity market risk at commercial banks and savings and loans, but that is a mistake in many of the following respects:

- Many banks hold equity securities of likely merger partners in anticipation of a future combination;

- Many banks lend to broker-dealers in securities with equity as collateral;

- Many banks have participated in highly subordinated lending where the "loans" have a degree of risk more consistent with equity risk than traditional bank lending; and,

- Many banks have been forced to own businesses for some period of time after loans have defaulted. The collateral for such loans has an equity-type risk.

A huge body of literature has developed around the theory and practice of equity portfolio risk management, and we will not attempt to summarize it here. From the perspective of institutions providing funds to the bank, however, an investment in common stock by the bank has most of the same characteristics as the loans analyzed in Section 10.1. A leveraged investment in equities is so inherently risky that the amount of leverage is tightly regulated for nearly every class of potential borrower except the banking industry. No banker in Japan or Germany can afford to ignore this reality, particularly in Japan where the 43% drop in equity markets from late 1989 through early 1992 severely depressed the market value of bank stocks, increased the cost of bank capital, depressed regulatory capital ratios, and effectively closed the market for equities in general.

Senior management would be making a large mistake not to include this equity risk under the same credit disciplines as a risky commercial loan. There is no difference in risk to the bank!

Like credit risk management discussed in Section 10.6, diversification of the equity portfolio (if the bank must hold one at all) is absolutely essential to avoid retaining risk that can be diversified away with no loss of return. Fortunately, the disciplines, techniques, and software for implementing the diversification of an equity portfolio are very advanced and widely available on an economical basis. For a cost of less than one basis point in return, any major financial institution can put these techniques to immediate use in diversifying away equity risk.

The late 1980s and early 1990s have seen an explosion in the depth and complexity of derivative products based on equity securities. Listed options and futures provide very economical hedging tools for those elements of an equity portfolio that cannot be sold for either economic reasons or political reasons. Even over-the-counter equity derivatives have the advantage of custom-tailored risk management—a benefit that may occasionally be worth the higher bid-offered spreads in the over-the-counter market.

10.8   FOREIGN EXCHANGE RISK

Many of the same comments that apply to equities pertain to foreign exchange risk as well. Many casual observers do not fully appreciate that the large profits realized by major international banks in foreign exchange trading result from carefully engineering cross-border arbitrages and a basic brokerage function rather than outright position taking. For most institutions, foreign exchange risk is not a major factor in day-to-day business. When cross-border capital flows are large, however, foreign exchange risk can take on a special prominence. This is definitely the case in Japan, where a large bank may find 40% of its assets denominated in a foreign currency. Even when every single asset is perfectly matched with funding in the same currency, accounting conventions and regulatory capital rules based on domestic currency accounting practices can play havoc with management attempts to satisfy the bureaucrats while trying to manage the real financial position of the bank.

In this section, we want to be especially careful to distinguish between these types of accounting anomalies and true economic risk. Real capital knows no bounds because of the currency of the initial public offering by the bank decades before. Twelve of the 13 largest bank holding companies in the United States have listed their stock in London and half have listings in Japan. Throughout most of the 1980s, the United States capital markets have been an important source of capital for banks from Europe and Asia as well as for domestic banks. Currency fluctuations impact true shareholder value in two major respects:

- Unhedged currency risks must be subjected to the same credit risk discipline as lending activities and stock market investments.

- Returns from currency trading and currency-related activities can be correlated with other risks the bank faces, even though most transactions are near-perfect arbitrages. The volume of trading activity, for instance, may move closely with interest rates and the level of the economy—in much the same way that major money center banks' bond trading activities create stock price movements that are very consistent with those of banks that take a lot of interest rate risk in their basic commercial banking business.

Perfectly match-funded foreign currency assets do not affect the true market value of the bank's capital. Any attempts to "hedge" these riskless assets because of the impact on accounting-based regulatory capital rules may actually **increase** the risk of the bank and destroy shareholder value.

The measurement of foreign exchange risk has two important aspects. One is the careful measurement of traditional currency mismatches by the maturity of the mismatch. A more recent and potentially more important risk is the risk of changes in the volatility of individual currencies versus the domestic currency. Dramatic changes in volatility can create large gains or losses in options-related derivatives products, a risk only a few Chief Credit Officers have managed with confidence. This volatility risk can be very great at a large international bank, when most options trading is based on the analytically convenient but completely false options model assumption that volatility is constant for the life of the option.

10.9 MEASURING FOREIGN EXCHANGE RISK

For those institutions that are comfortable with unhedged foreign currency exposures (a very small number of institutions in recent years), the basic techniques of interest rate and credit risk management can be applied directly to the measurement of foreign exchange risk. The reason for such a direct application is the fact that foreign exchange rates themselves are a "derivative" security. They are a product of interest rates in both countries and "other factors" that can be managed like credit risk. The basic techniques for managing foreign exchange risk include the following:

- Foreign exchange gap analysis,

- Foreign exchange rate "duration" analysis,

- Foreign exchange rate simulation analysis, and

- Foreign exchange rate volatility analysis.

Foreign Exchange Gap Analysis

Gap analysis for foreign exchange rates compares the "gaps" being born by the bank in each individual currency. For a bank based in U.S. dollars, the bank may have interest rate sensitivity gaps like the one shown in Table 10.1.

The same bank may also have assets and liabilities in yen. The yen interest rate sensitivity gap may look like the one shown in Table 10.2

Table 10.1
Interest Rate Sensitivity Gaps
(Based on U.S. Dollars)

	Maturity Under One Year	Maturity Over One-Year	Total
Assets	US$ 100	US$ 100	US$ 200
Liabilities	US$ 150	US$ 50	US$ 200
Interest Rate Gap	US$ (50)	US$ 50	

(assuming US$ 1 = 100 yen).

This example is simpler than a real situation in that the net gap in the base currency (in this example, U.S. dollars) adds up to zero. In general, this will only be true if all assets and liabilities were put on the books at the same exchange rate and that the current spot rate is unchanged from that rate. Otherwise, the net gap in the base currency will not be zero in each maturity.

Table 10.2
Yen Interest Rate Sensitivity Gaps

	Maturity Under One Year	Maturity Over One Year	Total
Assets	¥ 50000	¥ 15000	¥ 65000
Liabilities	¥ 45000	¥ 20000	¥ 65000
Interest Rate Gap	¥ 5000	¥ (5000)	
Gap in US$ Terms	US$ 50	US$ (50)	
NET GAP in US$	US$ 0	US$ 0	

In this example, one can see that the bank has effectively borrowed US$ 50 short-term and bought US$ 50 worth of short-term yen (5000 yen) with the funds. For over one-year maturities, the bank has borrowed 5,000 yen long-term and used the proceeds to buy an equivalent amount of long-term dollars (US$ 50). The offsetting hedging transaction would be to sell short-term yen and buy long-term yen forward. This would eliminate any residual currency risk. Like the analysis of interest rate gaps discussed in earlier chapters, this analysis is too crude for precise hedging, but it does alert management to major currency imbalances in the organization.

Foreign Exchange Rate "Duration" Analysis

The use of duration analysis for foreign exchange rate analysis rests on the same basic operational steps as in interest rate risk analysis. "Duration" can mean three things in this context: 1) the change in the value of a foreign currency bond with respect to foreign currency interest rates; 2) the change in value of a foreign currency bond with respect to domestic currency interest rates; and 3) the change in value of a foreign currency bond with respect to the spot rate of interest. All of these concepts are linked by a basic relationship that must hold or there would be an opportunity to make endless profits risklessly by arbitraging interest rates in the two countries on a fully hedged basis.

Let us define S as the spot rate of interest (expressed as the cost of country 2's currency in units of country 1 currency), $F(t)$ as the forward foreign exchange rate with maturity t, and $P_1(t)$ and $P_2(t)$ as the price of zero coupon bonds in the two countries that pay one unit of currency in t periods. Then we must have the following equation:

$$F(t) = S \frac{P_s(t)}{P_1(t)}$$

We can calculate each version of "duration" given above because every type of country 2 bond can be expressed as a country 1 bond using this relationship in place of the forward foreign exchange rate.

Calculation of the duration of a foreign currency bond with respect to its own currency is identical to the duration calculation that would be used for calculating home country duration. Only the interest rates would be different. Duration of the foreign bond with respect to country 1 interest rates is important because of the impact of country 1 interest rates on forward foreign exchange rates through the equation above. The steps in the calculation are as follows:

1. Multiply each foreign currency cash flow by the algebraic expression for the forward foreign exchange rate given above.
2. Being very careful about the impact of country 1 interest rates, take the derivative of the resulting expressions with respect to country 1 interest rates.
3. This derivative can then be substituted into the more traditional duration formula.

The same approach can be used when calculating the duration or elasticity of foreign bond prices with respect to the spot foreign exchange rate. While this topic deserves much more attention than can be devoted to it in this chapter, the key point is that the fundamental risk measures can be applied with only modest changes.

Foreign Exchange Rate Simulation Analysis

For many industrial applications of foreign exchange risk, the operations of a company in 100 countries is simply too complex analytically to reduce the problem to a simple formula. The same is true for the operations of a truly multinational financial institution with open positions in many currencies. Like the situation in interest rate risk analysis, it can be very helpful to use Monte Carlo simulation or its more modern cousin, latin hypercube simulation, to calculate the results of a very large number of scenarios. These scenarios would be based on assumptions about the probability distributions of the currencies and interest rates of the countries involved.

Typically, software used for these purposes produces probability distributions and relevant statistics for the variable in question; in a multinational bank, the variable might be the value of assets if exchange rates vary randomly. The standard deviation of asset values resulting from the simulation is one of a number of handy measures of risk that one can generate from a foreign exchange rate simulation.

Foreign Exchange Rate Volatility Analysis

Many bankers and corporate treasurers are using foreign exchange options to hedge currency risk. Others are using "delta hedging" based on the foreign exchange variants of the Black-Scholes options model to hedge options-type risk or to synthetically create foreign exchange options. Senior management should be aware that the value of these options will change dramatically if perceived market volatility changes, **even if foreign exchange rates themselves do not move!!** Delta hedging does not protect against these risks, since the Black-Scholes model assumes volatility is a constant.

Normal asset and liability management discipline requires continuous monitoring of this kind of obscure but potentially very large risk. Management should not rely solely on those responsible for running the positions for an assessment of volatility that will be used to judge their options hedging performance any more than Colonel Sanders asks foxes to keep his chicken inventory.

10.10 SUMMARY

Interest rate risk, credit risk, stock market risk, and foreign exchange risk all have one thing in common: fluctuations in each cause the value of the bank to change in an unpredictable way. The management disciplines for dealing with each risk are very similar. Moreover, each risk has an impact on the other, and all risks have a direct, quantifiable impact on the cost of funding to the bank. Management has to deal with all of these risks in an integrated way to keep shareholders in the "safety zone" where shareholder value is maximized.

APPENDIX 10A: AN OPTIONS THEORY APPROACH TO THE VALUE OF BANK DEBT AND EQUITY

This appendix describes how options pricing theory has been applied to evaluating the debt and equity of corporate entities. It is based on arguments presented in *Theory of Financial Decision-Making* by Jonathan Ingersoll (Ingersoll, Jonathan E., Jr., *Theory of Financial Decision-Making*, Savage, MD: Rowman & Littlefield, 1987).

We start by looking at a simplified case of a bank whose assets have a market value V. Because the business of the bank is risky, the market value of V is uncertain. This uncertainty could be due to interest rate risk, credit risk, foreign exchange risk, or stock market risk (for banks in Asia or Europe that hold significant equity investment portfolios). Let us assume that the bank issues a zero coupon bond with principal payment P that is due to mature at time T. We need to answer a key question: How should this discount bond be priced relative to the interest rate on a riskless (Treasury) discount bond with the same maturity T? In the market language of an American bank treasurer, what is the spread over treasuries for this zero coupon bond?

We start with a simple, fundamental relationship:

The Market Value of Assets V =
The Market Value of Debt D + the Market Value of Equity E

Let us assume that all of the firm's assets can be or will be converted to cash at time T. If the value of the firm's assets at time T is greater than the principal value of the zero coupon debt P, then the bonds will be paid off in full. From the equation above, this means that the equity holders of the firm will receive the following:

$$E = V_T - P$$

If the value of the assets V_T is less than the value of the principal amount of the debt P, then the firm is bankrupt and the equity holders receive nothing. The value of the equity of the firm is just like an option in the sense that the following:

$$E = Maximum \ [V_T - P, 0]$$

The equity of the firm is equivalent to an option with the following terms:

- The option is an option on the value of the firm's assets V.

- The maturity of the option is time T.

- The exercise price (or strike price) of the option is P, the principal value of the debt.

From the first equation, the value of the debt of the firm is as follows:

$$D = V - \textit{Option on V with strike price P maturing at T}$$

From the discussion of options theory in the previous chapter, this relationship means that the proper pricing for this debt issue depends on the following factors:

- The volatility of the underlying asset V.

- The riskless rate of interest.

- The time to maturity T.

- The principal amount of debt P.

- The initial market value of assets V.

The exact risk-adjusted pricing for the debt is given by a formula directly related to the options pricing formula given earlier. (See Appendix 10.B for details.) Note that the Bank for International Settlements (BIS) "risk-based weightings" do not appear in the list of factors above!

As shown in the previous charts, the proper risk-adjusted pricing for the debt of the firm changes in the following predictable ways when these factors change:

1. The spread over the riskless rate of interest increases as the volatility of V increases.

2. The pricing of the bond is always based on a spread over and above the riskless rate for the same maturity.

3. The spread increases as the leverage of the firm increases.

4. For a given principal amount of the debt P, the spread over the risk-free rate r decreases as r increases because the effective leverage of the firm is less.

5. The spread is a function of the maturity of the loan.

In this case, the leverage of the firm for purposes of evaluating pricing in this simple example is calculated by discounting the ultimate principal amount of the debt P by the risk-free rate r, and then dividing by the value of assets V:

$$d = \frac{Present\ value\ of\ principal\ P\ at\ risk\text{–}free\ rate\ r}{V}$$

(See Ingersoll, Jonathan E., Jr., *Theory of Financial Decision-Making*, Savage, MD: Rowman & Littlefield, 1987 for a more detailed explanation.)

The fourth bullet point on the previous page follows from this calculation for leverage d as shown. If r increases, leverage d decreases. Since leverage decreases, spread decreases.

APPENDIX 10B: PRICING RISKY LOANS AND THE BANK'S OWN COST OF FUNDS

During the 1980s, researchers in financial theory made tremendous progress in understanding the impact of interest rate volatility on the term structure of interest rates. From a finance theory point of view, reducing the analysis of risky credits to a simple formula is much more complicated—as any lending officer can appreciate. Nonetheless, the approach developed by Robert Merton and summarized by Jonathan Ingersoll shows the direct linkage between the risk of the underlying assets being financed and the pricing of the loan. From another perspective, the same formula shows how interest rate risk, credit risk, foreign exchange risk, and other risks figure directly in the cost of funds to the bank. Just as important, they show how a bank has to change its capital position to maintain a constant debt funding cost in the face of increasing credit risk.

For the mathematically inclined reader, the famous Black-Scholes call option pricing formula on an asset with value V, volatility σ, time to maturity t, strike price P, and riskless rate of interest r is as follows:

$$Call\ Option\ Value = V\,N\,(d_1) - Pe^{-rt}N\,(d_2)$$

$$where\ d_1 = \frac{\ln\left(\frac{V}{P}\right) + (r + .5\sigma^2)\,t}{\sigma\sqrt{t}}$$

$$d_2 = d_1 - \sigma\sqrt{t}$$

We know from Appendix 10A that the market value of assets must equal the sum of the market value of debt D and the market value of equity E. Since the value of equity is given by the value of the option given immediately above, the value of debt is:

$$D = V - V - N(d_1) + Pe^{-rt}N(d_2)$$

This expression can be rewritten using the relationship between call option pricing and put option pricing (the "put-call parity" relationship). The value of risky debt is as follows:

$$D = VN(h_1) + Pe^{-rt}N(h_2)$$

$$where\ h_1 = \frac{\log\left(\dfrac{Pe^{-rt}}{V}\right) - .5\,\sigma^2\,t}{\sigma\sqrt{t}}$$

$$h_2 = h_1 - \sigma\sqrt{t}$$

For a more detailed derivation and discussion of this complex topic, see Ingersoll's *Theory of Financial Decision-Making*.

Some readers may reach the appealing conclusion that this formula for risky zero coupon bonds can be used to value coupon-bearing risky bonds as a collection of risky zero coupon bonds. Unfortunately, this intuitive and appealing application is not correct since each interest and principal payment prior to maturity affects the probability of bankruptcy.

APPENDIX 10C: BINOMIAL OPTION PRICING APPROACH TO THE BANK'S OWN CREDIT RISK

In Appendix 10A, we showed how the level of the bank's asset risk figures directly into the cost of bank funds using logic from the options markets. In this appendix, we want to revisit this topic using another approach common in options analyses: the binomial approach. Recall that this approach was first introduced in Appendix 9A. In that case, the uncertainty pertained to the movement of the yield curve. In this case, the uncertainty revolves around the bank's asset volatility and the implications of that volatility on the bank's probability of default or failure.

First, we want to make some simplifying assumptions to make the basic points clearer. In any one-year period, we assume only two things can happen to a bond holder who holds the bank's bonds:

- Probability p   The bank is bankrupt, its assets are completely worthless, and the bank cannot and never will pay either principal or interest.

- Probability 1-p   The bank is healthy and pays interest and principal in full when due.

We call the probability p the probability of default. We also assume that the bond holder is completely "risk-neutral." That is, he or she does not mind bearing the risk as long as, on average, he or she receives fair compensation for the risk. The bond holder demands no compensation above and beyond the average expected amount of his losses.

What are the probabilities of default implied by the rates at which major banking companies are raising funds in the domestic U.S. market and in the Euro markets? Let us assume U.S. Treasury bill rates for a one-year maturity are such that an investor who buys Treasury bills with a market value of $1 will receive $1.06 in one year. If we assume this investor has the opportunity to buy a one-year bank certificate of deposit with a 0.01% probability of "default" as we defined it above, the investor will demand an interest rate of 6.01% to break even. This one basis point risk premium rises dramatically as the probability of default increases, as shown in Table 10C.1.

The break-even rate on the certificate of deposit for a risk-neutral investor given our definition of default (total loss of interest and principal) is as follows:

$$Breakeven\ rate = \left(\frac{\left[1 + \dfrac{riskless\ rate}{100}\right]}{\left[1 - \dfrac{probability\ of\ default}{100}\right]} - 1 \right) \frac{100}{T}$$

where T is the number of years to maturity (and T is less than or equal to one).

When the probability of default rises to 0.2%, the risk premium rises to 21 basis points. This is roughly the premium that a top quality bank would pay in excess of one-year Treasury bills in a market when rates are low. If there is a 1% probability of default, the risk premium jumps to 107 basis

Table 10C.1
One-Year Break-Even Funding Costs

Probability of Default	Breakeven One-Year Rate	Risk Premium
0.01%	6.01%	0.01%
0.10%	6.11%	0.11%
0.20%	6.21%	0.21%
0.30%	6.32%	0.32%
0.50%	6.53%	0.53%
1.00%	7.07%	1.07%
2.00%	8.16%	2.16%
3.00%	9.28%	3.28%
5.00%	11.58%	5.58%

points. Given the way break-even risk premiums are calculated, note two important observations:

- The risk premium is a very sharply rising nonlinear function of the probability of default, and

- The level of risk premiums is directly proportional to the level of the risk-free rate.

APPENDIX 10D: QUANTIFYING THE EFFECTS OF DIVERSIFICATION ON LOAN PORTFOLIOS

This appendix summarizes the quantitative aspects of the discussion in Section 10.3. The volatility of the loan portfolio encompassing two companies is expressed by the following formula:

$$Bank\ B\ Volatility = \sqrt{w_1^2\ \sigma_1^2 + 2w_1\ w_2\ \rho\ \sigma_1\ \sigma_2 + w_2^2\ \sigma_2^2}$$

$$= \sqrt{w_1^2\ (.15)^2 - 2\ w_1\ w_2\ 1\ (.15)\ (.25) + w_2^2\ (.25)^2}$$

In this formula, w_1 and w_2 are the proportions of the loan portfolio in loans to Rainy Day and Sunshine, respectively. The σs are the volatilities associated with each loan. For the mathematically inclined reader, we can solve for the risk-minimizing weights using the formula for volatility given above. Using a little calculus produces the minimum risk weights:

$$w_1 = \frac{2\sigma_2^2 - 2\rho\,\sigma_1\,\sigma_2}{2\,\sigma_1^2 - 4\rho\,\sigma_1\,\sigma_2 + 2\,\sigma_2^2}$$

$$w_2 = 1 - w_1$$

The Greek symbol rho (ρ) is the correlation coefficient between the returns on each loan.

CHAPTER 11

Liquidity Analysis

Chapter 10 analyzed the impact of credit risk, foreign exchange risk, and stock market risk on the cost of debt and equity for a bank. In every case, there is a direct link between the level of each type of risk and the bank's cost of funding, which in turn means that all of these risks have a direct impact on the risks and techniques that are more traditionally called "asset and liability management." There is another "traditional" asset and liability management topic: liquidity risk. It is safe to say that liquidity risk analysis is one of the least understood of all ALM areas.

Why is liquidity risk so misunderstood? **Liquidity risk is misunderstood because so many bankers have mistaken liquidity risk for the disease itself, when in reality it is only the symptom of a more fundamental problem.** Failure to distinguish between the symptom and the disease can get a doctor sued for malpractice. This chapter should protect bankers against a similar kind of problem.

Liquidity risk includes four basic kinds of analysis:

- Understanding how to measure the liquidity profile of a bank balance sheet;

- Understanding the impacts of the cost of bankruptcy and liquidation costs;

- Understanding the liquidity safety zone and the funding implications of these factors; and,

- Understanding their impacts on shareholder value.

Each of these topics will be discussed in this chapter.

11.1   WHAT IS LIQUIDITY RISK?

There is no universally accepted definition of liquidity or liquidity risk. This is, indeed, one of the reasons why it is so poorly understood: it means different things to different people. A precise definition of liquidity is not important; however, understanding its potential consequences and managing it well is critical.

Some of the concepts that are usually expressed on this issue are:

"Liquidity is having access to sufficient cash to maintain a 'business as usual' posture at all times."

"Liquidity is the ability to raise (or borrow) funds at a reasonable cost at all times."

"Liquidity buys time to work out problems."

The authors tend to favor the last because it emphasizes the point expressed in the introduction to this chapter. Any difficulty in a bank's liquidity or funding activities is only the symptom that reflects the existence of some other, more fundamental problem. The "buying time" perspective reflects the essential role that liquidity planning plays for a bank. It is often the only buffer between the bank and those that may be over-reacting to the "disease," whether the underlying problem is real, but overstated, or imagined.

No mention has been made about accounting or risk-based capital levels. Capital plays a special role as the "liability" with the longest maturity and as the only "liability" where no regular interest payments can trigger bankruptcy. Liquidity planning includes more than just capital, since "buying time" can be just as important in the short run as it is in the long run. How are liquidity and capital linked? A bank will have liquidity problems in the short run if the market believes that capital has been so impaired that in the long run the bank may not be able to pay off its liabilities. The two are linked symptoms of a disease somewhere else on the balance sheet, usually a loss due to high levels of credit risk or interest rate risk.

11.2   A SIMPLE BALANCE SHEET MODEL OF LIQUIDITY

In this section, a simple theoretical model of balance sheet liquidity is presented. This type of presentation is extremely effective in communicating to senior management and the board of directors. It is also useful for establishing liquidity policies and operating limits.

In this approach, all assets are allocated to one of two categories: "liquid assets" and "illiquid assets." All liabilities are classified as either "stable liabilities" or "volatile liabilities." Schematically, the balance sheet can then be presented as shown in Figure 11.1.

The focal point of this framework is the concept of "net liquid assets," defined as the difference between liquid assets and volatile liabilities. (This difference can also be referred to as the "liquidity gap.") When defined in this manner, there is a natural tendency to strive for a surplus of liquid assets over volatile funds. As a result, this definition is preferred over those that would calculate the ratio of liquid assets to volatile liabilities (or to total assets). This differencing, or netting, has the favorable attribute that an excess of volatile funding over liquid assets is a negative value, rather than a ratio that would result in a value less than 100%.

Figure 11.1
Balance Sheet Liquidity Model

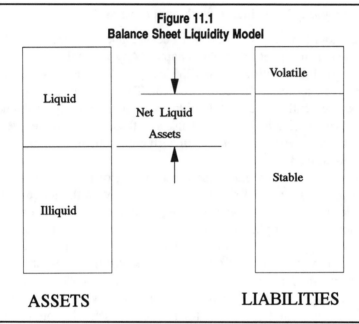

ASSETS   LIABILITIES

Psychologically, a 95% ratio of liquid assets to volatile funds may not sound too bad. But a negative net liquid assets value is usually taken much more seriously by ALCOs and boards of directors, as well it should.

This concept emphasizes that banks should understand when they are putting themselves at the risk of not being able to fund their operating cash needs. Any negative value for net liquid assets may be interpreted as such a potential circumstance. Simplistically, a negative value here means that assets readily convertible into cash may not be sufficient to cover the near-term maturities of deposits and debt.

Of course, it is important to establish appropriate criteria for the various balance sheet components. To use this concept properly, some careful thought must be given to the precise classifications of balance sheet components to the "liquid asset" and "stable liability" categories. The next section will discuss the liquidity characteristics of the main balance sheet categories. Some rather counterintuitive assessments are encountered!

11.3   BALANCE SHEET LIQUIDITY CHARACTERISTICS

Some balance sheet categories are relatively simple to categorize, while some are treacherous. The following is a very simplified discussion, in some cases augmented by utilizing a devil's advocate stand. This is an extremely serious topic; therefore, all asset and liability managers should spend some quality time getting acquainted and comfortable with these types of considerations. Because the consequences of insufficient liquidity can be so dire, we recommend that when in doubt, use a conservative assumption that, if anything, understates net liquid assets.

Many readers will notice that this presentation is very analogous to the "rate-sensitive assets" and "rate-sensitive liabilities" concept presented in many discussions of interest rate risk management. In interest rate risk analyses, the main classification feature is the expected time to the next repricing or rollover. In liquidity analyses, the main focus is on the effective maturity characteristic. Both techniques require selecting a time threshold by which items are determined to be sensitive or insensitive, liquid or illiquid, volatile or stable. For the net liquid assets measure, we recommend using either a three-month or six-month remaining maturity criterion. For the following discussion, assume that the threshold selected is six months.

Asset Accounts

A useful criterion for categorizing the various items on the asset side of the balance sheet is to ask whether the asset may be liquidated or pledged, and the bank still maintain a "business as usual" posture to the outside world. What is "business as usual"? Think of how your customers would react if your bank suddenly stopped cashing checks, or failed to deliver good funds at the closing of a mortgage transaction, or reneged on the requested drawdown of a loan commitment?

Cash and due from banks. Most bankers automatically classify vault cash, interbank clearing accounts, and required reserve balances at the Fed as liquid assets. We disagree! These balances are constantly monitored and decreased to the minimum levels required to carry out normal operations. No bank leaves material amounts of surplus vault cash, due from balances or reserve balances. Therefore, these balances usually cannot be substantially decreased in the event of a funding problem. By this reasoning, they are illiquid assets!

Federal funds sold and reverse repo. These are definitely liquid assets. One possible complication may be correspondent relationships that depend on your bank for short-term funding. Any balances of this type should be considered illiquid.

Placements and other money market assets. These are liquid to the extent they are less than the threshold of six months.

Investment securities. For this analysis, divide the investment portfolio into two important security types: those that can be pledged for repo borrowings in the open markets and those that cannot. Those that are eligible for repurchase agreement transactions should be entirely classified as liquid assets, even if they are currently all repoed or otherwise encumbered! (Net out the repoed securities by classifying their associated repurchase agreements as volatile liabilities. Similarly, collateralized borrowings that encumber eligible securities should be considered volatile.) For those not eligible for repo, only those maturing within the six-month threshold may be considered to be liquid assets.

A similar, yet simpler approach would be to classify all Treasuries and Agencies as liquid, and all other securities as illiquid. This simplification is quite useful in conducting peer comparisons where maturities during the next six months may not be available.

Trading assets. These assets are commonly repoed. As such, they should be counted as liquid assets. As with Treasury securities in the investment portfolio, the corresponding repurchase agreements will be classified as volatile liabilities.

Loans. Our general attitude is that all loans are illiquid. The standard argument against this extreme position is that all balances scheduled to mature within the six-month liquidity threshold should be considered liquid. However, treating all near-term maturities as liquid would violate the "business as usual" criterion. Implying that the funds generated from all scheduled maturities are available for purposes other than lending is tantamount to shutting down the bank's entire array of loan origination activities. Commercial and mortgage loan pipelines are often much longer than one month in duration. They cannot be shut down on short notice without severe disruption. Indeed, they really cannot ever be shut down without sending shock waves throughout the bank's customer base.

Likewise, consumer lending is being geared more and more toward cross-selling and relationship building. To cease accepting consumer loan applications would be just as shocking to this, the bank's most prized customer base. Our advice is simple: Do not count on decreasing loan origination volumes as a liquidity source.

A special argument is sometimes made about mortgages or some commercial loans that qualify as collateral for Federal Reserve discount window or Federal Home Loan Bank borrowing purposes. However, this approach would violate our "business as usual" criterion. Drawing down "lender of last resort" credit lines or backup lines would send clear signals to those entities that something is amiss. This distinction will be expanded in a later section.

The final special circumstance of loan securitization will be discussed in Chapter 12.

All other assets. These are generally considered to be illiquid assets.

Liability Accounts

Again, the liquidity threshold of six months will be an important factor in these evaluations. However, for retail deposit products, the law of large numbers and expected portfolio characteristics will also be considered.

Demand and savings deposits. Many banks classify all retail "nonmaturity" products as stable. These are products with no contractual maturity date. However, experience shows that there will be some deterioration of a retail deposit base as adverse publicity and downgradings progress. Several banks have analyzed the core deposit runoff experience of large regional banks that ultimately failed. Public regulatory reports can be examined to determine the extent of retail deposit loss as a function of rating agency downgrading. The idea would be to reflect the runoff seen at around the "C/D" credit rating stage. The percentages found by deposit product type would then be considered volatile liabilities.

If this is not practical, use the results from the seasonality analyses described in Chapter 9. That analysis, which is needed for interest rate risk analyses as well as for transfer pricing (see Chapter 14), splits demand deposit balances into core and volatile. The volatile percentage found there can be applied to the net liquid assets calculation. Under no circumstances should the bank blindly assume that all retail deposits are stable.

Retail certificates of deposit. Those balances that have more than six months remaining maturities are considered stable. As with the demand and savings accounts, it is reasonable to assume that a large percentage of the near-term maturities will roll over. Indeed, many banks automatically roll over maturing retail CDs, unless specific instructions are received otherwise. If the downgrade and runoff study described earlier is done, then appropriate assumptions can be established. Without this data, then assumptions consistent with the core versus volatile split for other retail accounts can be utilized.

Commercial demand deposits. These are usually related to long-established relationships. However, many corporations and businesses have strict credit rating minimum criteria for their relationship banks. Therefore, as a bank is downgraded, many strong business relationships may be lost. Also, corporate treasurers have absolutely no incentive to "stand by their bank" if their company's ability to conduct financial transactions is threatened. Therefore, the runoff estimates used for commercial DDA should be significantly higher than for retail DDA. (This should also be true for the volatile percentage determined for interest rate risk management purposes. As above, in the absence of other data, the split used in gap or duration analyses can be pressed into service here also.)

Large certificates of deposit. Only balances beyond the six-month threshold in remaining maturity can be counted as stable liabilities.

Foreign office time deposits. Balances beyond six months remaining maturity are "stable liabilities."

Federal funds purchased and repurchase agreements. As discussed for investment securities, these should all be counted as volatile liabilities.

Long-term debt. Any balances maturing within the six-month limit are volatile. Also, any debt beyond six months that requires collateral in the form of repo-eligible investment securities should be considered volatile.

Equity and other liabilities: These are stable liabilities.

This concludes our first liquidity tour of the balance sheet. Of course, no single definition or equation can be adequate for a subject as diverse and complex as this. The next several sections will dig through the layers and nuances of the liquidity management process.

11.4 MANAGING LIQUIDITY RISK: PERCEPTIONS AND REALITY

The asset and liability manager has to deal with two types of liquidity risks. One risk is the correct perception by the market that the ALM manager's bank is in financial trouble. A less common but still possible risk is the incorrect perception by the market that a bank has financial problems. The bank has to deal with both risks in a way that minimizes the expected liquidation costs and bankruptcy costs. (A description of the theoretical effects of liquidation and bankruptcy costs is presented in Appendix 10B.) These closely related but somewhat different problems will be addressed in reverse order.

The asset and liability manager is often the first to receive notice that the market does not think much of his institution. While there is plenty of sympathy for the underlying validity of the "efficient markets" school of financial theory, many banking colleagues have had to deal with the very real consequences of a market that does not want to lend money to their bank. This phenomenon has been observed in many markets, but New York and Hong Kong colleagues seem to be the most experienced in it. The first warning is funding or derivative products counterparties "turning down the name" of the manager's bank. A more easily observable signal is the resulting increase in funding costs that the bank faces on a daily basis relative to both the risk-free rate (U.S. Treasury rates in an American context) and to the funding costs faced by peer group banks. As mentioned in Chapter 10, this means the "implied volatility" of bank assets as viewed by the market has increased.

What should the asset and liability manager do to deal with the risk of market misperception? There are four aspects to the ALM manager's duties:

- Constant monitoring and reporting of market perceptions to the asset and liability committee in order to ensure that market signals are not missed.

- Ensuring that the financial condition of the bank is always clearly and accurately communicated to the investor community. Any hint of "stonewalling" is implicit confirmation of problems and may lead the market to believe that the situation is worse than it really is.

- Measuring the liquidation cost risk inherent in the balance sheet. (The term "liquidity risk" is avoided here to emphasize the fact that liquidity risk is derived from other risks and that the real concern of the asset and liability manager is that the bank pays costs to liquidate assets that could have been avoided.)

- Structuring the bank's balance sheet so that the bank is in the liquidity safety zone.

The first two points cannot be overemphasized, but they are so self-evident it is unnecessary to expand on them. The other two points need to be addressed in some detail. The emphasis is on managing the expected value of liquidation costs and postponing their payment for as long as possible.

11.5 MEASURING LIQUIDATION COST RISK

Unlike the risk-based capital adequacy guidelines, measurement of liquidation cost risk can be done with meaning and precision. There are three elements to this measurement: the costs of liquidation as a function of time, the liquidity gap for the bank, and liquidity duration. The last concept measures the change in the equity value of the bank that would result from a change in the implied volatility (increased risk) inherent in the bank balance sheet. Each of these measurement tools will be discussed in order.

Liquidation costs. The major elements of a bank's balance sheet can be converted to cash with varying degrees of efficiency depending on what the asset is and how long one has to convert the asset to cash. The costs of doing so are a function of brokerage and investment banking fees and the basic bid-offered spread in the market for the asset involved. The fees and bid-offered spreads are generally dominated by the ease or difficulty of determining the credit risk of the asset involved. In the case of short-term government securities, this risk is very literally close to zero. When it comes to consumer auto loans, it is almost literally impossible for anyone other than the bank to assess the risk of the assets involved because no third party has access to enough information to make the credit judgment. If the bank needs an investor to make a firm bid in a very short period of time, the bank can get one, but it will be a bid very heavily discounted in recognition of the lack of information on the risk. As stated in Chapter 12, there is a serious "moral hazard" risk in the sale of some assets: there is strong (short-term) incentive for the bank to sell its worst assets when sorting through its own consumer loan portfolio if the bank feels investors cannot measure the risk themselves. Investors recognize this risk and discount appropriately.

The costs of liquidating various categories of assets will depend on current market conditions, the institution itself, the time frame for liquidation, and the asset class. The authors believe most bankers would come up with a table of liquidation costs very similar to Table 11.1.

Table 11.1
The Cost of Liquidating Typical U.S. Bank Assets
Transactions Costs as a Percentage of Market Value

Asset	Time Available for Conversion			
	One Hour	One Day	One Week	One Months
U.S. Treasury Bills	0.031	0.031	0.031	0.000
U.S. Government Bonds	0.063	0.031	0.031	0.031
GNMA and FNMA Securities	0.125	0.063	0.063	0.063
Federal Funds Sold	0.125	0.000	0.000	0.000
Corporate Bonds	0.500	0.250	0.250	0.250
Corporate Loans	NA	NA	1.000	0.500
Whole Mortgage Loans	NA	NA	NA	1.000
Securitized Consumer Loans	NA	NA	NA	2.000
Other Consumer Loans	NA	NA	NA	NA

Note: NA means that liquidation is not available.

It goes without saying that there would be no transactions costs if the bank had the time to allow assets to mature and collect the underlying principal. Using charts like this, the bank can calculate the amount of cash and the amount of liquidation costs realized over a given time period. Unlike the BIS guidelines, these liquidation cost "haircuts" are readily observable to day-to-day market participants.

Liquidity gaps (also known as net liquid assets). Perhaps the best tool for supplementing measures of liquidation costs is a tool that was of only limited use in an interest rate risk context. That tool is the "gap" analysis, as described in Sections 11.2 and 11.3. When using the gap concept for interest rate risk analysis, assets and liabilities are classified in time categories according to their interest rate reset periods. In the liquidation cost context, assets and liabilities are classified by maturity. Using this classification, management can view the amount of cash that is made available with the passage of time without the payment of any liquidation costs.

Liquidity duration. The discussion of interest rate risk examined the concept of duration and interest rate elasticity at length. In that context, both tools measured the impact on shareholders' equity if the risk-free rates increased by 1% for all maturities. In the liquidation risk context, the same tools can be used. In this application, rates would rise not because the risk-free rates rise, but because the implied volatility of the bank's assets increases, driving up the marginal cost of funds to the bank through an increase in the bank's liquidity premium. While the basic calculation methods remain the same, there are a few differences in application in the use of liquidation risk elasticity. There are three steps in the process:

1. Calculate the present value of assets and liabilities using bank cost of funds rates as the discount rates.

   This mark-to-market calculation is different from the interest rate risk case, where the discount rates are the market yields that apply to the market for that particular asset (Treasury yields are used for Treasury securities, for example). If the resulting values are below true market values by more than the cost of liquidating the assets, it is cheaper to sell the assets than to keep them in a liquidity crisis.

2. Measure the change in the market value of equity from a change in the bank's cost of funds due to an increase in the risk premium paid by the bank to raise money.

   Like the interest rate risk usage of duration, we are implicitly assuming a "parallel shift" in the bank's risk premium. In other words, assume that the spread over the risk-free rate increases by the same amount at every maturity. If the LRE (liquidity risk elasticity) is zero, the bank has zero liquidity risk by this measure. If the LRE is sharply negative, it will pay the bank to shorten the maturity of its assets and lengthen the maturity of its liabilities, increasing liquidity, in order to reduce the amount of liquidity risk.

3. Take management action to control liquidity risk.

   These management actions are the subject of the next section.

Clearly, the LRE concept goes a significant step beyond the net liquid assets, or liquidity gap, approach. The remainder of this chapter will focus back on the net liquid assets idea. The LRE measure is very useful as a tool of strategic balance sheet management. It also serves to illustrate that the analytical concepts and tools described in earlier chapters for interest rate risk management are also applicable in other risk dimensions.

11.6   CONTROLLING LIQUIDITY RISK AND THE SAFETY ZONE

Once management has measured the amount of liquidity risk, the practical question is simple: what should be done about it? The true objective of liquidity risk management is the same when the bank is really in financial difficulties and when the market just thinks it is. The objective is simple: to buy time. This was asserted in Section 11.1. However, now we can more fully explain why this is important.

"Buying time" reduces liquidation costs because, as Table 11.1 shows, the more time management has to sell assets, the smaller will be the transaction costs that management pays in the process. This is particularly important when the market's perception of financial difficulties is incorrect. Buying time allows management to prove its case that nothing is wrong, in addition to allowing the treasury staff time to generate cash from less liquid assets at the smallest possible liquidation costs. As Hong Kong banks have proven over and over again, the best remedy for a run on deposits is to pay every depositor who wants his money until depositors realize there is no need to make a withdrawal in the first place.

When the institution truly is in difficulty, buying time reduces liquidation costs to a minimum and increases the possibility that the bank's fundamental problem resolves itself. One concrete example is the U.S. savings and loan crisis. If a savings and loan institution funded a 30-year fixed rate loan with 10-year fixed rate money, the institution might be bankrupt on a mark-to-market basis if rates rose dramatically after one year. Fortunately for the savings and loan association, however, it would have nine years in which it could wait (and hope) for a drop in rates to save the institution. As stated in the interest rate risk sections, it is better not to depend on good fortune for solvency. Nonetheless, a conservative posture from a liquidity risk point of view provides a second line of defense against many problems. Even postponing the inevitable sometimes has value.

What is the liquidity risk counterpart of the safety zone that was discussed in an interest rate context? The boundaries of the liquidity risk safety zone are fairly wide. One boundary of the safety zone is a balance sheet where the liquidity gap is positive at every maturity threshold. That is, the cash flow from liquid assets is always greater than the amount of volatile liabilities coming due. This means the bank will never have to pay liquidation costs unless the bank is truly bankrupt. Even if it is bankrupt, liquidation costs will be minimized.

The other boundary of the liquidity risk safety zone is less obvious and much more dependent on the institutional setting in which the bank operates. The bank should always be able to generate enough cash on its own to survive a market misperception of a crisis long enough for either (a) the government to come to the aid of the bank or (b) the crisis to end naturally, whichever is shorter. In the United States, most large banks would want to be able to survive based on their own resources for at least two weeks before they are forced to borrow from the Federal Reserve. In addition, they would want subsequent cash flow to be strong enough to pay down Federal Reserve borrowings quickly enough to avoid lasting government control of the institution. In the case of a more laissez-faire market like Hong Kong, the bank's financial posture would need to be much more liquid, since it is much less likely that a rescuer would be as benevolent at the U.S. government generally has been to bank shareholders.

These two extremes bracket the asset and liability management structure that defines the safety zone:

- On the "most liquid" side of the safety zone, the bank can meet all maturing volatile liabilities with the proceeds of liquid assets.

- On the "least liquid" side of the safety zone, the bank can generate only enough cash to stay afloat until the lifeguard arrives. This would be one to two to four weeks in a U.S. context and more in less benign environments.

11.7 DIVERSIFICATION OF FUNDING SOURCES

Apart from structuring the maturity of assets and liabilities, the bank has to emphasize the diversification of funding supplies in the same way that assets are diversified in order to minimize credit risk. The funding sources for each institution should be managed so that there is minimal impact if any one institution changes its mind concerning the credit risk of the bank. If any one institution provides more than 5% of the funding to the bank, that is cause for concern, particularly if the maturities involved are short term. While diversification of funding sources is a holy grail of treasury managers, diversity may have a price: What is a banker to do if the biggest supplier of funds consistently offers them at a price below market? There is no easy answer to this question, but we offer one anyway:

> **The asset and liability manager should seek to retain the cheapest funding on a risk-adjusted basis for the bank, regardless of maturity and regardless of source.**

If the interest rate risk characteristics are the only problem with the funds offered, the bank can change the interest rate risk characteristics using swaps, options, and futures. If the bank's closest correspondent bank offers fed funds at 0.25% below market, the bank should take the funds even if it pushes that source of funds beyond the risk limit (although this transaction must be approved in advance on a case-by-case basis by the Asset and Liability Committee or another management authority). The proper usage of such funds is limited; the bank should lay off the funds only in such a way that the liquidity risk of the bank is not increased. How can this be done? In this particular example, the funds should be invested in fed funds sold at going market rates. From a liquidity gap (net liquid assets) perspective, there is no additional risk. From a liquidation cost point of view, there would be no cost of liquidating the asset position.

When should attractive funding be turned down? Only in those cases when there is no "zero liquidity risk" investment alternative for placing the funds at a positive spread.

11.8   THE CONTINGENCY PLANNING PROCESS

No asset and liability management process is complete without a detailed contingency plan that shows a step-by-step process for who does what when the bank's (or more realistically, bank holding company's) funding is cut off. Most bankers will have close colleagues who have been forced to put such plans into action, either due to natural calamities like fires or earthquakes or due to adverse credit risk at their own institution. In times of crisis, there is no time to talk about who should do what—or worse yet, who should have done what. The detailed contingency plan makes the calculations of previous sections a practical reality.

The contingency plan is an exercise in "critical path" planning in the language of an industrial company. Many participants have to take action simultaneously for each part of the plan to be completed in proper sequence.

In an American context, almost every bank or bank holding company contingency plan will specify the following:

1. Senior executive (and two back-ups) responsible for contacting the local Federal Reserve Bank president and the chairman of the Federal Reserve Board in Washington D.C.
2. Senior executive responsible for contacting presidents of lead banks in commercial paper or other back-up lines of credit.

3. Senior executive responsible for contacting senior counterparts at one or two investment banking firms.

4. Decision process for activation of back-up lines of credit.

5. Decision process for sale of government securities and other liquid asset portfolios.

6. Decision process for borrowing from Federal Reserve Bank.

7. Precise instructions on asset sales over these timeframes:
   - One day
   - Two days
   - One week
   - One month
   - Six months

8. Reallocation of systems and consumer lending human resources to speed asset sales.

9. Lines of authority for sale of subsidiaries or assets to be securitized.

The contingency plan should demonstrate in a concrete way that the bank has sufficient internal cash flow to survive with no outside assistance for the minimum time period specified by the bank's senior management. Typically, the liquidity gap is a very important tool in the process of developing the liquidity plan.

As mentioned in Section 11.4, the asset and liability manager's task over the long run is to structure the balance sheet so that the costs of asset liquidation are minimized once a crisis has occurred. Once a liquidity plan has been put into action, however, speed of execution becomes the primary objective. There will be no time and the bank will have no negotiating power to pinch pennies on liquidation costs, lawyer's fees, and investment banking fees. The best way to manage those fees is to position the bank's liquidity risk position such that the contingency plan never needs to be put into action.

A few major banks have gone so far as to declare a "liquidity crisis" as a real-world drill to ensure that bank staff is prepared to execute the contingency plan. This drill is an expensive one, but it is one that may be worthwhile for those banks who are most aggressively taking liquidity risk.

11.9 SUMMARY: LIQUIDITY RISK AND SHAREHOLDER VALUE

There is no free lunch when it comes to liquidity risk, just like the interest rate risk case. The bank cannot create shareholder value by taking liquidity risk. The bank can only destroy value from taking liquidity risk outside of the safety zone. This value destruction is due to the potential costs of bankruptcy, which shareholders and debt holders cannot avoid through arbitrage actions for their own account.

The bank will maximize shareholder value by optimizing the expected liquidation costs and bankruptcy costs compared to the economic incentives for taking risk, like the tax deductions available for the costs of debt. One of the tools for controlling this risk is the securitization of balance sheet assets, the subject of Chapter 12.

APPENDIX 11A: JUST WHAT IS THE "LIQUIDITY PREMIUM" ANYWAY?

(This appendix is a continuation of Appendix 10C.)

Chapter 10 introduced the risk-premium that most banks must pay in funding the bank, referred to as the spread over Treasuries. This risk premium truly is the liquidity premium. What many bankers call the liquidity premium has a different definition. Let's say the bank decides to issue a floating rate certificate of deposit with a two-year maturity that pays interest at the risk-free rate plus a premium set by the market. We have already seen what this risk premium is in the one-year case. What many bankers call the liquidity premium is the difference between what the bank will have to pay on its floating rate two-year certificate of deposit and the cost of its own one-year cost of funding. In reality, this "liquidity premium" is simply a reflection that the risk of loss over a long time period is greater in the real world than it is over a short time horizon. We can see this in the following example.

Let us assume that the one-year Treasury rate is expected to stay constant at the equivalent of 6% per year. We also assume that the market expects the bank's probability of default in year two is twice as high as it is in year one. What would be the spread to the risk-free rate for a two-year floating rate certificate of deposit for the bank? The answers are contained in Table 11A.1.

To put the discussion in real-world terms, let's call the bank's one-year certificate of deposit cost LIBOR flat. If the bank's one-year probability of default is 0.10% (leading to a two-year probability of default of 0.20%), the bank can only issue a two-year floating certificate of deposit at 6.16%, a 5 basis point spread over LIBOR and a 16 basis point spread over the risk-free rate. This five basis point premium for two-year funds with a one-year floating rate is what many bankers call the "liquidity premium." In Table 11A.1 that LIBOR is only 11 basis points over the risk-free rate for a one-year maturity. If the probability of default is 50 basis points in the first year and 1% in the second, the cost of the two-year floating certificate of deposit is 26 basis points over LIBOR, a much higher liquidity premium.

What happens if the probability of default is the same in year one as it is in year two? Then there is no "liquidity" premium in the informal usage of the term, but there is a risk or liquidity premium over the risk-free rate that is the same as that of a one-year certificate of deposit.

Table 11A.1
Two-Year Floating Rate Break-Even Funding Costs

Year 1 Probability of Default	Year 2 Probabiltiy of Default	Risk Premium Over:		
		Break-Even Two-Year Coupon	Risk-Free Rate	One-Year Rate
0.01%	0.02%	6.02%	0.02%	0.01%
0.10%	0.20%	6.16%	0.16%	0.05%
0.20%	0.40%	6.32%	0.32%	0.10%
0.30%	0.60%	6.47%	0.47%	0.16%
0.50%	1.00%	6.79%	0.79%	0.26%
1.00%	2.00%	7.60%	1.60%	0.52%
2.00%	4.00%	9.23%	3.23%	1.07%
3.00%	6.00%	10.92%	4.92%	1.64%
5.00%	10.00%	14.43%	8.43%	2.85%

The break-even coupon can be calculated using the formula below when: (a) "default" means a total loss of interest and principal and (b) investors are risk neutral. We assume p_1 is the probability of default in year one and p_2 is the probability of default in year two. Just to simplify the notation, we assume the risk-free rate r_f is constant.

$$Coupon = \frac{(1 + r_f)^2 - (1 - p_1)(1 - p_2)}{(1 - p_1)(1 + r_f) + (1 - p_1)(1 - p_2)}$$

With a little bit of algebra, this reduces to the formula for the coupon on a one-year certificate of deposit given above. Note that in this formula, we are assuming interest rates are given as decimals and have not been divided by 100 to convert from percentage figures.

APPENDIX 11B: THE COST OF BANKRUPTCY AND LIQUIDATION COSTS

This appendix introduces some important "real world" considerations into the theoretical discussion from Appendix 11A. While this could be done in a precise way analytically, we will restrict ourselves to a logical argument rather than a mathematical one. The added consideration is a simple one that bankers and taxpayers have learned over and over again in the United States in the 1980s: Bankruptcy has a cost in and of itself. Debt holders lose more than just the difference between the true market value of assets and the value of principal plus accrued interest. They only receive a payout after the enormous costs of the bankruptcy proceedings themselves. In addition to court costs, legal costs, accountant's fees, and investment banking fees, there is the cost and inconvenience of waiting for payment beyond the scheduled maturity date. Even more important is the huge price paid, both financially and emotionally, by customers and employees.

What is the impact of these costs from a practical point of view? Until now, we have made the very defensible Modigiliani and Miller assumption that one cannot change the value of the bank by calling debt equity and equity debt. When bankruptcy has a cost, this powerful assumption is no longer true. As the possibility of bankruptcy increases, the expected value of incurring the costs of bankruptcy increases. This is a dead-weight loss to both debt and equity holders, not just an amount of money that passes from debt holder to equity holder (or vice-versa) without changing the aggregate value of the bank.

Because of the cost of bankruptcy, there is an optimal capital structure and liability maturity structure that results from the tradeoff from the increased tax deductions on additional debt versus the increased expected value of bankruptcy costs. The volatility of asset values is perhaps the single most important determinant of the expected value of bankruptcy costs, in addition to the impact volatility has on debt borrowing costs.

There is one more important real world consideration in managing liquidity risk. Many of the assets held by the bank cannot be converted to cash costlessly; there is a transaction cost in getting rid of them in order to make a cash payment. The amount of these costs is generally a function of how much time one has to convert them to cash, a phenomenon of which anyone who has had to sell his house in a hurry is painfully aware. If bankruptcy has already occurred, these liquidation costs are less important except for their impact on the time it takes to liquidate a bankrupt company in the most economical way. In the case of a solvent institution that suddenly has to liquidate assets unexpectedly, however, they become very important.

APPENDIX 11C: LIQUIDITY IN THE BANKING INDUSTRY

Tables 11C.1 and 11C.2 derive approximate net liquid assets to total assets ratios for all commercial banks by size range. The two tables pertain to 1985 and 1991 data to illustrate recent trends in balance sheet liquidity. One characteristic feature of these results is that liquidity ratios decrease with increasing bank size. The other striking feature is that the liquidity ratio for every bank size range has improved between 1985 and 1991.

Table 11C.1
Liquidity in the Banking Industry—1985 Data
(Values are Percentages of Total Assets)

	Under $300MM	$300MM to $5 Bn	Over $5Bn*	Ten Largest
ASSETS:				
Federal Funds Sold	5.55	5.11	3.17	3.71
Placements	2.86	4.02	7.85	7.75
Loans	54.21	59.73	62.96	62.99
Commercial	20.70	27.63	40.12	46.20
Real Estate	20.67	17.96	12.50	11.08
Consumer	12.84	14.14	10.34	5.71
Securities	27.17	18.30	9.41	4.19
Treasuries	3.82	7.95	4.06	1.94
Agencies	14.55	3.12	1.34	0.45
Munis	8.11	6.05	3.59	1.70
Other	0.69	1.18	0.42	0.10
Trading Account	0.03	0.29	1.24	3.55
Total Earning Assets	89.82	87.45	84.63	82.19
LIABILITIES:				
DDA	15.39	18.63	16.29	11.84
Interest Checking	8.02	5.35	3.10	1.47
Savings (Including MMDA)	21.05	20.70	13.09	9.76
Small CDs	31.33	18.44	10.03	4.34
Large CDs	11.63	13.58	12.26	8.21
Foreign Time	0.00	2.66	14.45	33.23
Federal Funds Purchased	1.60	8.59	13.17	7.75
Other Borrowings	0.63	2.58	5.00	6.44
Total Deposits and Borrowings	89.65	90.53	87.39	83.04

cont.

	Under $300MM	$300MM to $5 Bn	Over $5Bn*	Ten Largest
Liquid Assets	26.81	20.49	17.66	17.40
Federal Funds Sold	5.55	5.11	3.17	3.71
Placements	2.86	4.02	7.85	7.75
Treasuries and Agencies	18.37	11.07	5.40	2.39
Trading Account	0.03	0.29	1.24	3.55
Volatile Liabilities	13.23	24.83	39.88	49.19
Large CDs	11.63	13.58	12.26	8.21
Foreign CDs	0.00	2.66	14.45	33.23
Federal Funds Purchased	1.60	8.59	13.17	7.75
NET LIQUID ASSETS	13.58	−4.34	−22.22	−31.79

*Excluding 10 largest banks.

Source: "Recent Developments Affecting the Profitability and Practices of Commercial Banks." Federal Reserve Bulletin (July 1992) pp. 459-483.

Table 11C.2
Liquidity in the Banking Industry—1991 Data
(Values are Percentages of Total Assets)

	Under $300MM	$300MM to $5 Bn	Over $5Bn*	Ten Largest
ASSETS:				
Federal Funds Sold	5.52	4.65	4.59	2.80
Placements	1.53	1.80	4.28	4.13
Loans	54.22	61.09	60.89	63.03
Commercial	15.25	19.53	28.52	34.74
Real Estate	28.82	27.24	21.40	21.21
Consumer	10.15	14.32	10.97	7.08
Securities	30.03	20.82	16.17	9.23
Treasuries	9.30	5.88	3.73	1.31
Agencies	13.84	9.54	8.41	3.41
Munis	4.32	2.69	1.76	0.76
Other	2.57	2.71	2.27	3.75
Trading Account	0.06	0.56	0.94	6.02
Total Earning Assets	91.36	88.92	86.87	85.21
LIABILITIES:				
DDA	11.95	13.97	13.97	10.33
Interest Checking	11.07	8.02	5.59	2.96
Savings (Including MMDA)	19.23	20.69	17.87	13.56
Small CDs	35.39	24.92	17.73	5.78
Large CDs	10.01	10.32	11.17	6.23
Foreign Time	0.00	1.57	6.55	27.77
Federal Funds Purchased	1.33	7.26	10.24	6.57
Other Borrowings	0.52	3.04	5.42	9.88
Total Deposits and Borrowings	89.50	89.79	88.54	83.08

cont.

	Under $300MM	$300MM to $5 Bn	Over $5Bn*	Ten Largest
Liquid Assets	30.25	22.43	21.95	17.67
Federal Funds Sold	5.52	4.65	4.59	2.80
Placements	1.53	1.80	4.28	4.13
Treasuries and Agencies	23.14	15.42	12.14	4.72
Trading Account	0.06	0.56	0.94	6.02
Volatile Liabilities	11.34	19.15	27.96	40.57
Large CDs	10.01	10.32	11.17	6.23
Foreign CDs	0.00	1.57	6.55	27.77
Federal Funds Purchased	1.33	7.26	10.24	6.57
NET LIQUID ASSETS	18.91	3.28	−6.01	−22.90

*Excluding 10 largest banks.

Source: "Recent Developments Affecting the Profitability and Practices of Commercial Banks." Federal Reserve Bulletin (July 1992) pp. 459-483.

CHAPTER
12

Asset Securitization and Shareholder Value

Asset securitization began in the mid-1970s in the United States and has accounted for more than $1 trillion transactions to date. Of this sum, non-mortgage assets totaled $155 billion. In the United Kingdom, more than 12 billion pounds sterling have been securitized, and securitization in Japan will be enormously popular once that country's slow-moving financial regulators permit the concept.

In the words of one major international bank, "Securitization is good for Britain's economic health."[1] In the mind of others, securitization is a transparent accounting transaction that is nothing more than a scheme to avoid risk-based capital rules and a welfare plan for investment bankers. Which view is correct? This chapter will carefully answer that question from the same shareholder value perspective taken through this book.

12.1 ASSET SECURITIZATION: AN OVERVIEW

The rise of the securitization phenomenon in the United States is closely associated with the rise of capital ratio regulations, starting with the primary capital rules of the Federal Reserve Board in the early 1980s. The risk-based capital regulations have accelerated the trend and helped create an international interest in the process.

At this point, nine different categories of assets have been securitized:

- Residential mortgages;

- Commercial mortgages;

- Other commercial real estate loans;

- Credit card receivables;

- Commercial and industrial loans;

- Government guaranteed student loans;

- Trade receivables; and,

- Insurance policy holder loans.

---

[1] Barclays Briefing 87, "Securitization: Bridging the Gap." January, 1992.

The securitization phenomenon has helped make the economic roles of a lender very distinct and separable, particularly in the 1985-1991 period when securitization of nonmortgage assets grew most dramatically.

The first role is the origination function. The lender markets the availability of financing and physically makes the loan. The second role is that of credit analysis, evaluating the **initial** suitability of the borrower. The third role is the role of loan servicer, which is almost always performed by the original lender. The fourth role is that of credit support, the willingness to bear the risk of changes in the borrower's creditworthiness once the credit has been extended. Finally, the fifth role is that of funder, providing the ongoing financing to the borrower.

The improved "division of labor" in the performance of these roles is one of the primary benefits of securitization, in addition to the regulatory capital benefits. The following will emphasize the true economic role of each party in the transaction, as opposed to the formal legal, tax, or accounting pronouncements about which party performs which function. Without a focus on the true economic role, the shareholder value added from a transaction cannot be properly evaluated.

In marketing to potential issuers of securitized assets, investment bankers normally emphasize five points:

- The ability to "free up" regulatory and true equity capital;

- The ability to manage earnings by recognizing accounting gains associated with asset "sales";

- Asset and liability management related benefits;

- "Liquification" of assets; and

- Access to a AAA- or AA-rated funding source.

All of these advertised benefits will be focused on in this section. In analyzing the benefits, the key tax and regulatory issue in asset securitization is normally whether the assets have been "sold" for tax and regulatory capital purposes. Many types of securitization have become popular because the regulatory capital definition of a sale, for example, allows the asset to be removed from the bank's balance sheet when the issuer still bears all or most of its original risk. This distinction will be the primary focus of the following sections.

12.2 THE RISK-BASED CAPITAL RATIO IMPACT ON ORIGINATORS AND BUYERS OF SECURITIZED ASSETS

Asset securitization can be undertaken for two reasons: when there is a true economic benefit that accrues to the bank (independent of regulatory capital treatment) and when the only benefits to the transaction are the manipulation of regulatory capital treatment. The first types of benefits are easy to illustrate.

When the Bank of New England suffered heavy credit losses in 1990-1991, the ultimate bankruptcy or sale of the institution become almost inevitable. New senior management of the institution led by Lawrence Fish found it almost impossible to raise funds but needed to buy time in the hope of arranging a sale of the bank or delaying bankruptcy long enough for an improved economic climate to revive the credit quality of the bank's assets. The bank still owned a high quality credit card portfolio that, at that point, was worth more to third-party purchasers than it was to the bank itself. By selling this portfolio, the bank could stave off bankruptcy long enough to arrange the sale of the institution itself. In the language of our discussion of liquidity in Chapter 11, the bank reduced expected bankruptcy costs through the sale of assets and created (more precisely, preserved) shareholder value.

The second type of benefit has little or nothing to do with shareholder value. The primary function of many securitization transactions has been the manipulation of primary capital ratios. Perhaps the clearest example of these kind of transactions is a variation of the following "securitization" techniques:

■ The bank creates a special purpose legal entity.

■ The bank either transfers commercial loans to this legal entity or originates commercial loans on behalf of the legal entity.

■ The legal entity issues commercial paper to fund this loan portfolio.

■ Since the legal entity has effectively no capital, it can issue commercial paper only when it is backed by a letter of credit from the bank.

Under the original primary capital regulations issued by the Federal Reserve Board of Governors, banks' capital ratios were calculated including all assets (under generally accepted accounting principals) but excluding all off-balance sheet assets like letters of credit. Therefore, even this transparent scheme allowed banks to precisely manipulate their primary capital ratios.

Many securitization techniques are a more sophisticated variation on this basic theme, the "arbitrage" between regulatory capital regulations and the real world. As discussed below, such transparent transactions can have some shareholder value. More often, management mistakenly believes that achieving regulatory capital ratios through such manipulation has improved their capital position. Even more serious, management is sometimes allowed by regulators to postpone a much needed increase in true economic capital simply because regulatory capital ratios have been successfully manipulated.

This regulatory capital arbitrage advantage of securitization has become much more subtle as regulators and bankers have become more sophisticated. The ability to manipulate regulatory capital is centered around the definition of regulatory assets used in the capital calculation. If the bank can shift assets from a category where the risk-weighting ratio is 100%, for example, to a lower risk ratio category, it has improved its capital ratios. In addition, if the bank can "manufacture" earnings from capital gains on an asset sale, it achieves similar regulatory capital benefits. The most successful securitization transaction achieves true "sale" status for the asset. Regulatory, accounting, tax, and true economic definitions of a sale all revolve around one principal fact: the nature of the credit support for the securitized assets after the sale. This topic will be discussed in great detail in the following sections.

12.3 SECURITIZATION OF MORTGAGE LOANS

(Much of this section is derived from Chapter 2 of James M. Peaslee and David Z. Nirenberg, 1989.)

The mortgage loan market was the first market where securitization became a major factor, with total issuance of more than $850 billion. It is safe to say that the mortgage market provides the precedents, both structural and economic, for the securitization of other assets. There are four major categories of mortgage backed securities:

- Pass-through certificates;

- Pay-through bonds;

- Equity interests in owner trusts that issue pay-through bonds; and

- REMIC-related securities.

These structures have been created to repackage the cash flows from mortgage securities according to credit risk and maturity while minimizing the tax consequences of the repackaging.

The typical legal entity that is used as a vehicle for the issuance of pass-through certificates is the grantor trust. The grantor trust is generally not a taxable legal entity for federal tax consequences. Pay-through bonds are generally structured in such a way that there is little taxable income after the interest expense of the pay-through bonds is deducted from the income on the mortgages. The owner trust that issues the pay-through bonds is normally either a grantor trust or a partnership. The income in either case is allocated to the equity owners of the owner trust. REMICs are legally exempt from taxation. A discussion of each of the securitization structures follows.

Pass-Through Certificates

Pass-through certificates are usually issued by a trust that holds a predetermined pool of mortgages. The bank that owns these mortgages, which may be fixed or adjustable rate mortgages, transfers them to the trust and receives certificates from the trust in return. The bank or its agent then sells these certificates to the ultimate investors. In order to qualify as a trust for tax purposes, the trustee has tightly restricted powers to change the composition of the mortgages in the pool. Each certificate holder normally has a pro rata share in the pool of mortgages, for example, 1/10000. The trustee "passes through" receipts of principal and interest on the mortgages to certificate holders after deducting fees for servicing, administration, and any fees for guarantees or insurance of the pool. These guarantees can either be provided by private mortgage insurance organizations or by three well-known government-guaranteed or government-sponsored organizations:

- Government National Mortgage Association (GNMA);

- Federal Home Loan Mortgage Corporation (FHLMC); and,

- Federal National Mortgage Association (FNMA).

GNMA, a division of the Department of Housing and Urban Development, is guaranteed by the full faith and credit of the U.S. government. FHLMC ("Freddie Mac") and FNMA ("Fannie Mae") both are owned by the public, yet enjoy "quasi-governmental" status, known as "government-sponsored enterprises" (GSEs). While FHLMC and FNMA have no outright federal guarantee, a strong moral obligation to support their obligations is believed to exist.

Stripped Pass-Through Certificates

Another form of pass-through certificate is the stripped pass-through certificate. Under this type of certificate, the investor receives a different pro rata share of the principal payments and interest payments on the mortgages. The stripped certificate structure helps the sponsoring bank take advantage of differences in opinion about likely prepayment experience. The most radical classification of mortgage payments in a stripped transaction is the breakdown into principal only (PO) and interest only (IO) payments. Principal only payments are the mortgage-backed security equivalent of zero coupon bonds, but the ultimate maturity of the PO payments are dramatically affected by prepayment experience.

Senior and Subordinated Pass-Through Certificates

In the normal form of mortgage securitization, the certificates are supported by a guarantee or letter of credit from either the sponsor of a third party like GNMA, FNMA, and FHLMC. Occasionally, however, the pass-through certificates are broken into senior and subordinated classes. The senior certificate holders are protected to the extent that initial credit losses in the mortgage pool are born first by the subordinated certificate holders.

Pay-Through Bonds and Collateralized Mortgage Obligations

Pass-through bonds represent a pro rata interest in a pool of mortgages. Pay-through bonds are different in that the mortgages serve as collateral for the bonds; the bond holders have no direct ownership interest in the underlying mortgages. The mortgage payments received by the bond issuer and the bond payments themselves are usually structured to match as closely as possible however, complicated only by the uncertainty about the ultimate prepayment experience on the mortgages. The most popular form of pay-through bond is the collateralized mortgage obligation or "CMO."

The collateralized mortgage obligation is usually structured as an owner trust or special purpose corporation. The steps in the creation of a CMO are as follows:

1. The sponsor signs a trust agreement between the sponsor and the independent owner trustee.

2. The trust certificates are given to the sponsor in return for a nominal contribution of cash to the trust.

3. Mortgage collateral is transferred to the trust in return from the proceeds of the issuance of the collateralized mortgage obligations.

4. The sponsor may either keep the certificates of ownership of the trust or resell them.

5. The owner trustee pledges the mortgages as collateral to another institution acting as bond trustee on behalf of the investors in the CMOs as prescribed by the bond indenture for the CMOs.

6. The bond trustee collects the mortgages payments and makes payments to the CMO holders. Any excess is remitted to the owner trustee, who in turn pays it to the owner of the trust.

CMOs are usually divided into maturity classes and different priorities for the receipt of principal and interest. CMOs also allow for the payment of interest on a different basis (for example, interest paid on a floating rate basis tied to LIBOR) rather than the fixed rate on the underlying mortgages. CMO payments can also be made at different frequencies (quarterly instead of monthly, for example) from the underlying mortgages.

REMICs (Real Estate Mortgage Investment Conduits)

The pass-through certificate structure and the pay-through bond structure have some flaws. The grantor trust form used for pass-through certificates cannot be divided into multiple classes with various maturities. In addition, pay-through bonds cannot be structured in such a way that the mortgage payments are exactly the same as the bond payments. For these reasons, the REMIC structure was created in the Tax Reform Act of 1986. The rules regarding REMICs can be applied to a pool of mortgages according to function, rather than precise legal structure. Therefore, a REMIC can take any number of the following legal forms: a segregated pool of mortgages, state law trust, corporation, and a partnership.

The income from the assets of a REMIC is allocated to the owners of the REMIC in a pro rata way. Their interests specify the principal amount and interest payment (fixed or floating) just like a bond. There is one class of residual interests for all remaining cash flow. While these aspects of a REMIC help remedy some of the troubling aspects of pass-through certificates and pay-through bonds, REMICs are like the other financing techniques in that they can apply only to a fixed pool of mortgages.

12.4   SECURITIZATION OF OTHER ASSETS

The legal structure for mortgage securitization has a long history and is therefore very standardized. Securitization for nonmortgage assets is much less standardized, and there are many real economic differences that impact an issuing bank. Some of these include the following:

■ The charge-off rate of other assets is usually much higher and much less predictable than it is on mortgage assets.

■ The issuer himself normally bears the responsibility for determining the ongoing credit quality of securitized assets, not the trustee.

■ The issuer can and is often required to supply additional assets to the pool of securitized assets if selected assets in the pool fail to meet ongoing credit quality standards.

■ The federal government and organizations it sponsors do not normally participate in the credit enhancement of the securitized non-mortgage assets.

■ The form of credit enhancement and the identity of the institution providing credit support are keys to determining both the shareholder value of a transaction and the regulatory capital impact it has.

Excluding mortgage-related asset securitization, a total of $155.3 billion of assets have been securitized in the United States. Credit card receivables make up the largest proportion, with a 41.5% or $64.4 billion share of total securitized assets. The diagram in Figure 12.1 shows the pattern of cash flows associated with a typical credit card receivables issue. The complexity of the structure is necessary for two reasons: to achieve "sale status" for accounting and regulatory capital purposes and to avoid any adverse tax impacts on either the bank, the trust, or the holders of the participation certificates.

Auto loans and leases amounted to 38.5% or $59.8 million of the total. Home equity loans ranked third in importance, totaling $18.6 billion or 12.0% of the total. Figure 12.2 diagrams the cash flows for a typical home equity loan structure.

The remaining issuance of securitized assets consisted of manufactured housing ($5.3 billion or 3.4%), recreational vehicle loans ($1.3 billion or 0.8%), boat loans ($1.0 billion, 0.7% percent), and all other assets ($5.0 billion or 3.2%). Figure 12.3 summarizes the cumulative composition of these securitizations.

Figure 12.1

Cash Flows Associated with a Typical Credit Card Receivables Issue

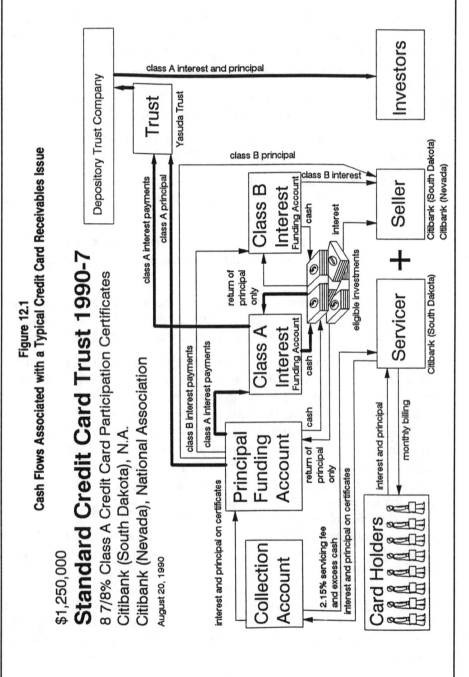

$1,250,000

Standard Credit Card Trust 1990-7

8 7/8% Class A Credit Card Participation Certificates

Citibank (South Dakota), N.A.

Citibank (Nevada), National Association

August 20, 1990

Figure 12.2
Cash Flows for a Typical Home Equity Loan Structure

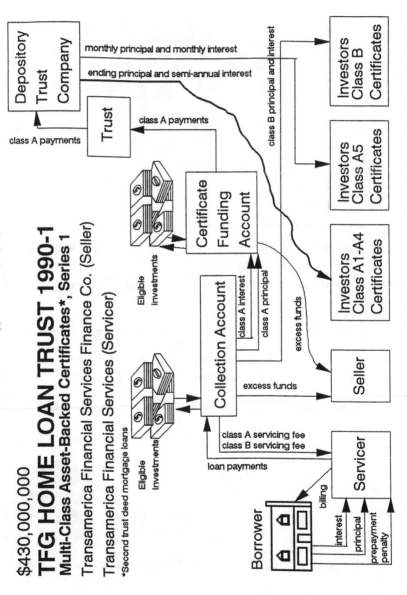

$430,000,000
TFG HOME LOAN TRUST 1990-1
Multi-Class Asset-Backed Certificates*, Series 1

Transamerica Financial Services Finance Co. (Seller)

Transamerica Financial Services (Servicer)

*Second trust deed mortgage loans

Figure 12.3
Cumulative Public Asset-Backed Securities
Issued Through December 31, 1991

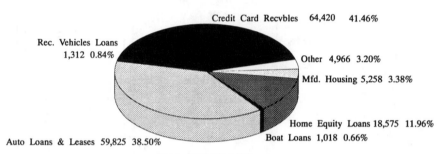

Credit Card Recvbles   64,420   41.46%

Rec. Vehicles Loans
1,312 0.84%

Other 4,966 3.20%

Mfd. Housing 5,258 3.38%

Home Equity Loans 18,575 11.96%

Auto Loans & Leases 59,825 38.50%

Boat Loans 1,018 0.66%

Total: $155,374 Million

Millions of U.S. Dollars
Source: Securities Data Company

The total amount of nonmortgage assets has skyrocketed since 1985 when total issuance was only $1.2 billion. Issuance jumped sharply to reach $42.4 billion by 1990 and $49.7 billion in 1991, as shown in Figure 12.4.

Figure 12.4
Public Asset-Backed Securities Annual Volume
Through December 31, 1991

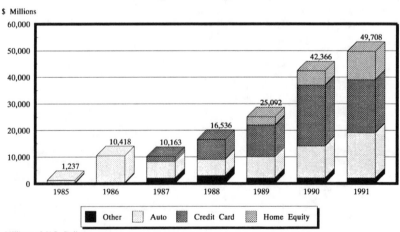

$ Millions

60,000

50,000

40,000

30,000

20,000

10,000

0

                                                                49,708
                                                   42,366
                                      25,092
                         16,536
            10,418   10,163
    1,237

1985   1986   1987   1988   1989   1990   1991

■ Other   □ Auto   ▨ Credit Card   ▨ Home Equity

Millions of U.S. Dollars
Source: Securities Data Company

In the case of mortgage securitization where credit support is GNMA or FNMA, it is very clear that securitization is an outright sale of assets from every perspective: financing, reporting, regulatory, tax, and shareholder value. The same is true when the only credit support needed to support the transaction is third-party credit support without recourse to the institution originating the assets. It is less obvious to determine from a shareholder perspective when a "sale" is a true sale if the only credit support in a securitization transaction comes from the originating bank itself. This is the subject of the next section.

12.5   SECURITIZATION AND CAPITAL RATIOS FROM A SHAREHOLDER VALUE PERSPECTIVE

Consider a situation where the bank places $100 million of its credit card receivables in a special purpose vehicle and agrees to add additional receivables whenever the cash flow on existing receivables is insufficient to meet the cash flow requirements of the $90 million in Class A certificates issued to investors by the special purpose vehicle. Assume that the bank owns the remaining $10 million in certificates, the Class B certificates. Given the structure of the transaction, the Class A certificates are rated AAA/Aaa by the major rating agencies because there is almost no chance that $100 million principal value of credit card receivables will be less than $90 million. Even then, the bank (if it is still solvent), has a legal obligation to add more receivables to the trust to ensure payment on the Class A receivables.

Let us also assume that the bank has managed to qualify this transaction as a "sale" for financial reporting and regulatory capital purposes. (*Note*: To avoid making this discussion overly detailed, we want to make clear that this is an assumption. It is not a description of what can be done under actual financial reporting and regulatory capital guidelines.) Has the bank created any value for its shareholders? If the market is not very sophisticated, it might not realize that the bank has the same credit risk it had before the securitization that it does after. The market might also not realize that the bank's regulatory capital ratios are not as good in reality as the reported numbers. Is not fooling the market sometimes good for the bank?

We think the answer to that question is no. Once management credibility is lost, it is gone forever. Especially in the area of accounting policy, the authors believe that this kind of transparent manipulation of regulatory capital numbers has only one defense. It is defensible only as the lesser of two evils. An extreme example helps to illustrate the point.

The ABC Bank has a regulatory examination on June 30. At that examination, the regulators insist that the bank make a new offering of shares by December 31 to bring its risk-based capital ratio from 7.99% to 8.25%. The regulators insist the issue take place, at the cost of $2 million in underwriting fees, or that the bank take some other action to raise its capital ratio on December 31, even though the bank has a signed, legally enforceable, irrevocable commitment from its largest shareholder to buy an equal-sized equity offering by the bank on January 2 with no underwriting fees at all.

In a case of regulatory irrationality like this, all would agree that cosmetic manipulation of regulatory capital numbers satisfies the regulators and saves $2 million in shareholder funds. Other than an extreme example like this, however, we are hard-pressed to imagine real economic benefits from regulatory capital prestidigitation. More often, such capital ratio magic generates revenue for investment bankers and lawyers and nothing at all for shareholders.

The analogous situation for installment loan securitizations commonly takes the form of an "interest reserve" requirement that is funded out of the initial cash flows of the loan portfolio. The interest reserve is truly an allowance for loan losses that can be five to ten times the expected present value of future losses. As with the "replenishment" obligation described above for credit card receivables, this interest reserve simply means that the issuing bank is providing virtually all of the credit support in this structure. Therefore, no credit risk has actually been removed from the bank!

12.6   THE IMPACT OF SECURITIZATION ON THE COST OF FUNDS

Securitization is often advertised as a "triple-A rated funding source" by investment bankers. Taken literally, there is no inaccuracy in this statement. Looking at the totality of the bank's funding costs, however, **it is often the case that a securitized transaction has no net impact on the bank's total cost of funds.** How can this possibly be true? A simple example will suffice.

Let us say, for example, the ABC Bank has decided to do an issue of securitized credit card receivables using the structure outlined in Section 12.5, a typical credit card receivables structure. The bank sells the assets via a special purpose vehicle called ABC Credit Card Trust. In reality, ABC Credit Card Trust will be backed totally by overcollateralization and the irrevocable legal obligation of the bank to provide additional receivables to the trust, if the receivables currently in the trust do not provide enough cash flow to meet the principal and interest the trust is obligated to pay on the Class A certificates issued by the trust. While this legal obligation may not be formally called a letter of credit, it has an identical economic meaning. The bank itself will hold the Class B certificates issued by the trust, the class of liabilities that are effectively subordinated to the Class A certificates. How are the debt holders of ABC Bank affected?

Consider the South Pacific Asset Management Company ("SPAMCO"). SPAMCO held 10% of ABC Bank's deposits before the securitization, a total of $95. As a result of the securitization of assets, ABC Bank will pay down $90 in deposits, including $9 in deposits held by SPAMCO. Because of SPAMCO's close relationship with ABC Bank, SPAMCO agrees to buy 10% of the Class A certificates issued by ABC Credit Card Trust (for $9). Table 12.1 outlines the ABC Bank balance sheet before and after securitization.

How is SPAMCO affected by the securitization of ABC Bank assets? On one hand, ABC Bank's investment bankers have told ABC and SPAMCO that the new CARDS issue is rated AAA/Aaa because $90 of Class A certificates are backed by $100 in credit card receivables and a legal obligation of ABC Bank to provide more collateral if $100 is not enough for the trust to meet its obligations on the Class A certificates. From SPAMCO's point of view, however, it still owns 10% of the ultimate liabilities of ABC Bank and its indirect liabilities issued by ABC Credit Card Trust. **In reality, nothing has changed!!**

Why? Before, deposits were backed by credit card receivables at a ratio of $1,000 of receivables to $950 in deposits, a ratio of 1.0526 to 1. After securitization, $860 in deposits are backed by $900 in credit card receivables, a ratio of 1.0465 to one. Therefore, the remaining receivables have a higher risk and higher cost. SPAMCO, a depositor and an investor in the Class A certificates, has the same risk and same return as before. The bank has the same liability cost in aggregate that it had before also, so it has gained absolutely nothing from the transaction.

This result should not be surprising to anyone who has been a student of finance at any time since 1958. That is the year that Modigliani and Miller published their famous "M&M Theorem." Modigliani and Miller demonstrated that there is a financial equivalent of the "no free lunch" when it comes to financial structure. The degree of financial leverage, or any variations in the form of financing, will not reduce aggregate financ-

---

Table 12.1
Effect of Securitization on Overall Funding Costs

ABC Bank Balance Sheet Before Securitization

Credit Card Receivables	1000
Deposits	950
Shareholders' Equity	50
Total Liabilities and Shareholders' Equity	1000

ABC Bank Balance Sheet After Securitization

Credit Card Receivables	900
Class B Certificates Issued by ABC Credit Card Trust	10
Total Assets	910
Deposits	860
Shareholders' Equity	50
Total Liabilities and Shareholders' Equity	910

Off-Balance Sheet Exposure

Effective Guarantee of Class A Certificates Issued by ABC Credit Card Trust	90

ABC Credit Card Trust, A Special Purpose Vehicle

Credit Card Receivables "Purchased" from ABC Bank	100
Class A Certificates Held by Investors	90
Class B Certificates Held by ABC Bank	10
Total Liabilities	100

---

ing costs except in special circumstances. In the more than 30 years since the original M&M article was published, these special circumstances are well understood. Increasing leverage can affect total borrowing costs only if there is some unhedgable benefit or cost that accrues to investors. The two most common factors that have an impact are the deductibility of interest payments for tax purposes (a benefit of leverage) and the costs of bankruptcy (a cost of leverage).

None of these factors apply in this case unless we think about the costs of bankruptcy, a factor discussed in Section 12.8. Therefore, any benefit from the collateralization of one class of liabilities is exactly offset by the higher financing costs that will result from the lower implied collateralization of the remaining asset classes. Unless there is third party credit support for a securitized transaction, there will not be any decrease in the cost of funds for the issuing bank. Even in the case of third party credit support, any potential benefit obviously depends on the price charged for the credit support.

12.7   THE COSTS AND THE PROCESS OF SECURITIZATION

Up to this point, most of the chapter has discussed the true benefits of a securitization transaction. To have the complete picture, you need to also consider the costs of a securitization. Costs can be broken down into the categories described in Table 12.2.

Table 12.2
Categories of Costs Associated with Asset Securitizations

Costs of management time at time of issuance

Costs of management time for monitoring of issuance

Legal costs

Accounting costs

Underwriting and other investment banking fees

Trustee fees

Cost of credit support

Cost of printing

Cost of external systems for pool selection and screening

Excluding underwriting fees, which vary by issuer and the nature of the securities offered, the remaining fees can easily exceed $500,000 per issue. First time issuers can expect underwriting fees of 25 basis points or more on outstandings. To some extent, as a percentage of the dollar amount of securities offered, costs will drop as the issue size increases and as an individual issuer continues to do similar financings.

The systems aspect of securitization is a potential stumbling block that has kept many an issuer from proceeding down the road toward securitization. Screening existing loan portfolios for assets suitable for securitization can be a routine task for banks that have succeeded in implementing sophisticated database management systems. For those who have not, however, it may take three to six months of internal work to access existing systems in the fashion needed to select and monitor a portfolio for securitization. In order to cut the time needed to achieve this task, several firms offer software products designed to link with existing systems to provide the necessary analysis and reporting. These systems generally cost $150,000 or more to purchase and install.

Another cost of securitization is more subtle. There are dramatic differences in funding from one legal entity with general obligations of that legal entity and in funding from one entity fragmented into many smaller legal entities, each of which is supported by assets pledged against liabilities of the individual legal entities. Clearly, it is much more likely that bankruptcy of some sort will occur if a large organization is effectively broken down into many smaller entities. This makes it more likely that shareholders will suffer the costs of bankruptcy, increasing the costs of securitization. There are clearly limits to the maximum degree of securitization than an individual institution can undertake.

12.8 SHAREHOLDER VALUE AND SECURITIZATION: A SUMMARY

We believe that a shareholder value perspective on securitization is very important, because there are have been so many misunderstandings about securitization. It is no accident that only seven institutions account for 82% of credit card securitization transactions, only seven issuers did 72% of all home equity loan securitization, and only six institutions account for 70% of auto loan securitization transactions. In some cases, securitization makes a lot of sense, and in others it makes none at all. The pros and cons of securitization can be summarized very simply:

- Securitization reduces assets in an accounting sense and therefore reduces regulatory capital ratios.

- When securitization produces a "sale" according to generally accepted accounting principals, the issuer may recognize a gain for financial reporting purposes.

- This fact by itself has no shareholder benefit except to forestall some hypothetical irrational act by regulators that is hinged on regulatory capital ratios or to postpone bankruptcy in the hope that rising asset values will rescue an institution that will otherwise soon go under.

- Assets are truly "sold" only when the true credit support for the special purpose vehicle used in securitization is provided by a third party. In a third party case, benefits to the seller depend on the nature and the cost of credit support.

- When there is no third party credit support (or when there is not an outright asset sale with no recourse to the seller), securitization does not lower the cost of funds to the issuing entity overall, even if the securitized issue has a better credit rating than the bank itself. The reason is the resulting increase in the cost of the remaining funds raised by the institution.

- Even if there are benefits to securitization, the costs of issuance are much higher than a normal debt financing.

For a few institutions, there is shareholder value in securitization—but the number is very few, as issuance statistics show. For the vast majority of institutions, shareholders would be better served if fundraising takes the form of traditional debt and deposit issues.

CHAPTER 13

Profitability Measurement

All of the topics presented until now pertain to asset and liability management issues as they are applied from the "top down." Indeed, it is our strong conviction that ALM activities are optimally assessed and managed at the level of the total bank or the consolidated multibank holding company. This allows for natural diversification and hedging effects, and it is consistent with a true shareholder perspective.

This view notwithstanding, there is also a legitimate need to understand the risk and shareholder value attributes of individual line departments and products. After all, this is the only way to understand why the organization is performing the way it is. This chapter and Chapter 14 present those principles that should be observed in dissecting the financial performance of the total bank. We will continue to be guided by the shareholder value and economic risk concepts presented throughout this book. However, we will now apply them to the realms of unit, product, and customer relationship profitability.

The authors have had the opportunity to observe several large banking companies attempt to implement profitability systems of various levels of sophistication and complexity. In the vast majority of cases, line managers developed either hostility or frustration with the results. Too often, the reports are used as "weapons" to "beat up" on certain units. It is only human nature that managers seek out erroneous assumptions or suspicious concepts to cite as defense mechanisms. "The system is flawed." "There are unjust allocations." "We are being hit with variances over which we have no control." These and a multitude of other rationalizations become the order of the day. In extreme cases, we have seen CEOs impose outright bans on ever mentioning cost accounting or transfer pricing in "their" banks.

Our attitude is that profitability measurement (as with any type of ALM analysis) should never be the final objective used to make summary judgments about line units or products. They are tools that should be employed to improve the bank's general understanding about its profitability and risk characteristics. They should raise constructive debate and discussion, rather than be used to plant land mines or booby traps.

In our opinion, a well-founded profitability system is essential to understanding why the organization performs the way it does. It can provide valuable guidance on performance measurement, product pricing, marketing strategies, customer segmentation, and goal-setting. In virtually all circumstances, the acceptance of the system will be a direct function of the commitment of senior management, and especially the CEO, to developing a fair system, as well as the observance of the principles outlined in this and the next chapter. In this spirit, we proceed.

13.1 GUIDING PRINCIPLES

We repeat our general caveat: We are not claiming that the approaches described in this and the next chapter are the only correct ones. We will present the general features that we have found to work best in our organizations. Our hope is that a full discussion of our experience will prove helpful for those attempting to deal with similar situations.

There are four critical principles upon which we have consistently relied when difficult issues or tradeoffs are encountered: shareholder value orientation; 80/20 rule; consistency across unit, product, and customer profitability measures; and variances derived only from unit's own actions. They have continuously provided solid guidance to our banks.

Shareholder value orientation. As described in earlier chapters, the shareholder value added (SVA) concept is the cornerstone of the profitability systems we have built. Indeed, it is quite practical to measure SVA for individual units or departments, for single products, and for customer relationships. Essentially all of the financial risk concepts presented in earlier chapters are distilled and incorporated in what will be described. To be sure, many shortcuts, simplifications, and approximations are included, but the spirit and integrity of SVA is well protected.

80/20 rule. Invoking a materiality concept in building such a system has helped to avoid endless controversy and nit-picking. All too many banks have succumbed to the temptation of comprehensiveness or exactness, only to find that they have spent significantly more time, money, and systems resources than they had anticipated, and that they have opened Pandora's box in terms of criticisms and complaints. As previously stated, we do not believe that the system should ever be used to make summary judgments about the "true" or "exact" bottom line of any unit or product. As such, precision is not the issue, but accuracy is. We have found that the relative performance rankings of units and products are rarely, if ever, swayed by extending cost allocations to the final penny. Getting generally in the right ballpark is good enough, and that we can do without time and motion studies, stopwatches, or monster mainframe databases. To emphasize this principle, many find it surprising to learn that the entire system we have used can be run on one microcomputer! The advantage this gives is that without truckloads of detailed allocations, the degree of contentiousness drops. We only make allocations or risk adjustments that will have a material effect on the ultimate **relative** SVA rankings. Moreover, the relative values obtained generally cover a very broad spectrum from terrific to horrible SVAs that are so different, it is obvious that further refinements will have little or no impact on identifying high and poor performers. This principle will be invoked repeatedly in the remainder of this and the next chapter.

Consistency across unit, product, and customer profitability measures.
Many banks have built separate unit, product, and/or customer profitability analytical systems. (These may not be full blown mainframe systems. They may simply be microcomputer spreadsheet analyses.) A common problem in such cases is the use of inconsistent allocations, assumptions, or transfer rates, such that it is impossible to reconcile the results in one system to those of another. This problem can best be addressed by tackling it at the very earliest design stage of such systems. Unless this is raised and heeded up front, it is often very expensive and time-consuming to go back and fix later. (This is true of most systems development projects.) We will explain how such consistency is maintained as topics are raised.

Variances derived only from unit's own actions. Profitability variances can hypothetically arise for any number of reasons: from a unit pricing differently than bank standards to the CEO traveling more than budgeted. To minimize the "unfairness" aspect of the measurements, we have guaranteed that the profitability variances in our system can only arise from actions under the direct control of the line unit or its management. Basically, no allocation variances will be allowed. This implies guaranteeing overhead allocation rates as well as product transfer pricing spreads. Surprisingly, this does not create much of a distortion. It has the benefit that overhead unit variances stay within overhead units and are not allocated out to the line units.

13.2   COMPONENTS OF THE PROFITABILITY SYSTEM

There are five basic components or modules of the profitability system. They are summarized in Table 13.1.

For each item listed in this table, we will always attempt to maximize compatibility with the shareholder value added concept, rather than with GAAP or regulatory standards. There are many details that will be altered from conventional practices to achieve this. Note that in the listing, several of the "items" are addressed for the sake of "risk-adjusting" a unit's or a product's returns. These include the transfer pricing, credit allocations, and capital allocations.

Table 13.1
Components of a Profitability System

Component	Item(s) Addressed
Budgets	Direct Revenues and Expenses
	Origination Volumes or Counts
	Retention (or Account Closure) Rates
Cost Allocations	Overhead and Product Support Costs
	Centrally Managed Costs (e.g., Facilities)
Funds Transfer Pricing	Net Interest Income
Credit Allocations	Loss Provisions
	Allowance for Credit Losses
Capital Allocations	Economic Capital

We emphasize that to implement the SVA measure, it is essential that all of the components and items listed in Table 13.1 be addressed. As each is described in the following sections, we hope that readers will come to accept that this can be accomplished with a modest, yet reasonable amount of effort through the judicious application of the 80/20 rule.

13.3 BUDGETING, ALM, AND SHAREHOLDER VALUE

Virtually all banks conduct some type of budgeting exercise. Budgets are usually built on a "most likely" set of business environment assumptions. Therefore, the ALCO or senior management team must stipulate budgeting assumptions about such items as interest rates for the coming year, growth in personal income, and housing starts and sales in the bank's market areas. Clearly, these assumptions should be consistent with those being used by the asset and liability management staff in analyzing the bank's overall ALM risk profiles. In rare cases, units are asked to budget based on some type of alternative set of assumptions to give the organization some feel for the sensitivity of its product originations and revenues to business conditions. Again, such alternative business assumptions should be consistent with the alternatives being analyzed by the ALM department to ensure that the "bottom-up" values generated in the budgeting process are consistent with the "top-down" forecasts being used by the ALCO.

We have generally sought to bring conventional budget activities more in line with SVA calculations and the guiding principles from Section 13.1 by removing any items not directly managed or controlled by the unit or its direct management. Fortunately, this usually means that the budgeting process is somewhat simplified and less onerous, especially for line unit managers. This includes removing any items that are centrally managed or controlled, such as facilities expense, benefits expense, and FDIC insurance premiums, from line units. It also includes removing any accounting deferrals, accretions, or amortizations, such as for FAS #91 loan fee and origination expense deferrals and amortizations, or amortizations of core deposit intangibles or goodwill.

These concepts are all budgeted, booked, and controlled centrally on a bank-wide basis. Facilities are usually managed by a Corporate Facilities unit, benefits by Human Resources, and FAS #91 or intangibles in a reconciling unit in the Controller's Department.

Our attitude about possibly removing the effects of purchase premiums and discounts is governed by the principle that only variances resulting from a unit's own decisions should stay with a unit. That is, if a unit is free to make its own decisions on purchasing assets at a premium or discount, then the amortizations of those items should stay with the unit. A good example is the investment portfolio, where portfolio managers routinely purchase securities at premiums or discounts. Similarly, if a loan servicing manager has discretion for purchasing and/or selling servicing rights and is free to negotiate the premium paid or received, then the amortization of the premium and gains on sales should be budgeted in and charged to that unit. However, if a loan servicing unit has no control over such decisions, then that unit should only be expected to budget and to be held accountable for its directly controlled operating expenses for a pre-specified, assumed level of account servicing volume.

Basically, the theme here is to ask unit managers only to budget and be held accountable for revenues and expenses that they directly manage and control. But, what about the balance sheet ramifications of their activities? How do we ask managers to budget and be held accountable for demand deposit balances or mortgage loan balances? The short answer is, we do not.

Line managers can and should only be held accountable for the numbers of new accounts originated, and, to a lesser extent, the numbers of deposit accounts closed or lost. The implication of this for the budgeting process is that they should not be asked to forecast portfolio volumes, but only the numbers of new accounts and, perhaps, closed accounts. Of course, there are some important refinements that should be incorporated, depending on the bank's marketing strategy. For example, if the bank is pursuing a retail relationship building strategy, then the numbers of households with more than three accounts may be an additional critical budgeting parameter.

Our fundamental point here is that branch and other line managers do control new accounts and, to a lesser extent, account closings. They cannot, however, be held accountable for the usage or balance levels of the accounts for transactions accounts or revolving lines of credit. Having them attempt to forecast their average portfolio balances will not be of any value to the bank as a whole. Portfolio balances are much more accurately and productively handled at the top-down or total bank level using portfolio totals from the profitability system and simulation models.

What about control over pricing? For fees and service charges, both of which are normal budget categories, managers have control and should be accountable. For rates and yields, managers oftentimes have limited control. This specific topic will be covered in Chapter 14 on "Transfer Pricing."

13.4   COST ALLOCATIONS

Cost accounting and transfer pricing have developed reputations almost as bad as duration. As with duration, we believe these to be "bum raps." Profitability measurement is impossible without all of the allocation and transfer pricing components presented back in Table 13.1.

As pointed out, some of this ill will is attributable to bad design or poor implementation. One common fault, in our humble opinions, is that banks try to get too detailed and too precise in their cost accounting activities. If perfection is sought, we can almost guarantee that the organization will regret it ever made the attempt. Here is where the 80/20 or materiality rule has the greatest benefit. We claim that precision is not necessary. If only significant items are allocated, then controversies tend to be far fewer in number and less contentious in degree. Therefore, we stipulate that a cost transfer should constitute greater than 3% of a unit's overall expenses before it will be recognized. (This threshold may vary from one bank to another.) This avoids such questionable practices as tracking how many telephone referrals were made from one department to another. It also allows the use of a PC-based cost allocation system.

This brings us to another important point about cost transfers. Many banks have opted to conduct such allocations in their mainframe general ledger systems. While we are not claiming that it is unwise to do this, we find that nine times out of ten, there are two predictable outcomes. First, the level of detail goes far beyond any reasonable application of the 80/20 rule. Thus, the amount of (immaterial) controversy and the staff expense associated with cost studies is very high. Second, such banks seem never to get beyond the cost accounting component of their profitability systems. That is, they cannot seem to figure out how to achieve transfer pricing and capital allocation results that are compatible with the level of detail they generate with their G/L cost allocations.

Another major problem with the general ledger approach is that it is straightforward to design for unit profitability measurement because the responsibility center (RC) hierarchy is usually reflected in the overall G/L system. Unfortunately, G/Ls are far from optimal to use for product or customer profitability purposes. This point will be considered further in the next section as we describe the strategy we have employed to maintain consistency across profitability dimensions.

13.5   A COST ALLOCATION STRATEGY

To achieve consistency in all three dimensions (unit, product, and customer relationship), it is essential that a lowest common denominator be identified that can be utilized in building up the cost transfers for all of the three measures. We generally choose some type of activity count—such as numbers of accounts—as that commonality concept. Therefore, we must allocate all costs to each product category on a "per activity count," or "standard unit cost," basis. The basic strategy is diagramed in Figure 13.1 and is described in the following paragraphs. For ease of presentation, we will only present the simplest set of procedures. Please be mindful that for actual situations, some additional complications must be addressed. For those versed in management or cost accounting, we recommend a single pass, full absorption approach. (However, reports will separate direct expenses from support and overhead allocations, so that direct and contribution margins can be determined.)

Designation of units. Every unit (or RC) in the bank must be categorized into one of three types: line, product support, or overhead. Some probable assignments are listed in Table 13.2.

Figure 13.1
Cost Allocations

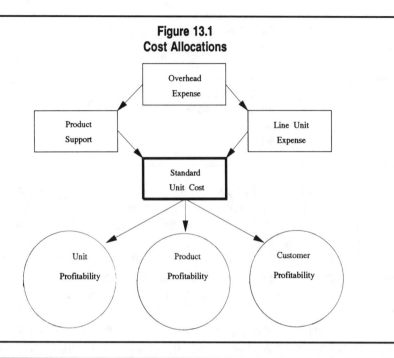

Table 13.2
Sample Unit Cost Category Assignments

Line

Retail Branch Group
Commercial Lending
Mortgage Originations
Cash Management
Trust
Mortgage Loan Servicing
Investment Sales
Insurance Sales
Investment (and Mortgage) Portfolio
ALCO/Treasury Unit (Interest Rate Mismatches)

Product Support

Item Processing
Teleservices (Balance Inquiry, Transfers, etc.)
Consumer Loan Servicing
Data Processing
Credit Administration
Marketing
Compliance

cont.

	Retail Administration
	Corporate Banking Administration
Overhead	Office of the CEO
	Controller's Department
	Human Resources
	Legal
	Audit

Line units are those that conduct origination or sales transactions with customers, or those that manage risky portfolios, such as the investment portfolio, or the ALCO or Treasury unit that houses the bank's interest rate mismatches (as will be described in Chapter 14 on "Transfer Pricing").

Product support units provide direct operational or back office support for certain products or services. Overhead units are those that provide general administrative services across a broad spectrum of units or departments.

Probably every reader of this book will have some debate about the classifications shown in Table 13.2. Is compliance a support or overhead unit? How about marketing or data processing? An interesting case is mortgage loan servicing. Some banks and thrifts buy and sell mortgage servicing rights and administer that area as a profit center. In such an instance, it probably should be considered a line unit. There are other circumstances where it only services in-house originated loans and none "for others." In this situation, it is better classified as a product support function.

Designation of Product Groups

Another prerequisite for generating standard unit costs is to designate the product groupings that will determine the level of product detail the system handles. In our experience, the use of from 30 to 50 product groups works well for a full service bank. Going to hundreds of products, as some banks have done, becomes cumbersome and conceptually impossible for most managers to grasp when they are asked to allocate their expenses across all products. Once again, the spirit of the 80/20 rule is at work!

We emphasize here that product groups are not limited to those items that appear on a bank's balance sheet. There are numerous services and activities sold by the bank that are not displayed in its footings. Among these are trust services; cash management services, such as lockbox, reconcilement, and payroll; sales of securities, annuities, and mutual funds; discount brokerage; savings bonds, cashier's checks, and safety deposit boxes; wire transfer; and contract collections. These are important business activities that should definitely find their way into any profitability system.

Special caution should be exercised for certain categories. For example, some banks and thrifts view their mortgage activities separately for originations, servicing, portfolio management, and loan sales. A variation on this approach defines "mortgage banking" as incorporating loan originations and secondary marketing activities (pooling, securitizing, and sales). Suppose a bank defines three product groups: mortgage banking, mortgage servicing, and mortgage portfolio management, where portfolio management refers to managing the balances that remain on the bank's balance sheet, usually by an ALCO or Treasury unit. Tremendous confusion will result if these "products" are not carefully defined when the cost surveys are conducted so that the data processing manager, marketing manager, and credit administration manager all understand the distinctions between them. Their tendency will be automatically to allocate any time related to mortgages in any way to the mortgage portfolio category.

Allocation of Budgeted Overhead Costs

The first set of allocations will be from the overhead units to all product support and line units. The values used should be budgeted dollars, not actual expenses! This is in keeping with our "only directly managed variances" principle. Any actual-to-budget expense variances for the overhead units should remain in the profitability reports with those units and not allocated across to the line units. The spirit of this approach is that line units do have input as to general overhead expense levels during the budget preparation and negotiation process, but not once the budgets are finalized and actuals start to flow.

Overhead expense is usually allocated based on some type of simple "generic" concept, such as full-time equivalent employees (FTE) or salary dollars. More specific allocations are usually based on percentage of time spent supporting specific groups or divisions. These more specific allocations should be researched and undertaken only if they are materially different from the generic method. (The 80/20 rule strikes again!)

Another form of "overhead" category in our system is facilities expense. As discussed in Chapter 2, the "ideal" handling of facilities expense would be to impute a current market lease rate on every branch or office building location. This would be a lot of work! Many banks simply allocate actual lease or depreciation amounts from their fixed-asset systems.

However, it is conceivable that some owned facilities may be fully depreciated, or that certain leases are at extremely advantageous rates compared to more recent leases. We suggest that one alternative is to create a handful (no more than five) of facilities categories, and to charge a standard per square foot all-in facilities rate for each category that would include utilities and leasehold improvements. Even simpler, charge a single bank-wide facilities rate per square foot, and recognize that some market "opportunity cost" distinctions are not being reflected.

Product Support Cost Allocations

After overhead costs are fully distributed among the line and product support units, the next step is to distribute product support expenses (including those overhead costs allocated to the product support areas). This is done on the basis of product surveys, where each product support unit manager is asked to allocate his or her total expenses on a percentage basis among the official list of product groups. This is usually in the range of 30 to 50 product categories for a full service bank. It is important to stress that in filling out the surveys, a long-term, or normalized, activity distribution should be reflected. Managers will have a tendency to overburden activity areas that have been commanding their recent attention due to special priorities or problems.

Also, product support managers should ignore any time they spend supporting overhead units. After all, if data processing gives a 10% allocation to the controller's department for general ledger support, controller's would have to turn around and redistribute those costs right back out to all other units, creating a series of simultaneous equations (for the mathematical reader) or multiple allocation passes (for hard-core cost accountants). As offensive as this may sound to the proponents of exactitude, we cite simultaneous equations and multiple passes to be violations of the 80/20 rule. Each bank should determine if this simplification causes a material error and deal with it appropriately.

For each product group, one activity basis is selected. This is most simply either numbers of accounts or balances outstanding. Total allocated product support and overhead expenses are then divided by the activity basis for the total bank to determine the "standard unit product support and overhead costs."

As discussed for the overhead allocations, only budgeted standard unit costs are used to determine the total product support allocation to a line unit. The budgeted standard cost is multiplied by the actual activity level of each product group to determine the total amount transferred to each line unit.

At this point, it is appropriate to ask: What about scale economies that should work to lower the standard unit cost factor? Again, we invoke the 80/20 rule. We presume that fairly reliable activity levels for every product group were estimated during the budgeting process, such that the standard unit cost factors based on budgeted product support expenses and budgeted activity levels are accurate enough. Nevertheless, many line managers, who always seem to be very optimistic about their production capabilities, will argue that if they were significantly to exceed their production targets, they should see a benefit in a lower standard unit product support cost factor.

Our attitude is that banks can only staff up for increased volumes and achieve scale economies if line units are willing to commit to those higher production amounts early on, such as during the budget process. Unexpected, or surprisingly large, positive variances to budgeted production targets usually do not create significant scale economies in the short run. (We assume here that there is no significant amount of unused capacity.) On the contrary, support areas must respond by staffing up quickly and incurring overtime, unexpected training costs, and managing through difficult quality and integrity challenges due to staff being constantly overburdened. It takes time to realize scale economies. Therefore, our reasoning is that it is usually unrealistic to expect instantaneous declines in standard unit costs. However, benefits should start appearing for sustainable increases in production during the next budget cycle. (*Translation*: If line units truly expect to overachieve their budget targets, they should commit to higher targets at the time the budgets are being created so that they can get the benefit of lower per unit support costs.)

Line Unit Expense Allocations

The last section described the generation of standard unit support costs. This section will address generating standard unit direct costs. The process is similar in concept to the previous discussion; however, for direct costs, actual expenses will be used rather than budgets, since line unit managers do control their direct expenses.

As above, line unit managers will be given the same expense surveys used for the product support surveys. They will be asked to allocate their unit's time spent on a "normalized" percentage basis across the spectrum of product groups. The most difficulty is often encountered with the retail branches, since they offer a wide array of products, and good historical information is usually not available to provide guidance. In our experience, retail senior management will want to shield their branches from the "distraction" of filling out such surveys. They will suggest that one of their administrative staff handle the survey input. However, we feel that unless line managers see and think about the surveys, much of the "mystery" of the system will linger and impede its acceptance. It is our conviction that the more "open" and accessible the system is for line managers, the easier it will be for them to air their concerns and understand its logic and structure.

The total actual line expense allocations to each product group should then be divided by the actual activity level to generate the standard unit direct cost factors. These can then be applied to the actual activity level within each branch to generate a standardized expense base against which to compare each branch's actual expense level. In a sense, we have created a direct expense model where the independent variables are the product activity levels, and the coefficients are the standard unit direct cost factors.

Cost Allocation Summary

This concludes our brief discourse on cost allocations. Many experienced cost accountants will react with a resounding, "Is that all?" Our answer is an equally resounding, "In principle, YES." Exactness, it is not. Neither does it require a staff of 20 professionals doing endless cost analyses.

Our attitude notwithstanding, we are not trying to be dogmatic about this. The system could certainly be refined if a material difference would ensue in the final performance calculations for any units or products. Nevertheless, we firmly believe that mainframe or general ledger level detail is not only excessive, it is counterproductive to the spirit and intent of practical, "let's just get in the right ballpark" profitability measurement.

A detailed case study example using the strategy presented in this section may be found in Appendix 13A.

13.6   INTERNAL FUNDS TRANSFER PRICING

An entire chapter will be devoted to this critical subject of internal funds transfer pricing (Chapter 14). For now, we will present only the most basic intentions and features of this critical activity.

The objective is to find a "risk-adjusted" net interest income value for every unit, product, or customer relationship. As with the cost allocation component, the lowest common denominator for all dimensions is the unit of product activity based on balances outstanding, usually expressed as a net transfer spread in percentage terms. This ensures the principle of consistency across all measurement dimensions.

The methodology adopted here is an extension of the coterminous, or matched-maturity, concept. It attempts to incorporate rate reset, final maturity, amortization, prepayment, and spread or basis risk dimensions. Recall that to measure shareholder value, it is important that results are fully risk-adjusted. As will be discussed fully in Chapter 14, there are many risk types that are overlooked in standard transfer pricing systems.

To maintain consistency with the other overall principles expressed early in this chapter, we guarantee every "generic" product a predetermined, fixed spread for an entire budget year. By generic, we are referring to the bank-wide average spread for products for which there is a "normal" or routine pricing strategy. We exclude large transactions (such as large commercial loan takedowns, purchases of investment securities, or issuances of large blocks of debt over $500,000), whose characteristics such as term and rate index are often very sensitive functions of current market or yield curve conditions. Large transactions are given "up-to-the-minute" transfer price quotes.

Guaranteed spreads are applicable more for retail or consumer activities, or for other aggregate portfolios of smaller account or transaction sizes. The net spread used in any particular year reflects a four-year moving average calculation that includes the prior three years of actual spread history and one year of forecasted spread. This smoothing serves to decrease the year-to-year volatility of the spreads used. Our attitude is that the bank should be kept "whole" over long-term rate cycles using this approach. However, it does complicate the reconciliation process in comparing the total bank actuals to the summation of the line units or product groups.

We have found that using these guaranteed spreads increases the "palatability" of the system, especially for the consumer-oriented line units. It is an essential concept if the principle of no unmanaged variances is to be achieved.

13.7   CREDIT ALLOCATIONS

These allocations refer to the income statement provision for credit losses as well as the balance sheet allowance for credit losses. The recommended approaches have absolutely nothing to do with BIS or risk-based capital standards!

In keeping with the shareholder value concepts of Chapter 2, both the allowance estimate and the provision allocation should reflect actual net chargeoff experience and future loss expectations. We have chosen to base these estimates around the bank's internal credit grading system for those loan products where such grading is usually conducted. For others, mainly the consumer or mortgage loans, the overall portfolio experience for each product is used.

Credit-Graded Loans

This category generally includes commercial, foreign, construction, and income property loans. Ideally, the bank has maintained a database of historical grade changes and chargeoffs for its loan portfolio. With such a database, it is possible, using a technique known as Markov chain analysis, to determine migration patterns and the ultimate loss expectations for each grade category and each product type. These patterns can then be used to estimate the present value of expected losses for each grade.

Unfortunately, to our knowledge, it is a rare bank that has such a database, although many institutions are in the process of creating such a resource. A common alternative is to work with the credit administration area to estimate such loss factors, perhaps by examining a sampling of the loan files. It is important that the loss factors be consistent with the bank's actual total chargeoff experience over the past several years when they are applied to the bank-wide totals of loan balances within each grade. These loss factors should then be applied to the balances within each grade for every product group in each line unit to determine the required allowance for credit losses. This takes care of the balance sheet credit allocation.

The provision for credit losses will be the sum of two concepts: actual net chargeoffs for the prior period and the amount needed to adjust for any change in the required allowance level. By this approach, units must recognize their actual losses and must also account for any degradation or improvement in the credit quality of their ongoing loan portfolio. On first hearing about this approach, some bankers complain that there is some sort of double counting involved here in that the allowance is supposed to absorb chargeoffs. They ask why a unit should be assessed a provision expense both at the time of booking a loan (in terms of creating an allowance equal to the present value of all future losses) and apparently a second time at the time of chargeoff. (This seems to be a common complaint of many bank executives during their regulatory "safety and soundness" examinations, too.)

Our view is that there is no double counting, at least not in the profitability system. Consider a simple situation where there are only two loan grades, 1 and 2, with the characteristics summarized in Table 13.3. We will consider four different situations.

Table 13.3
Example Annual Provision Calculations

	Grade 1	Grade 2	Total
Assumptions:			
Expected PV of Losses:	1.00%	2.00%	
Annual Chargeoff Rate:	0.30%	0.75%	
Starting Loan Balances:	1,000	1,000	2,000
Starting Allowance:	10.0	20.0	30.0
Situation 1: No Shift in Portfolio Quality			
Ending Loan Balances:	1,000	1,000	2,000
Ending Allowance:	10.0	20.0	30.0
Provision Calculation:			
Due to Allowance Change:	0.00	0.00	0.00
Due to Chargeoffs:	3.00	7.50	10.50
Total Provision:	3.00	7.50	10.50
Situation 2: Shift to Lower Portfolio Quality			
Ending Loan Balances:	800	1,200	2,000
Ending Allowance:	8.0	24.0	32.0
Provision Calculation:			
Due to Allowance Change:	−2.00	4.00	2.00
Due to Chargeoffs:	2.70	8.25	10.95
Total Provision:	0.7	12.25	12.95
Situation 3: Shift to Higher Portfolio Quality			
Ending Loan Balances:	1,200	800	2,000
Ending Allowance:	12.0	16.0	28.0
Provision Calculation:			
Due to Allowance Change:	2.00	−4.00	−2.00
Due to Chargeoffs:	3.30	6.75	10.05
Total Provision:	5.30	2.75	8.05
			cont.

Situation 4: No Shift in Quality; Liquidating Portfolio

Ending Loan Balances:	700	700	1,400
Ending Allowance:	7.0	14.0	21.0
Provision Calculation:			
Due to Allowance Change:	–3.00	–6.00	–9.00
Due to Chargeoffs:	2.55	6.38	8.93
Total Provision:	0.45	–0.38	–0.07

Note: The annual chargeoff rate is multiplied by the average balance in each grade category. The average balance is assumed to be the average of the beginning and ending loan balances.

In Situation 1, there is no change in the outstandings for either grade. This is not to say that nothing happened. It is fair to assume that there were chargeoffs, maturities, new originations, and rollovers. It happens that this represents a "steady state" condition where maturities and write-downs are exactly offset by the new originations and rollovers. As such, it is important that the beginning allowance level be maintained by a provision amount equal to the aggregate chargeoffs of $10.50. But, this is not a double counting.

The beginning allowance may be thought of as covering the expected present value of future chargeoffs from the loans on the books at the beginning of the year. The additional $10.50 provision is required to fund the present value of expected losses from the new loans and rollovers. How can we prove this?

Consider Situation 4 where, for whatever reason, the bank stops accepting new loans or rollovers. In theory, there should be no additional provision required, even though chargeoffs are expected to continue at their normal rate. Indeed, the required allowance at the end of the year has declined by $9.00 compared to the start of the year. This is approximately equal to the net chargeoff amount of $8.93 experienced by this liquidating portfolio. That is, the provision has been "self-funded" by the existing allowance.

Therefore, going back to Situation 1, the $10.50 required provision is only being assessed because new loans and rollovers are replenishing the portfolio that would otherwise have declined due to loans that are maturing or being written off.

Situations 2 and 3 demonstrate that shifts in portfolio quality will have predictable effects on the provision and allowance levels. For a loan portfolio that is shifting toward lower average grades (Situation 2), a portion of the higher provision (compared to Situation 1) is needed in anticipation of higher chargeoffs attributable to the downgrades. A portion is needed because a larger percentage of the new and rollover loans is in the lower grade category.

The implication of this discussion for building a profitability system is that we do advocate tracking line unit loan portfolios by credit grade. This is a significant complication and some may wonder if it represents a violation of our sacred 80/20 rule. We think not. As expressed early in Chapter 4, banks have historically not charged correctly for the credit risk they take. More shareholder value has been lost on poor credit evaluation and inadequate credit pricing than in all other risk activities combined. As discussed in Chapter 10, creating shareholder value requires finding lending opportunities where yields are higher than analytical pricing hurdles. In this section, we are asserting that diligent grade classifications and reinforcement of strong credit disciplines must be reinforced in the profitability system to achieve accurate measures of value creation.

Consumer and Mortgage Loans

Installment loans, mortgage loans, and consumer revolving lines of credit—such as credit cards and home equity lines of credit—are usually not monitored and administered using the credit grade approach. However, it is still possible to observe the principles outlined in the prior discussion on graded loans. For these ungraded categories, simply monitor the overall chargeoff rate and calculate a present value of expected losses for each product.

Off-Balance Sheet Credit Risk

While we have pointed out numerous times that regulatory capital standards are not accurate gauges of risk, the risk-based capital rules are quite correct in sensitizing bankers to the fact that unused loan commitments, standby letters of credit, foreign exchange contracts, and interest rate swaps do expose their institutions to additional credit risk.

It is beyond the scope of this book to delve into this subject. However, the authors are very sympathetic to the attitude that such exposures should be assessed for their risk implications. It is problematic whether this is best accomplished with credit allocations, capital allocations, or both. We have seen all three in practice.

13.8   CAPITAL ALLOCATIONS

As presented in Chapter 4, capital should be sufficient to protect any legal business entity or managerial business unit from unexpected cash flow volatility. As with all the other allocations, including cost, funds transfers, and credit, we want to approach this topic from a product perspective. How should capital be allocated among the product groups?

This is not a straightforward problem because we have specified that product groups include such diverse activities as safety deposit boxes, annuity sales, and trust services. None of these have direct linkages to the balance sheet or to regulatory capital standards. The key to our dilemma was provided in Chapter 4. All product groups do have one thing in common that is directly germane to the issue at hand, and that is **cash flow**.

We asserted that capital can be allocated using the volatility, or standard deviation, of a net cash flow stream. For profitability measurement, each product's net cash flows are obtained after removing all accounting artifacts, such as deferrals and amortizations, and after all of the allocation components described in this chapter. Yes, we must generate a set of historical net cash flows after conducting the cost allocations, transfer pricing, credit allocations, AND CAPITAL ALLOCATIONS. But, hold on just a minute! The astute reader should now be asking, "Weren't we doing this to derive what the capital allocation amount should be in the first place? How can we derive the needed cash flows if a necessary step is the capital allocation?" Good questions! We recommend generating these cash flows utilizing a simple set of "generic" capital allocations as discussed in Appendix 13B.

Cash flows will be derived for a minimum of three years of history and one year of forecast. The time periods analyzed will vary depending on the resources available. Clearly, the more time periods analyzed, the better. Ideally, cash flows will be analyzed over complete economic business cycles. We suggest the four years of quarterly cash flows as a minimum amount of analysis to conduct. (In our experience, quarterly cash flows have yielded very adequate results.)

The standard deviations of these cash flows are then calculated. The results may literally be used as crude, **relative** capital allocations. Finally, these relative capital allocations should be applied to the bank's **target** capital level, not its actual capital, to determine the final capital allocation for each product group. (This was presented in Chapter 4.)

Using a target, rather than actual, capital base is critical. Recall that accounting capital usually bears little relation to the actual market value or market capitalization of the firm. Also, there are numerous instances where capital is perceived to be too low or too high for management's future strategies or intentions. All of these issues are avoided by specifying that an "ideal" target capital level be utilized for all profitability measurement activities. This removes yet another source of "uncontrollable" variances.

Should Deposit Products Be Assigned Capital?

Implicit in this discussion is the assignment of capital to deposit products. This strikes many theorists as blasphemy. There is a perception that deposit gathering cannot cause a bank to fail, and therefore, there should be no capital allocated to it. This dispute is related more to differences in the perceived role of capital and not some horrendous misapplication of principle.

If capital is a cushion against failure, then one line of reasoning would assert that if one cannot cite an example where a specific business activity, like deposit gathering, caused or could cause a bank to fail, then there should be no capital allocated to it. There are many examples one can give to illustrate this point.

By our logic, any source of cash flow volatility can contribute to the chances of failure. If there is some source of cash flow volatility associated with deposit activities, and we know there are many, then capital should be allocated to deposits. Examples of sources of deposit cash flow volatility include transit problems (due to strikes or weather problems), operations breakdowns, business interruptions (earthquakes or fires), and kiting or fraud. Admittedly, the amount of capital allocated to deposits should be significantly less than to loans. Nevertheless, we assert that some allocation is proper, but we recognize that a lot of bankers may disagree. As asserted before, the only products or business units that should receive a zero capital allocation are those that have absolutely zero cash flow volatility.

13.9 SUMMARY

This completes our overview of the profitability system. To illustrate the concepts described in this section further, we provide two appendices. Appendix 13A shows a detailed cost allocation example. Appendix 13B presents a simplified case study of the entire system.

We acknowledge that for many readers, the system described in this chapter may seem unrealistically simple-minded. Our contention is not that this system delivers great precision. Rather, we assert that it provides results accurate enough to be useful. More importantly, it is not so complicated as to repel or horrify the managers from all the other areas of the bank. One does not need to be a "rocket scientist" to understand it.

The basic information flows and levels of detail are probably the minimum needed to achieve this goal. From here, it is a straightforward matter to add refinements and additional detail as warranted. However, we would advise that advocates of greater detail keep the materiality and 80/20 rules in mind before jumping ahead!

APPENDIX 13A: COST ALLOCATION CASE STUDY

We will present an example of the cost allocation techniques described in Section 13.5. This case study will be carried forward to Appendix 13B to illustrate several of the other profitability measurement components.

We assume a simplified bank that has six organizational units and four product groups. These are summarized in Table 13A.1.

Table 13A.1
Case Study Bank Units and Product Groups

Unit Name	Type
Administration	Overhead
Operations	Product Support
Treasury	Line
Corporate Banking	Line
Region A - Retail	Line
Region B - Retail	Line

Product Groups	Includes:
Commercial Loans	Commercial Loans
Demand Deposits	Demand Deposits Cash and Due From Bank Balances
Certificates of Deposit	Certificates of Deposit
ALCO	Investment Securities Interest Rate Mismatches

The Treasury department is considered a "line" unit in that it manages transactions with outside entities (securities dealers and other banks) and it manages a major risk portfolio consisting of all of the interest rate mismatches of the bank. (This last point will be discussed at length in Chapter 14.)

Next, we list those budget items that are pertinent to the allocation of expenses. These are presented in Table 13A.2. To simplify this example, we will assume that there are no variances to budgets. Notice that the equity account is budgeted by the Administration Department and that currency, float, clearing accounts, and the Federal Reserve account are all managed by the Operations Department under the "Cash and Due From Bank" account budget category.

Table 13A.2
Summary of Pertinent Budget Items

	Admin-istration	Operations	Treasury	Corporate Banking	Retail Region A	Retail Region B	Total Bank
Balance Sheet:							
Cash & Due		50					50
InvSec			200				200
Commercial Loans				750			750
DDA					100	100	200
CDs					450	300	750
Equity	50						50
Total Expenses:	6.0	7.0	2.0	10.0	7.5	7.5	40.0
FTE:	50	80	20	100	125	125	500
Memo: Salaries	2.00	2.40	0.80	5.00	3.75	3.75	17.70

There are five steps in this process: 1) allocation surveys, 2) overhead allocations, 3) product support allocations, 4) line unit allocations, and 5) standard unit cost factors. A brief discussion of each follows.

Step 1: Allocation Surveys

All three types of organizational units are surveyed. Overhead units will be asked to distribute all of their costs only among the product support and line units. For most, a "generic" allocation mechanism will suffice. For example, the office of the CEO may decide to allocate his or her time in proportion to each product support and line unit's salaries expense. Human resources may decide to allocate according to FTE staff count. If more specific allocations are necessary, then percentage allocations by unit can be conducted. Ideally, many of the overhead units will select a common "generic" approach. For this example, we will assume that the Administration Department utilizes salary dollars as their allocation basis.

Product support and line units will be asked to allocate all of their expenses across the array of designated product groups. Table 13A.3 summarizes the hypothetical survey results for the one product support and four line units in this example situation.

Table 13A.3
Allocation Survey Results
for Product Support and Line Units

	Operations	Treasury	Corporate Banking	Retail Region A	Retail Region B
ALCO	10%	100%			
Commercial Loans	30%		100%		
DDA/Cash & Due	50%			70%	70%
CDs	10%			30%	30%
	100%	100%	100%	100%	100%

Step 2: Overhead Allocations

From the overhead unit cost allocation survey, it was decided that the Administration Department expenses would be distributed according to salary expenses in the various product support and line units. There is $6.00 of budgeted expense in administration and $15.70 of salaries among the recipients. Therefore, the rate of allocation will be 38.22% of the salary dollars. From the salary detail in Table 13A.2, the following overhead allocations result in Table 13A.4.

Table 13A.4
Summary of Overhead Allocations
to Product Support and Line Units

	Operations	Treasury	Corporate Banking	Retail Region A	Retail Region B	Total OH
OH Allocations	$0.917	$0.306	$1.911	$1.433	$1.433	$6.000

Step 3: Product Support Allocations

The directly budgeted expenses of the Operations Department, as well as the allocated overhead expenses from the Administration Department to the Operations Department, are now distributed among the product groups based on the product support survey results submitted by the manager of the operations area. These are displayed in Table 13A.5. It is important not to commingle this unit's directly budgeted and allocated overhead expense dollars. They are tracked separately so that when the final unit or product reports are generated, the expenses can be displayed as to their origin: line, product support, and overhead. In Table 13A.5, the allocated overhead dollars are labeled "OH/PS," meaning overhead allocated to a product support unit.

Table 13A.5
Summary of Product Support Expense
Allocations to Product Groups

	Survey	Budgeted Expense	Allocated OH/PS
ALCO	10%	$0.700	$0.092
Commercial Loans	30%	2.100	0.275
DDA/Cash & Due	50%	3.500	0.459
CDs	10%	0.700	0.092
Totals	100%	$7.000	$0.917

Step 4: Line Unit Allocations

Next, the budgeted and allocated expenses of the line units must be distributed among the product groups. Again, survey results are utilized. Rather than show a separate table for the allocations of each individual line unit, we will summarize all of the line unit allocations in Table 13A.6. As discussed for the product support allocations, we again keep the directly budgeted dollars separated from the allocated overhead dollars.

Table 13A.6
Summary of Line Unit Expense
Allocations to Product Groups

	Line Unit	Survey	Line Budgets	Allocated OH/LN
ALCO	Treasury	100%	$ 2.000	$0.306
Commercial Loans	Corporate Bank	100%	10.000	1.911
DDA/Cash & Due	Retail	70%	10.500	2.006
CDs	Retail	30%	4.500	0.860
			$27.000	$5.083

The column labeled "Allocated OH/LN" represents overhead dollars allocated to the line units.

Step 5: Standard Unit Cost Factors

Table 13A.7 now summarizes all of the allocated costs by product group. In this table, the overhead allocations to the product support and line units have been added together in the column labeled "Overhead." Notice that all expenses for each of the three categories of organizational units as well as for the total bank are fully distributed or absorbed.

Table 13A.7
Summary of Total Cost Allocations
Across All Product Groups

		Allocated Costs ($)			
	Activity	Line	Product Support	Overhead	Total
ALCO	$200	$ 2.000	$0.700	$0.397	$ 3.097
Commercial Loans	$750	10.000	2.100	2.186	14.286
DDA/Cash & Due	$200	10.500	3.500	2.465	16.465
CDs	$750	4.500	0.700	0.952	6.152
Totals		$27.000	$7.000	$6.000	$40.000

Table 13A.7 also shows the activity levels of the product groups. Notice that for the Demand Deposit group, the activity base is the gross outstanding DDA balance of $200. It would have been equally acceptable to have used the net DDA balance of $150, assuming that float is not unusually distributed between the two regions.

Finally, the standard unit cost factors are generated by dividing each expense value in Table 13A.7 by its respective activity level. The results are shown in Table 13A.8

Table 13A.8
Summary of Standard Unit Cost Factors

	Standard Unit Cost Factors			
	Line	Product Support	Overhead	Total
ALCO	1.000%	.350%	.199%	1.549%
Commercial Loans	1.333%	.280%	.291%	1.905%
DDA/Cash & Due	5.250%	1.750%	1.233%	8.233%
CDs	.600%	.093%	.127%	.820%

This completes the calculation steps for the cost allocation component of the profitability system. Please keep in mind that this entire presentation was based on budgeted expense and activity levels.

Standard Expense Ratios

At this point, it is possible to construct a "standardized" budget expense level for each line unit using the standard unit cost factors in Table 13A.8. Actual budgets may then be compared to these standards; the ratio of budgeted to standard expense is called the standard expense ratio. An efficiency ratio below 100% indicates a line unit that is more efficient at offering its product mix, all other things being equal. A ratio above 100% suggests a degree of inefficiency, or higher expense, given a particular mix of product activity.

This form of analysis is pertinent for any set of units that offer a similar mix of products. Generally, it will be most applicable to the retail branch system and to loan production offices. Table 13A.9 presents the standard expense analyses for the two retail regions of the case study bank.

Table 13A.9
Standard Expense Ratio Analysis

Standard Expense Calculations:

Region A	Activity	Standard Unit Cost (Line Unit)	Standard Line Expense
DDA/Cash & Due	100	5.250%	$ 5.250
CDs	450	.600%	$ 2.700
			$ 7.950

Region B			
DDA/Cash & Due	100	5.250%	$ 5.250
CDs	300	.600%	$ 1.800
			$ 7.050

Standard Expense Ratio:

	Actual Expense	Standard Line Expense	Standard Expense Ratio
Region A	$ 7.500	$ 7.950	94.3%
Region B	$ 7.500	$ 7.050	106.4%

Notice that for this analysis, only the line unit standard unit cost factors are used. When multiplied by the activity level in each line unit, a "standardized" line expense is generated for each product group. These are summed, yielding a standard direct expense amount for that unit.

The particular results in Table 13A.9 indicate that Region A is more efficient than Region B in delivering its particular mix of product activities. There may be very reasonable explanations as to why this is the case. This analysis should not be used to make summary judgments. It does indicate discrepancies and inconsistencies in the direct or budgeted expense profiles of comparable line units and should aid management in directing its questions and tracking of performance.

APPENDIX 13B: PROFITABILITY CASE STUDY

This appendix continues the example presented in Appendix 13A. In that discussion, the focus was on allocating expenses across all product groups and among the line units. We will now present the other steps necessary to generate a full set of profitability reports.

We begin by showing the budgets that most banks prepare. They are shown in Table 13B.1.

Typically, organizational units budget their direct revenues, direct expenses, headcount, outstanding balances, and rates or yields for the coming year. A complete income statement and the calculation of formal performance measures are usually only prepared at the total bank level.

Table 13B.1
Unit and Total Bank Budgets
(All Values Are $ Millions)

	Admin- istration	Operatio ns	Treasuries	Corporate Banking	Retail Region A	Retail Region B	Total Bank	Rate/ Yield	Interest Income (Expense)
Balance Sheet:									
Cash & Due		50					50	0.00%	0.00
InvSec			200				200	8.10%	16.20
Commercial Loans				750			750	8.50%	63.75
DDA					100	100	200	0.00%	0.00
CDs					450	300	750	4.80%	(36.00)
Equity	50						50	0.00%	0.00
Revenues & Expenses:									
Fees:				4.0	4.0	2.0	10.0		
Expenses:	6.0	7.0	2.0	10.0	7.5	7.5	40.0		
Memo:									
FTE:	50	80	20	100	125	125	500		
Salaries	2.00	2.40	0.80	5.00	3.75	3.75	17.70		

Income Statement:

Interest Income	79.95
Interest Expense	36.00
Net Interest Income	43.95
Noninterest Income	10.00
Noninterest Expense:	
Salaries	17.70
Other Expense	22.30
Total Expenses	40.00
Pretax Income	13.95
Taxes at 34%	4.74
Net Income	9.21

Performance Measures:

ROA	0.92%
ROE	18.41%

SVA Calculation:

Net Income	9.21
Hurdle Income	7.50
SVA	1.71

Balance Sheet Allocations

To begin the profitability measurement process, certain balance sheet categories should be allocated, including items such as cash and due from

bank balances (including required reserve balances), equity, and the loan loss allowance (which is not being considered in this example). For cash and due from bank balances, a simple approach is to allocate the amounts in proportion to demand deposit balances. Also, very simple capital allocations will be assumed, as shown in Table 13B.2. In practice, the standard deviation methodology described in Chapter 4 is recommended.

Table 13B.2
Balance Sheet Allocations

Balance Sheet Allocations (Excluding Equity):
(Amounts for each unit are balances in $ millions)

	Treasury	Corporate Banking	Retail Region A	Retail Region B	Total Bank	Capital Factor	Capital Allocation
Cash & Due			25	25	$ 50	1.00%	$ 0.50
InvSec	200				$200	1.00%	2.00
Commercial Loans		750			$750	4.00%	30.00
DDA			100	100	$200	1.00%	2.00
CDs			450	300	$750	1.00%	7.50
						Total	$42.00

Equity Allocations:
(Amounts for each unit are equity allocations in $ millions)

To Units:	Treasury	Corporate Banking	Retail Region A	Retail Region B	Total Bank
Cash & Due			0.25	0.25	$ 0.50
InvSec	2.00				2.00
Commercial Loans		30.00			30.00
DDA			1.00	1.00	2.00
CDs			4.50	3.00	7.50
Mismatching	8.00				8.00
Total Equity	10.00	30.00	5.75	4.25	$50.00

cont.

To Product Groups:

	Balance	Capital Factor	Capital Allocation
ALCO:			
Investment Securities	200	1.00%	$ 2.00
Mismatching			8.00
Total ALCO			$10.00
Commercial Loans	750	4.00%	30.00
DDA/Cash & Due From:			
Cash & Due From	50	1.00%	0.50
DDA	200	1.00%	2.00
Total DDA/Cash & Due			2.50
Certificates of Deposit	750	1.00%	7.50
		Total	$50.00

Notice that the procedure requires two different types of allocations. The first is illustrated in the upper panel of Table 13B.2. It relates to the capital allocations based on balance sheet items and any balance sheet equivalents for such off-balance sheet items as unused loan commitments, standby letters of credit, interest rate swaps, and foreign exchange contracts. The capital factors used here are arbitrary, although the results are plausible.

The capital factors are applied to each unit's balances, resulting in the equity allocations displayed in the middle panel of Table 13B.2. In addition, there must be allocations for other risk-taking activities. In this example, the only other risk-taking activity is the interest rate mismatching for the bank, which is the responsibility of the Treasury unit.

In determining the amount of equity to allocate for interest rate mismatching, we offer one possible approach. The interest rate elasticity of equity for this hypothetical bank is about –8%. (For those intrepid readers who understand duration calculations, we offer calculating the duration and interest rate elasticity of equity for this hypothetical bank as an exercise, assuming that all items are "bullet" or zero coupon transactions.) This implies that for every 100 basis points that rates rise, the net market value of equity will decline about 8% of $50 million, or $4 million. If we assume that a realistically conservative equity allocation is enough to cover an instantaneous rate shock of 200 basis points, then the equity allocation for mismatching should be about $8 million. Another approach would be to calculate the standard deviation of equity values as a function of the expected standard deviation of interest rates.

Also shown in the lower portion of Table 13B.2 are the capital allocations to the formal product groups.

Transfer Pricing

We will assume very simple transfer pricing parameters. These are presented in Table 13B.3, where all interest-bearing items are considered to be fixed-rate items with the maturities indicated. For noninterest-bearing items, the "maturity" is the assumption used for transfer pricing purposes. A full explanation of transfer pricing issues may be found in Chapter 14.

Table 13B.3
Transfer Pricing Bankwide Summary and Allocations

Bankwide Summary:

	Balance	Maturity Years	Rate/ Yield	Transfer Rate	Net Spread	Net Interest Income
Assets:						
Cash & Due From Banks	50	1.00	0.00%	7.00%	−7.00%	$(3.50)
Investment Securities	200	2.00	8.10%	8.00%	0.10%	0.20
Commercial Loans	750	0.50	8.50%	6.50%	2.00%	15.00
Liabilities & Equity:						
Demand Deposit Accounts	200	1.00	0.00%	7.00%	7.00%	14.00
Certificates of Deposit	750	0.25	4.80%	6.00%	1.20%	9.00
Equity	50	2.00	0.00%	8.00%	8.00%	4.00
			Total Allocated Net Interest Income			$38.70
			Mismatching Income			5.25
			Total Net Interest Income			$43.95

cont.

Net Interest Income by Product Group:

	Balance	Spread	Net Interest Income
ALCO:			
Investment Securities	200.00	0.10%	$ 0.20
Mismatching			5.25
Equity Allocation	10.00	8.00%	0.80
Total ALCO			6.25
Commercial Loans	750.00	2.00%	15.00
Equity Allocation	30.00	8.00%	2.40
Total Commercial Loans			17.40
DDA/Cash & Due From:			
Cash & Due From	50.00	−7.00%	−3.50
DDA	200.00	7.00%	14.00
Equity	2.50	8.00%	0.20
Total DDA/Cash & Due			10.70
Certificates of Deposit	750.00	1.20%	9.00
Equity Allocation	7.50	8.00%	0.60
Total CDs			9.60
		Total	$43.95

Net Interest Income by Line Unit:

	Treasury	Corporate Banking	Retail Region A	Retail Region B	Total Bank
Cash & Due			−1.75	−1.75	$−3.50
InvSec	0.20				0.20
Commercial Loans		15.00			15.00
DDA			7.00	7.00	14.00
CDs			5.40	3.60	9.00
Equity	0.80	2.40	0.46	0.34	4.00
Mismatching	5.25				5.25
Totals	6.25	17.40	11.11	9.19	$43.95

Notice that the allocated net interest income total of $38.70 to the balance sheet items in the top panel of Table 13B.3 is different from the $43.95 displayed in the total bank income statement in Table 13B.1. This difference, as explained in detail in Chapter 14, is attributable to the interest rate mismatching in this bank's balance sheet. The amount of the "mismatch" earnings is $5.25. It will be allocated to the unit responsible for interest rate risk management, the Treasury unit.

Also, although equity is not a formal product group, there is an "earnings credit" for allocated equity dollars. Under the assumptions used, this amounts to $4 million as indicated above. It is allocated among the line units in proportion to the capital allocations derived in Table 13B.2.

Product Support and Overhead Allocations

We will utilize the standard unit cost factors presented in Tables 13A.7 and 13A.8 to determine the product support and overhead allocations to the line units as displayed in Table 13B.4.

Table 13B.4
Product Support and Overhead Expense Allocation to Line Units

Product Support Costs:

	Treasury	Corporate Banking	Retail Region A	Retail Region B	Total Bank
ALCO	0.70				$0.70
Commercial Loans		2.10			2.10
DDA/Cash & Due From			1.75	1.75	3.50
Certificates of Deposit			0.42	0.28	0.70
	0.70	2.10	2.17	2.03	$7.00

Overhead Costs:

	Treasury	Corporate Banking	Retail Region A	Retail Region B	Total Bank
ALCO	0.40				$0.40
Commercial Loans		2.19			2.19
DDA/Cash & Due From			1.23	1.23	2.46
Certificates of Deposit			0.57	0.38	0.95
	0.40	2.19	1.80	1.61	$6.00

Unit Profitability Reports

The results from Tables 13B.1, 2, 3, 4 are now combined to generate the unit profitability report shown in Table 13B.5.

Table 13B.5
Unit Profitability Reports

	Treasury	Corporate Banking	Retail Region A	Retail Region B	Total Bank
ALLOCATED BALANCE SHEET:					
Assets					
Cash & Due			25.00	25.00	$ 50.00
InvSec	200.00				200.00
Commercial Loans		750.00			750.00
Transfer Assets	(990.00)	30.00	555.75	404.25	0.00
	(790.00)	780.00	580.75	429.25	$1000.00
Liabilities					
DDA			100.00	100.00	200.00
CDs			450.00	300.00	750.00
Equity	10.00	30.00	5.75	4.25	50.00
Transfer Liabilities	(800.00)	750.00	25.00	25.00	0.00
	(790.00)	780.00	580.75	429.25	$1000.00
Memo:					
"Average Assets"	105.00	390.00	290.38	214.62	1000.00
ALLOCATED INCOME STATEMENTS:					
Net Interest Income	6.25	17.40	11.11	9.19	$43.95
Fees		4.00	4.00	2.00	10.00
Direct Expenses	(2.00)	(10.00)	(7.50)	(7.50)	(40.00)
Direct Margin	4.25	11.40	7.61	3.69	26.95
Product Support	(0.70)	(2.10)	(2.17)	(2.03)	(7.00)
Contribution	3.55	9.30	5.44	1.66	19.95
Overhead Expense	(0.40)	(2.19)	(1.80)	(1.61)	(6.00)
Pretax Income	3.15	7.11	3.64	0.05	13.95
Taxes @ 34%	(1.07)	(2.41)	(1.24)	(0.02)	(4.74)
Net Income	2.08	4.70	2.40	0.03	$9.21

cont.

PERFORMANCE MEASURES:

Return on Assets	1.98%	1.21%	0.83%	0.01%	0.92%
Return on Capital	20.8%	15.7%	41.7%	0.7%	18.4%
Efficiency Ratio	49.6%	66.8%	75.9%	99.6%	74.1%
SVA Calculation:					
Net Income	2.08	4.70	2.40	0.03	$9.21
Hurdle Income	1.50	4.50	0.86	0.64	7.50
SVA	0.58	0.20	1.54	(0.61)	$1.71

Notes: ▪ "Average Assets" is the average of all assets, excluding transfer assets, and all liabilities and equity, excluding transfer liabilities.
▪ The efficiency ratio is defined as total expenses, including allocated product support and overhead, divided by the sum of net interest income and noninterest income.
▪ "Transfer Assets" for all units except the ALCO unit will equal the amount of "real" liabilities and equity. The ($990) amount in the ALCO unit reflects the "contra-transfer assets" that are the offsets of the other transfer asset amounts shown on that line.

There are several important observations at this point.

SVA is the best measure of shareholder value. It yields the clearest picture of performance on a fully risk-adjusted basis. None of the other measures even qualitatively correlates. The next best is return on allocated capital or return on allocated equity. (This is NOT return on accounting capital.) The reason we assert that SVA is superior to any ROE concept is that it indicates the amount of value added in dollar terms. An activity may have a huge ROE, but very little SVA, depending on the magnitude of its cash flows relative to other activities.

Mismatch earnings are not locked in. Please do not be fooled by the positive SVA value in the Treasury unit. This is purely coincidental and is by no means assured in future periods. Recall that the vast majority of the net interest income in the Treasury is attributable to mismatch earnings. These are still very risky earnings and will rise and fall in future periods as a complicated function of shifts in future yield curves. This point will be discussed further in Chapter 14. In the meantime, the positive SVA in Treasury should not be interpreted as true value creation or as any reason for ALCO members to congratulate themselves on making good forecasts of interest rate movements.

A negative SVA is not always bad news. Comparing Regions A and B, there is no doubt that Region B needs some attention. Appendix 13A indicated that Region B has an apparently high expense base relative to Region A. From Table 13A.9, it was seen that on a "standardized" expense basis, Region A should be incurring about $1 million less in direct expenses than Region B. However, their expense budgets are exactly the same. This is probably a major factor in the difference in SVA between these two units. However, we do not believe that the manager in charge of Region B should be chastised over this result. Because of this profitability system, we are now in a position to better understand the magnitudes of and the reasons for the performance differences. Also, under the SVA system, managers are not only rewarded for positive SVAs, they are also rewarded for improvements in SVA. Therefore, the Region B manager has a strong positive incentive to improve his or her SVA results.

Any SVA above zero is good. In examining the unit SVAs, there is a natural tendency to conclude that Region A is performing better than the Corporate Banking unit. While its SVA is higher, the staff in Corporate Banking should still be highly complimented and rewarded. ANY positive SVA is a job well done, since this indicates that the unit is exceeding the risk-adjusted hurdles set by the markets.

Product Profitability Reports

The product profitability reports in Table 13B.6 are compiled using the results presented in Tables 13B.1, 2, 3, 4.

Many of the same comments presented for the unit profitability statements are applicable here. Again, the net income, ROA, and efficiency ratio measures do not correlate well with SVA. Hence, none of them give a true reflection of shareholder value creation.

Table 13B.6
Product Profitability Reports

	ALCO	Commercial Loans	Demand Deposits	Certificates of Deposit	Total Bank
ALLOCATED BALANCE SHEET:					
Assets					
Cash & Due			50.00		$ 50.00
InvSec	200.00				200.00
Commercial Loans		750.00			750.00
Transfer Assets	(990.00)	30.00	202.50	757.50	0.00
Total Assets	(790.00)	780.00	252.50	757.50	$1000.00
Liabilities					
DDA			200.00		200.00
CDs				750.00	750.00
Equity	10.00	30.00	2.50	7.50	50.00
Transfer Liabilities	(800.00)	750.00	50.00	0.00	0.00
Total Liabilities & Equities	(790.00)	780.00	252.50	757.50	$1000.00
Memo:					
"Average Assets"	105.00	390.00	126.25	378.75	$1000.00
ALLOCATED INCOME STATEMENTS:					
Net Interest Income	6.25	17.40	10.70	9.60	$43.95
Fees	0.00	4.00	6.00	0.00	10.00
Direct Expenses	(2.00)	(10.00)	(10.50)	(4.50)	(27.00)
Direct Margin	4.25	11.40	6.20	5.10	26.95
Product Support	(0.70)	(2.10)	(3.50)	(0.70)	(7.00)
Contribution	3.55	9.30	2.70	4.40	19.95
Overhead Expense	(0.40)	(2.19)	(2.46)	(0.95)	(6.00)
Pretax Income	3.15	7.11	0.24	3.45	13.95
Taxes @ 34%	(1.07)	(2.41)	(0.08)	(1.18)	(4.74)
Net Income	2.08	4.70	0.16	2.27	$9.21

cont.

PERFORMANCE MEASURES:

Return on Assets	1.98%	1.21%	0.13%	0.60%	0.92%
Return on Capital	20.8%	15.7%	6.4%	30.3%	18.4%
Efficiency Ratio	49.6%	66.8%	98.6%	64.1%	74.1%
SVA Calculation:					
Net Income	2.08	4.70	0.16	2.27	$9.21
Hurdle Income	1.50	4.50	0.38	1.13	7.50
SVA	0.58	0.20	(0.12)	1.14	$1.71

CDs result in the greatest SVA, but this does not mean that CDs are superior to commercial loans. It may mean that the local competitive CD pricing situation is permitting unusually high risk-adjusted returns. The results do indicate that demand deposits may need some attention, perhaps with respect to its fee schedules for the noninterest-bearing product, or regarding its expense characteristics.

CHAPTER 14

Transfer Pricing

Internal funds transfer pricing is practiced to some degree by every bank. Some have elaborate mainframe systems with automated data feeds from their applications systems. At the other extreme, some bankers denigrate the concept, but practice it nevertheless. They do so whenever they consider whether to make a loan or buy an investment security. They do so whenever they think about the spread they are earning on a commercial loan. They do so whenever they are considering the margin implications of their retail CD pricing strategy.

Every banker should understand the basic principles of transfer pricing. They are an essential part of any type of profitability measurement, pricing analysis, or risk-adjustment for any balance sheet product. Those that criticize the topic are usually only upset about others who get carried away by theoretical or implementation complexities. We agree. Those that desire "precise" transfer pricing are violators of the 80/20 rule!

As with the other aspects of profitability measurement, there are a myriad of different, legitimate perspectives on this topic. In the context of this book, the main objective of internal funds transfer pricing is to risk-adjust the net interest income or margin for a line unit or product for profitability analysis purposes. Emphasizing the principles elaborated on in Section 13.1 will provide important guidance in developing the procedures described in this chapter. The discussion that ensues is not the "only" way; rather it is one of many possible paths. Other perspectives may be found in *Banker's Treasury Management Handbook* (Binder, Barrett F., ed., Boston, MA: Warren, Gorham and Lamont, 1988).

14.1   OBJECTIVES OF TRANSFER PRICING

There are four main objectives in any complete transfer pricing system: remove interest rate risk from line units and products, reflect "risk-adjusted" spreads over long-term interest rate cycles, centralize all interest rate mismatches of the bank in one (ALCO) unit, and provide consistent guidance in product pricing analyses.

Remove interest rate risk from line units and products. Line unit managers may have some discretion of product pricing, but they have no control over market yield curve shifts or unusual behavior of index rates, such as the Prime rate. In the spirit of leaving only controllable variances in their profitability reports, it is essential that the transfer pricing system remove all unmanageable interest rate risk from their results. This requires guaranteeing a net spread to the unit for every product over each budgeting cycle, generally a one-year period.

Reflect "risk-adjusted" spreads over long-term interest rate cycles. Even if a net spread on a product is guaranteed for one year, if that spread shifts unexpectedly between years, the sudden adverse effect on a line unit could be substantial. Therefore, determine spread relationships over full interest rate cycles, making the year-to-year changes in net spreads minimal. However, this practice will result in greater volatility in the ALCO or Treasury unit where all interest rate mismatches are transferred. This will be discussed later.

Centralize all interest rate mismatches of the bank in one (ALCO) unit. Transfer pricing does not actually remove interest rate risk from a bank. It transfers it from one unit to another, a concept explained in the next section. For now, it is most effective to transfer all interest rate mismatches in the bank into one unit for analysis and management. This is usually an organizational unit referred to as the ALCO unit or Treasury unit.

Provide consistent guidance in product pricing analyses. The detailed procedures to be described for transfer pricing in the profitability system are not exactly applicable to product pricing analyses or pricing spreadsheets. There are some critical differences that will be described. Nevertheless, the general principles are the same and maintaining consistency with these is essential.

14.2 OVERVIEW OF "MATCHED-MATURITY" TRANSFER PRICING

The concept of matched-maturity transfer pricing is best illustrated by example. Consider a "bank" with the balance sheet shown in Table 14.1. The reader will immediately notice that this "bank" has no equity. Transfer pricing equity will be discussed in a later section.

Table 14.1
Transfer Pricing Case Study
Matched-Maturity Method

Item	Unit	Balance	Maturity (Years)	Rate	Interest Income (Expense)
Asset:					
Commercial Loan	Corporate	$100	1.00	9.0%	$9.00
Liability:					
Certificate of Deposit	Retail	$100	0.25	5.0%	(5.00)
			Total Bank:	4.0%	$4.00

Note: Assume that each transaction is a "bullet" or zero coupon item, where all interest and principal is paid at maturity. All items are fixed rate transactions. The dollar net interest income and expense figures will occur only if interest rates remain stable over the course of one year.

Bankers over the years have devised numerous shortcuts for determining how to split the bank's total 4% net interest margin between the two line units. Briefly, some of the more popular method are as follows:

Do nothing. By this approach, there is no internal transfer pricing and there is no attempt to divide or allocate the total bank net interest income among the line units. Generally, for budgeting activities, the net interest income budget is housed in a finance or Treasury unit. Line units are only expected to budget product outstandings and portfolio rates or yields.

Single market (or single pool) rate. This is the simplest method for determining a net interest spread or net interest income for a line unit. Unfortunately, no single market rate can ever be appropriate. Yet, it is surprising how many banks do a crude form of transfer pricing using the federal funds rate or a moving average of a short-term LIBOR or CD rate.

Multiple pool rate(s). This is basically a "gap" approach to transfer pricing where each product is classified in one of several pools with differing maturity ranges. Indeed, alignment of this approach with the bank's interest rate gap bucket definitions has significant advantages. The transfer rate assigned to the product is the respective pool rate for its maturity range.

This approach is really not at all bad. Keeping its limitations in mind, acceptable results can be obtained with a very modest effort.

The co-terminus, or matched-maturity, method may be considered to be a much more detailed and refined version of the multiple pool approach. Its basic tenet is that every incremental customer transaction should be "matched" with a corresponding hypothetical internal funds transfer. This matching concept should include the following attributes:

- The transfer funds should mirror the expected cash flow pattern of the original transaction, including amortizations and/or prepayments.

- The interest rate assigned to the transfer funding should be consistent with the marginal cost of a large block of wholesale funding at the bank's current marginal funding rate(s) for the cash flow pattern expected.

Using the example from Table 14.1, to apply the matched-maturity method, we must determine the marginal cost of funds for each maturity listed. Assume that the relevant rates are 6.0% for three-month funds and 7.0% for one-year funds. With this information, we can generate the necessary funds transfers as shown in Table 14.2.

Table 14.2
Matched-Maturity Funds Transfers
for the Case Study Situation in Table 14.1

ASSETS	LIABILITIES
Corporate Banking:	
100 One-Year Loans at 9.0%	100 One-Year Transfer Liabilities at 7.0% *
Retail Banking:	
100 Three-Month Transfer Asset at 6.0% **	100 Three-Month CDs at 5.0%
ALCO Unit:	
100 One-Year Transfer Asset at 7.0% *	100 Three-Month Transfer Liabilities at 6.0% **

Note: * and ** denote matched pairs of funds transfers.

Notice that for each actual customer transaction, there is a matched pair of funds transfer entries. For the one-year loan, a transfer liability is booked for the same amount and maturity. This transfer liability carries the one-year transfer rate of 7.0%. An offsetting transfer asset entry is made on the books of the ALCO unit. It will have the same balance, maturity date, and interest rate as the transfer liability. This matched pair of transfer entries ensures that when the books of all units are consolidated, all internal funds transfers are eliminated.

An analogous pair of entries is booked in response to the three-month CD. In this case, a three-month transfer asset is entered for Retail Banking and an offsetting transfer liability is created for the ALCO unit. The result is that each unit now has a "balanced" balance sheet and a "locked-in" net interest spread for each product. Most importantly, the basic interest rate mismatch being undertaken by this bank is now transferred into the ALCO unit, the area responsible for interest rate risk management, and the mismatch spread is accurately quantified. **Management should always understand what portion of their net interest margin is attributable to such interest rate mismatches. These "earnings" are very volatile.** The final division of the overall bank's margin of 4% is diagrammed in Figure 14.1.

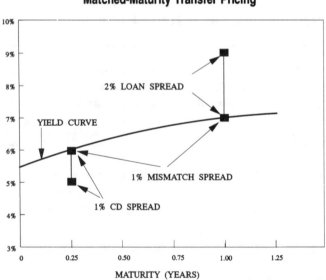

Figure 14.1
Matched-Maturity Transfer Pricing

It is critical to understand that the mismatch spread of 2% is by no means assured beyond the initial three-month period where the CD rate is known. The risk of this balance sheet mismatch will become apparent at each rollover date of the CD over the life of the loan.

14.3 ADVANTAGES OF THE MATCHED-MATURITY TRANSFER PRICING METHOD

For the simple example just described, the advantages of the matched-maturity transfer pricing method are substantial. They include the following:

The marginal spread for each product is accurately measured. In theory, for each new transaction booked by the bank, a concurrent transfer rate is assigned. The spread between the yield of the transaction and the transfer rate represents the true profitability contribution of that product to the bank's overall net interest margin, and therefore, is the correct spread to incorporate in product or unit profitability analyses.

The earnings attributable to interest rate mismatching is correctly identified. Bankers rarely appreciate the magnitude of their spreads that are truly at the mercy of the markets and shifts in the yield curve. In our experience, when this is elucidated using such a transfer pricing system, most senior managers gain a much greater sensitivity and concern over the magnitude of these "earnings at risk," and they usually act to manage it more conservatively. It is only with a matched-maturity approach to transfer pricing that any reasonable estimate of the magnitude of these mismatch earnings can be accomplished.

Each product spread is independent of any other balance sheet element. This is a critical point. Many, many bankers mentally "allocate" certain deposit transactions to be the funding source for certain types of loans for the purpose of estimating their "lending spreads." For example, they might reason that MMDA deposits "fund" Prime-based loans. This approach means that any spread that should rightfully be assigned to the efforts expended in gathering advantageous MMDA deposits is usurped as a subsidy for the lending activities of the bank. Aside from the unfairness aspect, this reasoning only works as long as the volumes of these "linked" balance sheet categories stay close to one another.

In contrast, the matched-maturity method is valid at all times, whatever the relative levels of any loan or deposit category. For example, return to the case study situation in Table 14.1. Suppose that the Corporate Banking manager renounced any transfer pricing and "claimed" the retail CDs as the proper cost of funds for commercial loans. By this logic, the entire margin of 4% should be allocated to Corporate Banking and none for Retail Banking. The lenders would probably show very high current profits, and might reason to themselves that they could afford to lower their pricing to achieve greater market share.

Assume they conclude that they could double their outstandings by lowering their loan rate to 8% from 9%. Their "analysis" would look something like the upper panel in Table 14.3.

Table 14.3
Contrast Between Faulty and Correct Pricing Analyses

"Faulty" Pricing Analysis:

	Original	Pro Forma	Increment
Loan Rate	9%	8%	
"Cost of Funds"	5%	5%	
Spread	4%	3%	
Volume	100	200	100
Net Interest Income	$4.0	$6.0	$2.0

Matched-Maturity Pricing Analysis:

	Original	Pro Forma	Increment
Loan Rate	9%	8%	
Transfer Rate	7%	7%	
Spread	2%	1%	
Volume	100	200	100
Net Interest Income	$2.0	$2.0	$0.0

There are two errors in the upper panel. First, it assumes that loan originations are the only source of net interest income, whereas Table 14.2 demonstrates that only a portion derives from lending; the rest is attributable to deposit-gathering and balance sheet mismatching. Secondly, it assumes that $200 of CDs can be generated at the same rate as the bank generated the first $100 of CDs. However, this is easier said than done. As the lenders are recognizing, doubling the outstandings of any product usually requires some type of major rate concession. The assumption that the bank can also double its CD volume with NO rate concession at all is quite unrealistic.

Using the matched-maturity method, it becomes instantly clear that this pricing alternative would be detrimental to the bank. Outstandings might double, but there would be no incremental revenues. Indeed, this would be the actual result if the bank chose to match-fund the incremental $100 of loan growth using wholesale funding at the wholesale CD rate of 7%. Only the matched-maturity method depicts this reality.

Therefore, one of the major advantages of the matched-maturity approach is that it accurately separates the bank's net interest income for each product and for any balance sheet mismatching. Any of those individual spreads are completely independent of the existence of any of the others and may be achieved on a stand-alone basis. Referring back to the original situation in Table 14.1, the bank could offer the commercial loans, but not accept the CDs, if, for example, it wanted to exit retail banking. It could achieve the spread of 2% funding with one-year wholesale CDs at 7%. Alternatively, it could fund with three-month wholesale CDs at 6% and earn the loan spread of 2% and the mismatch spread of 1%.

Conversely, it could offer the retail CDs, but not make commercial loans, and still earn the CD spread and/or the mismatch spread. Finally, it could earn the mismatch spread, and not offer any other product! It would do so by issuing $100 of three-month CDs in the wholesale markets at 6% and investing the proceeds in a one-year maturity Eurodollar CD or Eurodollar deposit earning 7%. Presto! It has a risky 1% net interest margin on the mismatch with no commercial loans or retail CDs.

14.4 SELECTING A TRANSFER PRICING YIELD CURVE

This is a critical aspect of the matched-maturity method. All product spreads will be based on the difference between the product's rate or yield and a corresponding point on this transfer pricing yield curve. Generally, a CD or LIBOR yield curve will be selected because these rates generally best reflect the characteristics of bank marginal funding costs. These are more appropriate than a Treasury yield curve, because banks cannot directly fund themselves in the wholesale markets at the Treasury rate.

What are the attributes of an "ideal" yield curve for transfer pricing activities? It would reflect a realistic, all-in cost of large blocks of wholesale funding consistent with the target credit rating of the bank. Unfortunately, there are several issues with this concept that require resolution.

Funding versus investment rate. In the real world, there may be a significant rate difference between the cost of a large block of wholesale borrowings and the yield earned on a large block of new investment securities. Therefore, one could argue that the transfer rate associated in funding a loan as a "cost of funds" is quite different from the transfer rate associated with the "earnings credit" given to a block of new deposits. Actually, the difference may not be too large. Most banks tend to invest in government or AAA-rated securities at yields substantially less than their cost of wholesale funding (since so few banks can borrow at a AAA-rate). However, for transfer pricing, focus on an incremental investment rate consistent with the (target) credit rating of the bank. This might be an A or BBB corporate bond yield. Most banks' actual investment purchases are of extremely high credit quality for liquidity management purposes, or to "balance out" or "average out" the credit risk of the loan portfolio. However, the hypothetical "earnings credit" that should be given to the bank's deposits should reflect the yield related to the overall "average" credit rating of all earning assets. This would be a rate significantly higher than a Treasury or AAA yield.

All this notwithstanding, the vast majority of bankers have a much easier time accepting a funding perspective rather than an investment perspective in considering transfer pricing methods. This will tend to give a slight "windfall" to the deposit gatherers, but probably does not violate the 80/20 rule.

Identifying "All-In" Cost Adjustments

There are several adjustments that must be considered to quoted CD market rates before they can be used for transfer pricing. They include:

360-day rate basis. Secondary market CD, LIBOR, and federal funds rates are quoted on a 360-day year basis that must be converted to an actual, or 365-day, basis for internal bank use. Also, many banks will run their systems on a monthly interval, necessitating converting a "bond equivalent" semiannual coupon concept into a monthly coupon-equivalent interest rate.

FDIC insurance premium. All domestic deposits are assessed a BIF or SAIF insurance premium. Quoted CD rates must be increased by a yield equivalent amount to adjust for this. For consistency, this implies that all deposit generating units should also be allocated their share of the bank's insurance expense in the cost allocation component of any profitability system. Thus, for a hypothetical branch that only raises deposits but makes no loans, it will bear the BIF insurance premium for its deposits as an interest expense, but this will be exactly offset by the transfer earnings credit that has been "grossed up" by the insurance premium rate.

Required reserves. When they exist, Federal Reserve Bank reserve requirements must also be considered. However, if CD rates are being used, and there are no reserve requirements on CDs, this issue can be ignored in generating the yield curve. Also, if LIBOR is used, then reserves are not relevant.

Commissions. If wholesale funding sources were used, the bank would expect to pay a normal level of commissions or fees to the dealers or brokers. These should be factored into the yield curve as well.

14.5 TARGET VERSUS ACTUAL CREDIT RATING OF THE BANK

There is one final adjustment to quoted market rates that must be discussed. It relates to the bank's credit rating in the marketplace as discussed in Chapters 10 and 11. The concepts of LIBOR and secondary CD rate quotes apply to "prime" or top-tier banking companies. All others will face an additional spread over these rates that generally increase for longer maturities.

This issue is most critical for long-term (over one year) maturities where the bank's funding spreads (over Treasuries) should always be a major focus of management attention. In a sense, these spreads represent a market assessment of the overall riskiness of the bank and its debt. Larger banking companies have widely known ratings published by the rating agencies. These are often the most accessible guides for establishing realistic borrowing spreads for such entities. Another good source for large bank holding companies are the various investment houses that will provide borrowing spread quotes upon request.

However, a serious dilemma arises here. Suppose that for years a bank has operated as a high quality, AA-rated bank. However, over the past couple of years, it has run into serious credit quality problems, such that its formal rating has slipped into a BBB category. Management has improved its credit policies and strengthened its credit administration practices. It is absolutely dedicated to re-establishing its AA stature as soon as possible. Therefore, it claims that its current BBB-rating is only temporary. Should the bank use a "target" AA yield curve for transfer pricing purposes (since it is anticipating regaining this rating), or should it use a current BBB yield curve? The difference in transfer rates could be as high as 100 basis points!

This issue of the "target" versus "actual" credit rating in determining transfer rates has become a raging controversy in recent years because so many banking companies have been severely downgraded in the late

1980s and early 1990s. There are two viewpoints that each have powerful arguments.

Viewpoint #1: Actual credit rating. In a world where market discipline is exercised and rational economic forces can prevail, using current actual credit ratings should always prevail. In such a "rational" world, the proof is in the proverbial pudding. In other words, the markets are reflecting management's proven behavior in allowing the bank's credit quality to deteriorate. The cost of funds will not improve merely on the basis of promises, but only after the markets are convinced that the bank's behavior has really changed and increased credit quality can be realistically anticipated.

Viewpoint #2: Target credit rating. If management is truly committed to improving the bank's credit quality and is only allowing loans consistent with a long-run AA rating onto its books, then this is the correct "incremental" cost of funds and the bank should employ the AA yield curve. There are two other arguments that are commonly expressed in support of this approach:

- Using a BBB yield curve would create a huge windfall in the profitability of the deposit gathering activities because of the "artificially" high earnings credits they would receive. This would allow the deposit pricers to increase the bank's posted deposit rates in an effort to gain market share from the competition. However, any incremental deposit dollars raised would certainly not be invested at a BBB yield. Hence, the transfer spreads being advantageously assigned to incremental deposit dollars would not reflect actual total bank incremental earnings. This violates a tenet of transfer pricing that it should generally reflect actual "match-funded" bank spreads.

- While viewpoint #1 is legitimate in a world where BBB banks actually use BBB funding, the reality is that the vast majority of BBB banks **never use a single dollar of BBB funds.** One of the most important effects of FDIC deposit insurance and the "too big to fail" corollary is that they obviate market discipline for insured depositories. Banks and thrifts simply do not pay their rational economic cost of funds because of the protection that FDIC insurance provides. Moreover, for large blocks of incremental, long-term funding, there are officially established avenues of subsidized funding available. For example, the Federal Home Loan Banks routinely provide **AA or better** long-term funds to banks and thrifts. It is not unusual for the

FHLBs to offer "specials" in the form of long-term funds at or below LIBOR or even below Treasuries! Therefore, while it may be theoretically correct to use a BBB yield curve, in the real world, it just does not actually happen.

In our experience, it is only realistic to use the actual credit rating at the bank holding company level, where FDIC insurance and subsidized funding are not available and market discipline is freely exercised. At the bank level, it is extremely difficult to get management to accept a BBB cost of funds if the bank never borrows a single dollar at a BBB rate. Also, adopting a BBB yield curve for a bank (as opposed to a bank holding company) would severely distort deposit pricing activities. Therefore, we have generally accepted the use of an AA yield curve for bank transfer pricing activities.

Two points must be emphasized. First, the bank's return to AA quality must be a high probability. Second, the right marginal cost of funds for AA credits is an AA cost of funds. If asset quality is below AA, a higher cost of funds should be used.

14.6 APPLYING THE 80/20 RULE TO TRANSFER PRICING

In considering the implementation of a matched-maturity transfer pricing system, banks often become anxious about the amount of data, analysis, and capital and human resources required to design, program, operate, and maintain it. Hypothetically, a bank could attempt to perform a transfer pricing analysis on every separate loan and deposit account in the bank. For an amortizing automobile or mortgage loan, funds transfers would be required for the expected principal paydown pattern for every month of the life of the loan. This can quickly require an unbelievable amount of data processing resources to analyze and report!

Here is another place where the application of the 80/20 rule can bring sanity out of chaos. For most product groups, transfer spreads should be determined only for the bank's total portfolio of each group, and not for the unique profiles of originations and maturities within each line unit. Notice the stipulation that a bankwide **spread** be determined for each product group. We are not advocating determining a single transfer **rate** for an entire product group.

14.7   USE OF GUARANTEED PRODUCT SPREADS

Going one giant step further, we also advocate **guaranteeing** the spread for each product for the entire budget year. Why do this? It is the only way to be consistent with our profitability principle that variances should only arise from controllable events. Many shifts in transfer pricing spreads are not controllable by line unit managers. Examples include a shift in the spread between the Prime rate and its optimal funding mix (as discussed in Chapter 9), the effect of prepayments on mortgage loans, or general disintermediation effects of market rate shifts on retail deposits. None of these are controllable by line managers, but they all could have substantial effects on current transfer pricing "maturity" assumptions and the resulting product spreads.

Another major advantage of this approach is that, for most products, transfer pricing analyses need only be updated once per year in preparation for the budgeting cycle. The exception is an important one. We assign "up-to-the-minute" transfer rates for large transactions (over $500,000). These are generally either very large loan drawdowns, purchases of investment securities, or the issuance of a large block of debt. In either case, the spread in these instances can be a very sensitive function of market yield curve conditions at the precise time the transaction is effected. For these large items, a log is maintained in the Treasury unit of the pertinent transfer rate for each, and that transfer rate is permanently linked to that specific asset or liability transaction.

Returning to the situation for most products, there is one more aspect of this once-per-year updating that is crucial. The guaranteed spread for a coming year is a four-year moving average spread, consisting of three years of actual history and one year of forecast based on the bank's simulation model. This long-term averaging serves the useful role of further smoothing year-to-year performance volatility, without hindering the bank's overall interest rate risk management activities.

As a specific example, return to the example of Prime-indexed loans. Chapter 9 showed that the variance minimizing funding portfolio consists approximately of 40% federal funds, and 60% 90-day LIBOR tractor funds (which is simply a 90-day moving average of the 90-day LIBOR rate). Historical data from 1975 through the first four months of 1992 were analyzed for a hypothetical product that is priced to yield Prime "flat" (i.e., no spread over Prime). The calculated annual spreads generated against the "optimal" transfer pricing portfolio are shown in Table 14.4. Notice that there are consecutive years where there can be large year-to-year differences in the spread.

Table 14.4
Spreads Between Prime Rate and "Optimal" Funding Portfolio

Year	Annual	Four-Year Moving Averages
1975	1.03%	
1976	1.31	
1977	1.04	
1978	0.80	1.05%
1979	1.09	1.06
1980	1.61	1.14
1981	1.99	1.37
1982	1.86	1.64
1983	1.38	1.71
1984	1.40	1.66
1985	1.60	1.56
1986	1.43	1.45
1987	1.33	1.44
1988	1.60	1.49
1989	1.60	1.49
1990	1.80	1.58
1991	2.49	1.87
Overall Average	1.49%	

Also shown in Table 14.4 are the four-year moving averages of the annual data points. Using the annual spreads, the largest year-to-year change in spread was 0.69%, compared to the average spread of 1.49%. With the moving averages, the largest change between two years was only 0.29%. Conceptually, the use of the moving averages not only gives line managers a more stable bottom line or SVA, it also reinforces the notion that their pricing strategies should take longer term interest rate cycles into consideration. Pricing should not be based solely on current, perhaps unusual, market rate relationships.

14.8 ADVANTAGES AND DISADVANTAGES OF THE 80/20 RULE

The savings to the bank of employing the recommendations in this chapter can be staggering. We offer one rough quantification of the benefit. Suppose that two banks have decided to build new transfer pricing systems. Both have about 100 line units and the same full-line retail and corporate product set. One decides that precision and detail are to be achieved at any cost, the other opts for the recommendations just presented.

To estimate the difference in the "size" of the respective system data storage requirements, we can make the crude estimates displayed in Table 14.5.

Table 14.5
Calculation of Hypothetical System Complexity Levels

	Detailed Approach	80/20 Rule Approach
Number of Line Units Analyzed:	100	1
x Number of Product Groups Analyzed:	100	40
x Frequency of Analysis (Per Year):	12	1
x Average Number of Origination Periods/Product	20	3
x Average Number of Maturity Buckets/Product:	10	2
= Number of Storage Elements Needed:	24,000,000	240

The 80/20 rule results in a system that is about 100,000-fold less complex! Aside from the clear logistical advantages of the simpler approach, there is the critical advantage of the ease of understanding and gaining a good intuitive "feel" for a data set numbering 240 versus one numbering over 20 million by managers with a nontechnical background.

There are two disadvantages of this simplified approach. First, the four-year moving average spreads are not directly applicable to product pricing analyses. Any spreadsheet used for understanding the profitability implications of product pricing strategies should have **current period** transfer rates only. A different situation exists for indexed products, such as Prime-based loans. The authors believe that VERY long-term spreads between the index rate and the transfer funding portfolio should be employed if the product being analyzed has a maturity greater than one or two years. This is evident from Table 14.4. Notice that in 1991, the spread for this index increased to 249 basis points, well above its long-term average of about 150 basis points. Unless management is convinced that this wider spread is indicative of a permanent new spread relationship between the Prime rate and other market rates, pricing spreadsheets should reflect the long-term value of 150 basis points.

The second disadvantage is that the use of four-year moving averages in the profitability system does complicate the total bank net interest income reconciliation process. This would be a major problem if the profitability system were being used for total bank interest rate risk management analyses. Fortunately, it usually is not. Long-term, moving average spreads will definitely distort the estimation of mismatch earnings for the ALCO unit IN THE SHORT RUN. However, these short-term errors will all wash out over extended periods. That is, a four-year moving average of the calculated mismatch earnings will be useable. The authors believe that this issue is quite a small sacrifice to make for the advantages listed and recommend that others give these arguments serious consideration.

14.9 PREPAYMENT RISK

Chapter 9 introduced the seriousness of prepayment risk on asset and liability management analyses. Other types of embedded options features were discussed as well. There are two fundamental methods for incorporating and reflecting prepayment risk in transfer pricing systems. (Of course, there is always the third option of simply ignoring prepayment risk, referred to as the ostrich strategy.) The two methods may simplistically be referred to as the "after-the-fact" and "before-the-fact" approaches.

After-the-fact approach. This is applicable to larger-sized transactions, especially where an economic prepayment penalty is charged to the borrower. Transfer rates are assigned based on the contractual amortization or maturity schedule. If and when a prepayment occurs, the original transfer funds are "sold" back to the ALCO unit with a mark-to-market prepayment loss (or gain) passed to the line unit in the form of a cost allocation. In theory, the unit will collect a similar amount from the customer at the time of the prepayment, such that the unit's profit and loss statement will not be adversely affected. This prepayment fee collected by the ALCO unit through the cost allocation can be used to offset by the ALCO unit manager actually to prepay any matched funding it may have originally undertaken to fund the loan.

Before-the-fact approach. This is recommended for loan products where there is generally no prepayment penalty assessed. These include mortgage loans and installment loans. The concept is incrementally to increase the funds transfer rates by an amount that will compensate the ALCO unit over the expected average life of such loans for the prepayments that may occur. A methodology referred to as the "option-adjusted spread" (OAS) calculation provides a usable estimate. In determining the transfer rates, the contractual amortization patterns should be adjusted for the long-term expected average prepayment rate. This will significantly lower the "expected maturity" of the loans, and thus the starting transfer rates. The OAS spread is then added onto the basic transfer rates as an adjustment. These spreads are readily available from investment firms for mortgage loans, including adjustable rate mortgages (ARMs).

Please keep in mind that even ARMs have significant OAS adjustments. This may not be apparent at first. ARM prepayments do pick up when fixed mortgage rates drop because of refinancing activity into fixed mortgages or conversions. Also, ARMs have annual and lifetime caps that may limit the extent of any interest rate resets, such that the bank's margin is "squeezed" in periods of extreme rate volatility. The ARM OAS adjustment compensates the bank for these risks.

A question often asked at this point is: "Shouldn't the bank buy some prepayment protection with the proceeds of this OAS spread being collected from the line units for these risks?" Indeed, this question should be seriously discussed in the ALCO. There is no simple answer. Unfortunately, there is also no "pure" off balance sheet hedging instrument available, even if the bank wanted to hedge itself. However, the Federal Home Loan Banks do make available long-term fixed or floating rate advances with prepayment (or "call option") privileges. Also, larger banking firms can issue callable debt in the wholesale markets. It may well be prudent to spend some of these OAS "dollars" on such protection. In any event, the responsibility and risk involved in this decision should be borne by the ALCO unit, not by line units.

14.10 THE LIQUIDITY COMMITMENT SPREAD

Another source of funding risk that should be considered relates to the mismatch between the repricing sensitivity period of a transaction and its ultimate maturity. The best example of this (again) is Prime-based loans. The weighted average sensitivity of the "optimal" funding mix of 40% Federal Funds and 60% 90-day CD tractor is only about 27 days. However, the average maturity of most Prime-based loans can often be five years or more.

To understand the issue, it is easiest to consider the following question: If five-year Prime-based loans were the only earning assets in a bank, what type of funding strategy should it adopt to "match fund" these loans? Our answer is NOT to use 40% federal funds and 60% 90-day CD or LIBOR tractors. Why not? After all, this would indeed best address the **interest rate sensitivity** aspect of this bank, but it would leave the bank woefully exposed to **liquidity risk**. (This is an appropriate place to scream, "Remember Continental Illinois!")

The concept of matched funding must encompass ALL risk dimensions: maturity as well as rate sensitivity. Of course, for fixed-rate loans, maturity and sensitivity are pretty much the same. But, for floating rate loans, the difference is significant.

The correct hypothetical answer to the question posed is to raise 60% five-year floating rate debt indexed to three-month CDs or LIBOR, and staggered into three pools (or tranches) that reset each month in sequence; and 40% five-year fixed rate debt swapped into a federal funds equivalent all-in cost. The net characteristics of such a funding strategy would match both the rate sensitivity and the maturity characteristics of the loans being funded.

How would this elaborate strategy affect the all-in cost of funding? We estimate that it would raise the cost of funds about 20 to 30 basis points above the cost of "plain vanilla" federal funds and CD or LIBOR funding. One can think of this incremental cost as a sort of "commitment fee" being paid to the markets to guarantee that the funding will remain in place for the full five-year term. Any bank that funds five-year Prime-based loans only with short-term funds is accepting the huge risk that should any unexpected problem arise as to its credit quality, there could be a future "run" or "flight" away from this bank's name by the wholesale markets, triggering a liquidity crisis, or even insolvency, for the bank.

Including this aspect of funding into the transfer pricing system need not be complicated using the 80/20 rule. We have adopted the approach that a "generic" liquidity commitment spread of 25 basis points will be applied to any transfer rate for any product group that has a rate reset less than one year, but expected maturity greater than one year. Table 14.6 summarizes those product groups that commonly receive this increment to their transfer funding rates. For deposits, the increment increases its transfer spread and its profitability. In essence, those deposit categories are being compensated for the liquidity protection they provide.

Table 14.6
Products Associated with a Liquidity "Commitment" Spread

Assets

    Prime-Based Commercial Loans

    Other Money Market Rate-Indexed Commercial Loans

    Floating Rate Consumer Loans:

        Home Equity Lines of Credit

        Variable Rate Credit Cards

        Guaranteed Student Loans

    Adjustable Rate Mortgages

Liabilities

    T-Bill Indexed or Floating Rate Retail Deposits:

        Money Market Deposit Accounts

        Interest-Bearing Checking Accounts

    Variable Rate Individual Retirement Accounts

    Variable Rate Retail CDs (Over One Year)

    Floating Rate Long-Term Debt

14.11 SPREAD OR BASIS RISK

The final source of transfer pricing risk to be considered is again related to Prime-based loans. It also pertains to any other item that is indexed to a rate other than the bank's transfer pricing CD or LIBOR yield curve, such as Treasury Bills or the COFI (Cost of Funds Index). We are referring here to the topic of spread or "basis" risk. The Prime rate or the Treasury Bill auction rate are not perfectly correlated with typical transfer pricing (CD or LIBOR) rates. This additional risk should not be ignored.

To introduce this topic, review Figure 9.2. Notice on the x-axis that while there is some reduction in spread volatility using the "optimal" funding mix of 40% federal funds and 60% 90-day LIBOR tractor, there is still a substantial amount of volatility remaining. The standard deviation of this residual "basis" or spread risk is about 48 basis points. Recall from the same figure, as well as from Table 14.4, that the average spread was 149 basis points.

Using a normal distribution assumption, these values provide an indication of the dispersion or volatility characteristics of the Prime rate funding spreads as shown in Table 14.7.

Table 14.7
Probability Distribution of Prime Rate Spreads
Assuming a Normal Distribution Function

Assumptions:

Average (Mean) Spread	149 Basis Points	
Standard Deviation	48 Basis Points	
With a Probability of:	**Spread Will Be Greater Than:**	**and Less Than:**
68.3%	101 Basis Points	197 Basis Points
95.4%	53 Basis Points	245 Basis Points

The 68.3% probability refers to the range of spreads calculated as the mean (average) spread plus or minus one standard deviation. The 95.4% line refers to a range of the mean spread plus or minus two standard deviations. Put another way, there is less than a 5% chance (about one year in every 20) that the spread will be less than 53 basis points or greater than 245 basis points. These statistics are quite consistent with the one observation of 249 basis points for the 17-year period analyzed (Table 14.4).

Hopefully, this discussion has left the impression that there is still quite a substantial level of margin risk, even with an "optimal" funding portfolio. Indeed, there is! From the 68.3% line, it is clear that more than 30% of the time, the Prime rate's spread will be either lower than 101 basis points or more than 197.

How should such risk be incorporated in the transfer pricing rates for Prime-based loans? Some banks leave this risk with the units that make such loans. They establish a transfer funds rate based on the "optimal" funding mix, ignoring both the liquidity "commitment" spread presented in the last section as well as this spread risk. The attitude that goes along with this approach is something like: "The line units are creating this basis risk for the bank, so they should bear the consequences."

While this approach certainly has some legitimacy, it is not compatible with the "no uncontrollable variances" principle. Line managers have no control over the detailed behavior of the Prime rate. Indeed, in many banks, it is the executive management in the persons of the CEO and either the Chief Credit Officer or the Chief Financial Officer who determine the specific timing of Prime rate changes. Therefore, one could make the perverse argument that the CEO should bear the consequences of this spread risk!

Our recommendation is to "charge" for this spread risk, then guarantee whatever spread remains. A simple approach is to charge one standard deviation. Hence, for Prime-based loans, a charge of 48 basis points would be assessed for this risk. For products based upon other indices, studies similar to that described in Chapter 9 and summarized in Figure 9.2 would be conducted. (There is nothing magic about using one standard deviation. If this seems too onerous, then one-half standard deviation can just as easily be adopted.)

Even simpler would be to adopt a "generic" spread risk increment of about 25 basis points for any indexed product. This would be applied to any product with an optimal funding portfolio standard deviation of 20 basis points or more.

14.12 A SURVEY OF TRANSFER PRICING ADJUSTMENTS

A brief survey of some common bank products and the transfer pricing considerations appropriate for each is presented in Table 14.8. The column labeled "Rate Sensitivity" refers to the initial basic estimated maturity or rate reset characteristic that is the focus of all presentations on "matched-maturity" transfer pricing, which was discussed in Sections 14.2 and 14.3.

Notice that an OAS adjustment is made only for those products that display "economic" prepayment risk. Auto loans have relatively stable prepayment rates that are not sensitive to interest rate movements. The estimated rate of such prepayments will be dominated by "demographic" factors, such as the sale of the car, or an insurance settlement after an accident. This can be factored into the initial estimate of the "effective" paydown pattern used to establish the basic sensitivity characteristic by scheduling out the contractual amortization pattern and adjusting it for an estimated demographic prepayment rate of a little above 1% per month for a "seasoned" portfolio. Demographic prepayments occur steadily and do

Table 14.8
Survey of Transfer Pricing Elements

Product	Rate Sensitivity	Prepayment OAS	Liquidity Commitment	Spread Risk
LOAN PRODUCTS:				
Prime-Based Loans	Yes	No	Yes	Yes
"Capped" Prime Loans	Yes	Yes	Yes	Yes
Fixed Rate Commercial Loans	Yes	After-Fact	No	No
Fixed Rate Mortgage Loans	Yes	Yes	No	No
Adjustable Rate Mortgages	Yes	Yes	Yes	Yes
Guaranteed Student Loans	Yes	No	Yes	Yes
Credit Card (Fixed Rate)	Yes	No	No	No
Automobile Loans	Yes	No	No	No
DEPOSIT PRODUCTS:				
Non-Int. Bearing DDA	Yes	No	No	No
Interest DDA (Floating Rate)	Yes	No	Yes	Yes
Money Market Deposit Account	Yes	No	Yes	Yes
MMDA (With a Rate "Floor")	Yes	Yes	Yes	Yes
Retail CDs	Yes	No	No	No

not change because of interest rate shifts. Economic prepayments occur specifically because interest rates have lowered enough to drive borrowers to refinance.

The "after-fact" notation for fixed rate commercial loans signifies that there is usually a full, explicit prepayment penalty fee. Therefore, it is appropriate to make an "after-the-fact" mark-to-market adjustment for any associated transfer funding (or real funding). This is especially applicable if the bank has assigned "up-to-the-minute" transfer rates for large loan drawdowns.

The OAS adjustment for the "floored" MMDA product is to reflect the potential value of a rate floor on any deposit product for the depositor, or "squeeze" on the bank's margin. It would lower the "earnings credit" assigned to MMDAs through the transfer pricing system. Likewise, "capped" Prime loans should also be assessed an OAS adjustment.

Interestingly, there are home equity lines of credit that are indexed to the Prime rate that have interest rate floors at or near 10%. Such a product should have an OAS spread **added** to its basic transfer pricing spread in recognition of the value to the bank of that feature.

14.13 TRANSFER PRICING ITEMS WITHOUT MATURITIES: DDA AND EQUITY

Many of the concepts presented in Chapters 8 and 9 are pertinent here. For noninterest-bearing demand deposits, the "core" and "volatile" portions can be estimated as described in those chapters. The volatile portion should be assigned a short-term effective maturity transfer rate, perhaps a 30-day tractor. The core portion should receive the "generic" long-term tractor assumption as described in Section 9.3. Assuming that the bank has selected a four-year tractor for its generic long-term category, then a typical transfer pricing assumption might be: 20% 30-day tractor transfer rate and 80% four-year tractor transfer rate.

Likewise, for equity, the generic long-term tractor provides a convenient assumption. For purists, one could argue that the **duration** of net equity should determine the transfer rate maturity assumption.

14.14 HEDGING STRATEGY FOR THE LARGE TRANSACTION BOOK

Section 14.7 stipulated that for large transactions (over $500,000), we track up-to-the-minute transfer rates. Typically, the "up-to-the-minute" concept applies only to the underlying Treasury rate quote. To this, the bank's target credit rating spread-over-Treasuries is added to generate the full transfer rate. In many regional banks, these large transactions are managed for interest rate and liquidity risk separately from the rest of the balance sheet. We think this is quite prudent.

For such a "large transaction book," generally managed by the Treasury unit, there are excellent hedging and risk management strategies available. This is because these types of transactions tend to be few in number, very explicit in their terms, and have full economic prepayment adjustments or accurately priced call privileges. Examples include large commercial loan takedowns, purchases of investment securities, and the issuance of large blocks of debt or wholesale CDs.

One durable strategy is described here. It recognizes the need to maintain both long- and short-term casn flows within the safety zones. It also shows how both duration and gap analyses can complement one another.

The basic procedure for a book of large, fixed rate transactions is as follows:

Analyze quarterly cash flows using gap analysis and duration (IRE) analysis.
If the book contains a large number of short-term (under one-year) transactions, quarterly buckets may not be detailed enough. Some banks use weekly short-term buckets. However, quarterly buckets work quite well for transactions over one year. The strategy will be to use gap analysis to measure all mismatches under two years. Mismatches beyond two years will be analyzed with the interest rate elasticity (IRE) concept from Chapter 8.

Hedge all gap mismatches under two years with financial futures. The futures markets are ideal for hedging time periods of two years or less. A range of weighted gap mismatches should be established. Whenever the gap profile under two years becomes larger than the target range (or safety zone), that is a signal to the Treasury staff to execute some incremental futures transactions. The safety zone should be small enough to be prudent, but large enough to prevent large numbers of one-contract trades.

Hedge the net IRE of all cash flows over two years with swaps. A swap book is used to manage the IRE of all long-term cash flows. For large books, this management process will entail a substantial number of transactions, establishing a pattern of regular participation in the markets. With this constant presence, Treasury staff will become quite proficient at buying and selling their positions. Again, a conservative, yet practical safety zone should be established for the large transaction book's IRE.

Also, the Treasury unit manager should not overlook the liquidity safety zone! Limits should be placed on the use of short-term wholesale CDs (or commercial paper in the case of holding company activities). Whenever the limit is reached, the treasurer should be issuing long-term debt that can be swapped into whatever rate reset characteristic is desired.

14.15 SUMMARY

Transfer pricing is not a simple subject. However, it is possible to adhere to the profitability principles presented in Chapter 13. In particular, the

80/20 rule decreases the complexity of transfer pricing systems by incredible degrees! This allows the ALM staff to get beyond the basic sensitivity aspect of the matched-maturity approach, and to deal with other risk topics such as OAS adjustments, liquidity commitment fees, and "basis" or spread risk.

As radical as some of the suggestions in this chapter may appear, we would respectfully encourage readers to consider them well. They simplify an extremely complex topic. Even if only employed during the development of initial prototype versions of what may be intended to be much more "sophisticated" transfer pricing systems, we believe they will dramatically facilitate the understanding and acceptance of these critical concepts by a very broad cross section of bank management and staff.

CHAPTER 15

Putting It All Together

This completes our overview of the world of asset and liability management. The approaches described in this book provide a set of relatively simple implementation procedures that are consistent with the shareholder value perspective and corporate financial theory. In closing, we take this opportunity to review some of the most important principles presented in this book. They include the following:

Shareholder value perspectives should be understood. Many bankers profess their commitment toward shareholder value concepts. However, unless they truly analyze the implications of their strategies on the market value of equity and overall bank volatility risk, a healthy dose of skepticism is warranted. A shareholder perspective can be analyzed, understood, and achieved if the basic foundations and principles presented in this book are observed.

The 80/20 rule pays large dividends. This is our golden rule. It has served to keep attention focused on the "forest," rather than become mired in the "twigs" of analytical complexity and detail. Theoretical soundness and simplicity of implementation are not incompatible. Yet simplicity can become the key to establishing a broad base of understanding and acceptance. Indeed, this rule is often essential if a broad, internal consensus is to be achieved.

Market signals are useful for pricing risk. The cost of capital, the hurdle ROE, the borrowing spread over Treasuries, and many other "risk pricing" dimensions can be derived from available market information. However, strict adherence will not always be possible. A corollary of the 80/20 rule is that precision in measuring hurdle rates is not important. General consistency with approximate hurdles can work quite well.

There is no free lunch. Higher returns are usually associated with increased risk. However, it is always worthwhile to explore any available diversification opportunities. This goes beyond straightforward credit risk diversification as described in Chapter 10. It implies that interest rate and liquidity management for multibank holding companies are best practiced at the consolidated corporate level to take advantage of any natural internal hedging effects.

Be consistent in all evaluations. It is terribly hypocritical to monitor the riskiness of the market value of equity for ALCO purposes, but to have all internal incentives based on some type of accounting earnings measure. If the bank is committed to understanding and managing its shareholder value, then it is essential that many levels of the organization be evaluated with performance measures that are consistent with SVA. In this respect, the profitability measurement principles described in Chapters 13 and 14 are critical.

Teams play fair if the game is fair. One of the constants of human existence is organizational politics and internal competition. If the criteria used to judge performance are arbitrary, unclear, or unfair, politics and internal competition can be very destructive. Using the approach outlined in this book, any bank can lay out the rules of a game that are simple, fair, and obviously good for the organization. This kind of performance measurement does exactly what you would expect: the banking units focus on maximizing shareholder value and have no incentive to concentrate on minimizing the accomplishments of their internal "competition." This important cultural benefit can be one of the strongest benefits of a rational shareholder value management system.

Everything depends on everything else. One of the many conclusions of this book is that the organization's many activities simultaneously impact each other. The level of credit risk affects the bank's cost of borrowing. This in turn affects the profitability of deposit gathering. Higher deposit gathering profits increase the returns from a larger branch system. This in turn increases the need for capital. Finally, a bank that proves it can generate shareholder value will get the capital it needs. These links are intuitively understood by most senior bankers but they have traditionally been hard to quantify. With the techniques described in this book, the links between units will be concrete and clearly visible to all bankers in an organization. The result is better strategic planning, better execution, and better performance from the entire organization.

Please let us know your point of view. We appreciate that there are many legitimate alternative perspectives on all of the asset and liability management issues presented in this book. We sincerely welcome hearing about alternatives that you believe are improvements on the approaches described here. After all, asset and liability management is a continuous learning curve . . . and we are climbing it along with all of you!

BIBLIOGRAPHY

Binder, Barrett F., ed.: *Banker's Treasury Management Handbook.* Boston, MA: Warren, Gorham and Lamont, 1988.

Black, Fischer and Scholes, Myron.: "The Pricing of Options and Corporate Liabilities." *Journal of Political Economy.* May 1973, pp. 637-654.

Cates, David C.: "Liquidity Lessons for the '90s." *Bank Management.* April 1990, pp. 20-25.

Cox, John C. and Rubinstein, Mark: *Options Markets.* Englewood Cliffs, NJ: Prentice-Hall, 1985.

Fabozzi, Frank J. and Konishi, Atsuo, eds.: *Asset/Liability Management.* Chicago, IL: Probus Publishing, 1991.

Ho, Thomas S. Y. and Lee, Sang-Bin: "Term Structure Movements and Pricing Interest Rate Contingent Claims." *Journal of Finance* 41: 1011-1029, 1986.

Hull, John: *Options, Futures, and Other Derivative Securities.* Englewood Cliffs, NJ: Prentice-Hall, 1989.

Ingersoll, Jonathan E., Jr.: *Theory of Financial Decision Making.* Savage, MD: Rowman & Littlefield, 1987.

Jacobs, Rodney L.: "The Rate Maturity of Prime and Other Indexed Assets and Liabilities." *Journal of Bank Research.* Summer 1984, pp. 108-114.

Kaufman, George G.: "Measuring and Managing Interest-Rate Risk: A Primer." *Economic Perspectives.* Federal Reserve Bank of Chicago, January/February 1984, pp. 16-29.

Matz, Leonard M.: *Bank Solvency. A Banker's Guide to Practical Liquidity Management.* Rolling Meadows, IL: Bank Administration Institute, 1986.

Merton, Robert C.: "On the Pricing of Corporate Debt: The Risk Structure of Interest Rates." *Journal of Finance* 29: 449-470, 1974.

Merton, Robert C.: *Continuous Time Finance.* Cambridge, MA: Basil Blackwell Inc., 1990.

Modigliani, Franco and Miller, Merton: "The Cost of Capital, Corporation Finance, and the Theory of Investment." *American Economic Review.* 48: 261-297, 1958.

Peaslee, James M. and Nirenberg, David Z.: *Federal Income Taxation of Mortgage Backed Securities.* Chicago, IL: Probus Publishing Co., 1989.

Stewart, G. Bennett III.: *The Quest for Value. A Guide for Senior Managers.* New York, NY: HarperCollins, Publishers Inc., 1991.

Toevs, Alden L. and Haney, William C.: "Measuring and Managing Interest Rate Risk: A Guide to Asset/Liability Models Used in Banks and Thrifts." in Platt, Robert B., ed. *Controlling Interest Rate Risk. New Techniques and Applications for Money Management.* New York, NY: John Wiley & Sons, 1986.

Index